Electoral Competition and Institutional Change in Mexico

Electoral Competition
and
Institutional Change
in
Mexico

CAROLINE C. BEER

UNIVERSITY OF NOTRE DAME PRESS

Notre Dame, Indiana

Chapter 3 is a revised version of "Assessing the Consequences of
Electoral Democracy: Subnational Legislative Change in Mexico,"
Comparative Politics 33 (July 2001), and appears here by permission
of *Comparative Politics*.

Library of Congress Cataloging-in-Publication Data
Beer, Caroline C., 1972 –
Electoral competition and institutional change in Mexico / Caroline C.
Beer.
p.   cm.
"From the Helen Kellogg Institute for International Studies".
Includes bibliographical references and index.
ISBN 0-268-02766-8 (cloth : alk. paper)
ISBN 0-268-02767-6 (pbk. : alk. paper)
1. Representative government and representation — Mexico.
2. Democracy — Mexico.   3. Elections — Mexico.   1. Mexico   Politics
and government — 1988 –   I. Helen Kellogg Institute for International
Studies.   II. Title.
JL1281 . B44 2003
320.972 — dc21

2003004349

To my mom and dad

CONTENTS

FIGURES

ACKNOWLEDGMENTS

This book would not have been possible without the assistance and encouragement of many people too numerous to mention. I am deeply grateful to all who contributed to this undertaking. The members of my dissertation committee — Karen Remmer, Neil Mitchell, Ken Roberts, and Jonathan Fox — deserve special thanks. As the director of my dissertation, Karen was involved in nearly every aspect of the design and production of the dissertation from which this book evolved. I would like to thank her for her mentoring and friendship. Few graduate students are fortunate enough to have a mentor who reads and comments on multiple drafts of dissertation chapters in a single afternoon. Ken Roberts and Neil Mitchell also patiently read many drafts and provided valuable insights that improved the research immeasurably. Jonathan Fox's insights into the Mexican polity added considerable depth and richness to the final product.

I would like to thank all of my teachers, especially those in the political science department at the University of New Mexico. I am particularly grateful to Mark Peceny. Without his kind words and unwavering support, I might not have had the confidence to finish. Ken Coleman and Bill Stanley also provided important help along the way. At Oberlin College, Eve Sandberg's faith in my abilities was instrumental in my going to graduate school in the first place.

I would not have been able to carry out successfully my field research without the generous support of my friends and colleagues in Mexico. Luis Miguel Rionda arranged my affiliation with the Centro de Investigaciones en Ciencias Sociales at the University of Guanajuato (CICSUG). His kindness in the early days of my field research helped me to get this project off the ground. The researchers at CICSUG provided me with a stimulating and enjoyable environment for carrying out my fieldwork.

Juanita Vallejo, Cecilia Romo, and Maria del Carmen Ramos Flores warmly welcomed me into their homes during my long stays in Mexico. For this and for their meaningful friendships, I express my heartfelt appreciation. My understanding of Mexican politics benefited enormously from the many enjoyable conversations I shared with Boris Marañon, Regina Henríquez, Ana Maria Ruíz Marín, Maria Elena Ruíz Marín, Joel Sánchez, Baltazar Reyna Reynoso, Alvaro López Lara, Nicolás Loza Otero, Pablo Vargas, and Javier Alvarez Isasi.

Moises Arce, Erik Wibbels, Eric Jepsen, Judy Palier, Ann Mettler, and Jessica Barthelow added fun and distraction to the long days of graduate school. Their friendships then and now have given me much needed encouragement. The political science department at the University of Vermont provided a lively and supportive home for me while I finished this book. Candace Smith and Carol Tank-Day helped me in immeasurable ways on a daily basis. Josh Forrest and Rod Camp read and commented on the entire manuscript. I appreciate their generosity in sharing their time with me.

At the University of Notre Dame Press, Jeffrey Gainey, associate director of the press, efficiently and competently shepherded this manuscript through the publication process. Elisabeth Magnus did a fine job copy-editing the manuscript. I would also like to thank Scott Mainwaring, the general editor of the Helen Kellogg Institute for International Studies series at the University of Notre Dame Press.

Parts of this book have been published elsewhere. An earlier version of chapter 3 appeared in "Assessing the Consequences of Electoral Democracy: Subnational Legislative Change in Mexico," in *Comparative Politics* 33: 421–40, July 2001. Parts of chapter 6 appear in "Electoral Competition and Fiscal Decentralization in Mexico" in *Decentralization and Democracy in Latin America,* edited by Alfred Montero and David Samuels, University of Notre Dame Press, forthcoming. I thank these publishers for permission to reprint my work here.

Several institutions provided financial support for this project. I gratefully acknowledge the financial support of the National Science Foundation (under grant SBR-9809180), the International Dissertation Field Research Fellowship Program of the Social Science Research Council with funds provided by the Andrew W. Mellon Foundation, and a Doctoral Fellowship from the Latin American Institute of the University of New Mexico.

I thank my parents for educating and encouraging me from the very beginning. Their steadfast love and support have made so many things possible in my life. My deepest thanks go to my husband. Without him, nothing else would matter.

CHAPTER ONE

Introduction

The wave of democracy that politically transformed much of the Third World and the former communist bloc left Mexico lagging far behind. In the late 1980s, as Mikhail Gorbachev was preparing for the first-ever free elections in Russia, Carlos Salinas was elected to the Mexican presidency on the basis of extensive electoral fraud. "Mexican exceptionalism," which has long provided a major theoretical foundation for the study of the Mexican polity, was used to explain Mexico's latest resistance to broader regional and global trends (e.g., Needler 1995). After more than seventy years of uninterrupted one-party rule, many doubted that the Institutional Revolutionary Party (Partido Revolucionario Institucional, PRI) would ever give up power. But slowly, and sometimes imperceptibly, small enclaves of democracy began to emerge in Mexico and then grew at an accelerated pace. Each successive round of elections returned another victory to opposition parties. In 1989, the PRI governed all thirty-one states and the Federal District. By the year 2000, opposition parties had ruled eleven state governments and the Federal District, and in July of that year they conquered the biggest prize of all, the presidency. Contrary to many expectations, the most recent global wave of democratization has also encompassed Mexico and has done so from the bottom up.

Recent research has taught us much about the dynamics of democratic transitions (Bratton and van de Walle 1997; Crawford and Lijphart 1995; Dawisha and Parrott 1997; Higley and Gunther 1992; O'Donnell, Schmitter, and Whitehead 1986) as well as the process of democratic consolidation (Lijphart and Waisman 1996;

1

Linz and Stepan 1996; Mainwaring, O'Donnell, and Valenzuela 1992; Shugart and Mainwaring 1997). Yet important questions about regime change remain unanswered: What are the consequences of democratization? In what ways do competitive elections alter the nature of the political system? How does electoral competition influence the long-term distribution of power across political institutions? How does the breakdown of a one-party system play out at the subnational level? Is the process uneven across subnational units?

This book addresses these questions by analyzing the impact of electoral competition on politics in the Mexican states. Building upon a long tradition of research on politics in the U.S. states (e.g., Erikson, Wright, and McIver 1993; Key 1949; Lockard 1959), as well as recent theoretical contributions in the comparative field (e.g., Przeworski 1991; Rueschemeyer, Stephens, and Stephens 1992), the central thesis is that electoral competition has important institutional consequences that lead to strengthened representative institutions and a greater separation of powers. A greater separation of powers, in turn, helps to promote improved executive accountability and the rule of law. More competitive elections generate changes in institutional behavior that alter political recruitment patterns, legislative roles, and the policy-making process, leading to the selection of more locally connected candidates, stronger and more professional legislatures, and a closer nexus between the supply and demand for public goods. This research departs from standard studies of democratization in three major ways. First, by focusing on subnational politics it stresses the uneven nature of democratic transition across subnational units and the bottom-up dynamics of transition. Second, it reverses the causal arrows of the dominant institutional literature by focusing on the causes of institutional change rather than the consequences of institutional constraints. Third, emphasis is placed on the consequences of democratization rather than the causes.

While the dominant approach to the study of democratization has stressed top-down models of elite strategic negotiation (Higley and Gunther 1992; O'Donnell and Schmitter 1986; Przeworski 1991), this analysis takes advantage of the drawn-out transition to democracy in Mexico to analyze the bottom-up dynamics. The initial struggles for democracy in Mexico took place at the state and local level. In many countries the process of democratization has been extremely uneven across geographical units (O'Donnell 1994). While a few studies have addressed subnational trends (e.g., Fox 1994a, 1994b; Gay 1994; Hagopian 1996; Kohli 1987; Oxhorn 1995; Putnam 1993; Snyder 2001a; Stoner-Weiss 1997), the bulk of existing research on democratization has focused on national-level politics and has ignored the enormous regional and local variation in the process of reform. The first important contribution of this book is to take subnational politics seriously and draw out the causal connections between subnational political variation and national regime change. Scholars have tended to assume that democracy is constant across subnational units, yet as Hagopian (1996) points out with reference to Brazil, a transition to democracy at the national level does not necessarily lead to democratization at the subnational level. As evidenced by the history of the U.S. South, even in a well-institutionalized national democratic context, levels of political participation, electoral competition, and policy performance may vary widely across subnational units (Key 1949). In Mexico the situation has been reversed, with subnational democratic enclaves leading the transition to national democracy.

Moreover, analysis of subnational politics is particularly timely and relevant because in the Latin American context democratic governance at the national level has not successfully addressed problems of pervasive inequality and poverty (Petras and Leiva 1994; Tokman and O'Donnell 1998). In response, international financial institutions have increasingly prescribed decentralization to solve the region's intractable problems, assuming that shifting policy responsibilities to state or local governments will result in more efficient and responsive government performance. Hence, subnational governments took on much greater responsibilities during the 1990s and are spending an increasing percentage of their nation's public resources. Yet in many cases regional disparities continue to grow and subnational authoritarian enclaves remain resistant to change (Fox 1994a; Fox and Aranda 1996; Hagopian 1996; Snyder 1999b). In most cases very little is known about how subnational governments function.

In addition to shedding new light on subnational politics, this book also makes an important contribution to the study of institutions and institutional change. Research on institutions has been dominated by analysis of the consequences of institutional change rather than its causes. This research reverses the causal arrows of the dominant institutional literature by focusing on the causes of institutional change rather than the consequences of institutional constraints. Dominant institutional models seek to explain how varying institutional arrangements influence political outcomes. In these models, institutions are held constant. Yet in many political systems (especially democratizing systems), institutions are not constant but rather are being reformed on a continual basis. To address this gap in the literature, this book explores the ways in which politics influences the development of institutions, and it highlights the utility of a dynamic institutional approach.

Finally, this book makes an important contribution to the study of democratization by explicitly focusing on the consequences of regime change. With a few notable exceptions (e.g., Hunter 1997; Weyland 1996, 1997), prior research on democratization has treated democracy as the dependent variable and bracketed questions about the political consequences of regime transitions (e.g., O'Donnell et al. 1986). Democracy has been defined narrowly in procedural terms as a system with fair elections, universal suffrage, and freedom of association, leaving its substantive impact open to empirical analysis (Karl 1990). As a result, major reservations have been expressed about the meaning, significance, and quality of democracy in the contemporary developing world (e.g., Huber, Rueschemeyer, and Stephens 1997; O'Donnell 1994, 1996). Given the current constraints imposed upon new democracies by the requirements of the global market, the conditionality of international financial institutions, and the trend toward insulated and autonomous technocratic policy making, observers have even suggested that the move toward competitive electoral systems is not reflected in policy formation or increased government responsiveness to citizens' concerns (Conaghan, Malloy, and Abugattas 1990; Przeworski, Stokes, and Manin 1999; Stokes 1997; Veltmeyer and Petras 2000).

Systematic research on these issues remains limited, however, not to mention complicated, by the coincidence of democratic transitions with unprecedented levels of economic crisis in most emerging markets and developing nations (Remmer 1995). The sheer depth and prevalence of economic difficulties limit the usefulness of before-and-after comparisons because it is difficult to isolate the economic from the political causes of policy outputs. Cross-national studies are also problematic for assessing the impact of democratic transitions, especially within the Latin American context, where there is limited variation. The only major Latin American countries that were not democratic in the 1990s were Cuba, for which very little information is available, and Mexico, which was in the midst of a process of transition.

The Mexican states, in contrast, provide a useful set of units for comparative analysis of the consequences of democracy. There are substantial methodological advantages to focusing upon the subnational level of analysis (Lijphart 1975; Linz and de Miguel 1966, Snyder 2001b). In particular, comparison of subnational units is valuable because it increases the number of available cases and controls for some systemic sources of variation (King, Keohane, and Verba 1994; Putnam 1993). Furthermore, if democratization is uneven across subnational units, using averages of these heterogeneous subunits without controlling for dispersion is methodologically unsatisfactory because nationally aggregated data may hide important subnational variation (Linz and de Miguel 1966). Moreover, national means may provide the same values for one country with substantial regional inequality as for another with relative equality across subnational units, thus possibly misrepresenting the similarities between the two cases. Subnational comparison often allows for more precise coding and more accurate measurement of variables than aggregate national-level data and also allows for a more complex understanding of spatially uneven processes (Snyder 2001b).

There are also significant theoretical reasons for disaggregating political systems by focusing on subnational politics. Classic theorizing has assumed that political systems are largely homogeneous across nation-states. Yet in many Latin American countries the legality of the democratic state has not penetrated many peripheral areas, and the full rights of citizenship have not been extended to all citizens (O'Donnell 1993). Authoritarian enclaves, usually in rural areas, exist in many democratic countries across the region. These areas can exert influence on national politics in territorially based systems of representation because the authoritarian elites from these enclaves become members of the national legislature and then may trade their votes for control over bureaucracies and policy arenas. Coerced votes in rural areas may also be enough to swing presidential elections. Irresponsible economic management at the subnational level can derail national efforts at reform (Remmer and Wibbels 2000).

Mexico typifies the heterogeneous character of many Latin American states. Although Mexico was still in the process of transition to democracy throughout the 1990s, some areas outpaced national politics by institutionalizing democratic practices in many areas of governance, particularly in states where opposition parties had assumed power (Mizrahi 1995a; Rodriguéz and Ward 1995b). In other areas, authoritarian enclaves remain resistant to change, lagging far behind the national government in terms of enforcing the full rights of citizenship (Bruhn 1997; Fox 1996). The Mexican states thus provide a useful laboratory for a comparative analysis of the impact of democratic reform. Within the parameters established by the national political system, the Mexican states evince substantial variation in levels of electoral competition, as well as the rules of the game shaping incentives and opportunities for democratic contestation. The federal structure allows for comparison of the impact of electoral competition across states and through time while many structural and cultural variables are held constant.

Furthermore, because consecutive reelection is prohibited for all elected offices, Mexico provides a least likely case for testing the consequences of electoral competition. Most accounts of the consequences of elections stress the incentives created by the quest for reelection. Theoretically, elections generate accountability because politicians strive to please their constituents in order to win reelection (Mayhew 1974). In Mexico, the links between electoral competition and accountability are much weaker. Hence, if there are significant changes in representative institutions in Mexico as a result of increased electoral competition, in spite of the prohibition on consecutive reelection, then we should expect to see similar changes in most other contexts.

Mexico is a useful case because of its slow-motion transition. Whereas many complex causal linkages were obscured in the rapid transitions characteristic of Eastern Europe and other parts of Latin America, the causal linkages can be isolated and traced over time in Mexico. Moreover, because Mexico's one-party hegemony has historically coexisted with high levels of participation in the electoral arena (i.e., universal suffrage), the transition to a more democratic political system mainly involved the growth of competition, or, in the vocabulary of Dahl (1971), the shift from a participatory hegemony to a polyarchy. The study of democratization in the Mexican states is thus limited to the study of growing competition, facilitating the process of comparison over time and across political units.

Finally, the study of democratization at the subnational level in Mexico is interesting empirically and theoretically because comparative evidence regarding the relationship between national-level democracy and subnational political institutions and processes remains extremely limited. With a few important exceptions (e.g., Cornelius, Eisenstadt, and Hindley 1999; Fox 1994a; Rodríguez and Ward 1995b; Snyder 2001a), research on Mexican democratization has focused overwhelmingly on politics in the nation's capital, even though many of the most important struggles for democracy have taken place at the state and local levels. The few studies that have focused on subnational politics usually include just one or a very small number of cases, thus making generalization difficult. The neglect of subnational phenomena in the democratization literature represents a significant lacuna that leads to inaccurate interpretations of political conditions and overlooks important trends. Not only is the emphasis on the nation as a unit of analysis largely arbitrary (Lijphart 1975), but also subnational politics is interesting and important in its own right. National-level analyses have overlooked the importance of the interplay between local and national politics. As Mexico's experience with democratization makes clear, local politics can have important consequences for national politics. Moreover, decentralization processes in Latin America and other parts of the globe are enhancing the importance of understanding subnational political processes.

Method of Analysis

Reliance on purely quantitative or qualitative analyses alone may not be able to provide complete answers to many important political questions. Large-N statistical analyses often obscure the important details of complicated processes. Operationalizations may not measure what the researcher intends to measure, and a myriad of biases built into data published by politically motivated governments create problems of validity in statistical research. Still, large-N analysis offers important opportunities to develop theoretical models by testing hypotheses across many cases. On the other hand, in-depth comparative case studies may not allow for high levels of generalization, but they do provide a more textured examination of trends and relationships that can bring to light problems with statistical data.

This book combines both large-N statistical research and detailed small-N comparative analysis to address variations in subnational politics in Mexico. It uses subnational comparisons both as a methodological tool and as a theoretical tool. A broad cross-sectional analysis of the impact of electoral competition on subnational institutional changes across all thirty-one states is combined with in-depth analysis of politics in three central Mexican states: Guanajuato, Hidalgo, and San Luis Potosí. The latter analysis revolves around in-depth field research and over seventy interviews, including forty-two interviews with members of state congresses, archival research, and day-to-day observation of legislative sessions and committee meetings. These data are complemented by a mail survey of members of state congresses from across the country using a survey instrument that draws questions from a survey of national legislators in the former Soviet Union (Colton 1996) as well as surveys and interview research of the U.S. state legislators (e.g., Jewell and Whicker 1994; Thomas 1994). The book also draws upon an original database of governors' career paths in the thirty-one Mexican states and published economic data on state expenditures and revenues.

The three states chosen for in-depth analysis are Guanajuato, Hidalgo, and San Luis Potosí. These states were selected because all have roughly similar structural conditions, yet the patterns of political competition vary widely across the three states. The three states are all situated in the central region of the country, creating commonalities and eliminating the confounding effects of the northern border. The GDP per capita in Guanajuato in 1993 was N$9,864 new pesos, compared to N$9,476 in Hidalgo and N$9,963 in San Luis Potosí (Instituto Nacional de Estadística, Geografía, e Informática [INEGI] 1996, 3), while per capita state GDP varied from

N$6,400 (Oaxaca) to N$34,508 (Campeche) nationally. The median per capita state GDP was N$11,693. In addition, the agricultural sector makes up similar proportions of the three states' economies: 9.81 percent of Guanajuato's GDP, 9.04 percent of Hidalgo's GDP, and 12.77 percent of San Luis Potosí's GDP (INEGI 1996, 52), as compared to a national range of 1.44 percent (Nuevo León) to 25.61 percent (Zacatecas). Agriculture makes up 6.76 percent of the national GDP. Furthermore, all three states are below the national mean for urbanization (Nacional Financiera 1995, 13–15). Finally, all three states lie within one standard deviation of the national mean for measures of industrial production (INEGI 1996, 52), illiteracy (INEGI 1992, 103–7), the proportion of the population that is indigenous (INEGI 1992, 42–55), and the proportion of the employed population that works in the agricultural sector (INEGI 1992, 368–94). Thus none of the three states can be considered a statistical outlier in terms of standard measures of socioeconomic development.

Reflecting a long tradition of opposition strength, Guanajuato became the second state in the country to be ruled by a governor from an opposition party. The opposition National Action Party (PAN) took over the governor's seat in a negotiated transition in 1991 and won a plurality in the state congress in 1997. Hidalgo, on the other hand, is a relatively noncompetitive state. The ruling PRI won over 95 percent of the vote in all state and local elections in Hidalgo until the mid-1980s (Vargas González 1998). As late as 1986, the PAN failed to run a candidate for governor in the state (Gutiérrez Mejía and Vargas González 1994). In the gubernatorial elections of 1992 the PRI won 85 percent of the vote, while both of the major opposition parties garnered less than 5 percent each (Banamex 1996). By 1999, the gubernatorial elections were more competitive, with the PRI taking only 53 percent of the total vote. Nonetheless, the PRI maintained a 21-point advantage over the runner-up PAN candidate, who garnered 32 percent of the vote (SourceMex, Feb. 24, 1999).

The third state, San Luis Potosí, falls between these extremes of competitiveness. While the electoral arena is relatively contested, especially in the capital city, the PRI has thus far maintained control of both the governorship and the legislature. In 1958 the city of San Luis Potosí elected the first opposition mayor in a state capital. In 1991 the results of the highly competitive elections for governor were contested and resulted in a political crisis in which the governor-elect was forced to resign (Bezdek 1995; Pansters 1996). The PRI's candidate for governor in 1997 won just under 46 percent of the vote (see figure 1.1 for a map of the cases selected).

In sum, the research taps multiple streams of evidence and nests case studies of three states within a broader comparative framework that tests

Figure 1.1.   Cases Selected for In-Depth Analysis

the hypotheses across all thirty-one of the Mexican states. This research design combines systematic quantitative data with richly textured qualitative analysis to transcend the limitations of each technique. Such a combination arguably represents one of the most promising methods for social science research (Coppedge 1999; King et al. 1994; Rogowski 1995; Tarrow 1995). Empirically, this book introduces new types of data that have not previously been employed in studies of subnational politics in Mexico. Too often researchers choose questions based on the availability of easily accessible data, thereby leaving important questions unanswered. This book, in contrast, provides extensive new data sources, including three original data sets with observations from across the states of Mexico. These data allow for systematic analysis of political phenomena that previously were dealt with only descriptively.

Democratization in Mexico

The process of democratization in Mexico has been marked by a complex interplay between opposition victories in subnational elections and important democratic advances in the national political arena. Since 1929, elections have been carried out at consistent intervals for legislative and executive positions at the municipal, state, and national levels (with the important exception of the mayor of Mexico City), but the elections were not typically competitive. Electoral fraud was pervasive, and the rights and opportunities of opposition parties were severely circumscribed. As a result, from the revolution until the year 2000 the ruling PRI and its predecessors won every presidential election. Until 1988 the PRI had only ever lost one senate seat to an opposition party. The PRI also managed to maintain a two-thirds "supermajority" in the national chamber of deputies until 1988, enabling it to pass constitutional reforms without consulting other parties. Furthermore, the PRI won every gubernatorial election in the country until 1989.

The existence of regularly scheduled elections in Mexico, even though they were often not free and fair, had important consequences for the process of democratization. The struggle for democracy in Mexico revolved around elections. The democratization process took the form of constant iterations of electoral fraud, opposition protest, and electoral reform. As elections became more competitive, fraud became more necessary, and opposition forces increased their capacity to monitor elections, organize disruptive protests, and push for further reform of electoral law, bringing Mexico ever closer to conducting more meaningful elections. To the extent that negotiation between the opposition and government revolved around reforming laws and providing more equitable legal treatment of opposition parties and voters (rather than promoting clientelistic payoffs to opposition organizations), the conflict ultimately brought greater agreement upon a set of rules for the selection of leaders. The rule of law in Mexico has been strengthened as rules and institutions have replaced fraud and protest as a means of selecting leaders.

Meaningful electoral competition began to emerge first at the municipal level. While there were a handful of opposition successes before 1980 (Meyer 1995), the most important advances for opposition forces at the municipal level took place during the early 1980s (Cornelius 1987; Rodríguez and Ward 1995ba). At the national level the presidential elections of 1988 marked a watershed in the process of democratization. After a split within the ruling PRI, Cuauhtémoc Cárdenas, the former governor of Michoacán and son of the popular President Lázaro Cárdenas, ran against the PRI's official candidate Carlos Salinas de Gortari, a technocrat who had never held an elected office. After elections marred by irregularities, the PRI claimed victory for its candidate but lost much of its popular support and legitimacy. The long-ruling party also lost its "supermajority" in the national chamber of deputies, thereby forcing it to compromise with other political forces in order to reform the constitution. In response to the growing political instability following the elections of 1988, the PRI initiated a number of far-reaching electoral reforms to liberalize the electoral system (Molinar Horcasitas 1991, 1996).

The elections of 1988 had other democratizing consequences as well. Many claim that the opposition party PAN was able to win the gubernatorial elections in the state of Baja California and actually take control of the governor's office as a direct result of the PRI's legislative losses in 1988. Because the PRI was unable to reform the constitution without the support of another party, some have argued that it negotiated with the PAN to allow the opposition party victory to stand in Baja California in exchange for the PAN's legislative support (Lujambio 1998, 174). Hence, in response to the upsurge of opposition strength from the municipal level, combined with increased opposition party leverage at the national level, competitive politics began to take hold in a number of state governments in the early 1990s (Crespo 1995). By 1995 the PAN controlled governorships in Baja California, Chihuahua, Guanajuato, and Jalisco.

The midterm elections of 1997 marked another important milestone in the process of democratization. Cuauhtémoc Cárdenas, candidate for the opposition Party of the Democratic Revolution (PRD), won the first-ever elections for the mayor of Mexico City. Also in 1997, the PRI lost its majority in the national chamber of deputies for the first time since the party's founding. As a result, a diverse opposition coalition took control of the chamber of deputies, and the legislative branch began to exert real influence on the political process. By the year 2000, an opposition party had governed eleven of the thirty-one states, along with the Federal District, and, most important, the PAN's candidate Vicente Fox had won the presidential elections. Figure 1.2 provides a map of the relative levels of electoral competition across the states in the 1985 and 1997 federal legislative elections. The level of electoral competitiveness is measured by the PRI's margin of victory over the runner-up party. The lighter states are the more electorally competitive. Both maps show the tremendous diversity in patterns of electoral competition across the states. The most competitive states tend to be those along the northern border, such as Baja California and Chihuahua, as well as a few states in the central western area, especially Jalisco and Guanajuato. The least competitive states are concentrated in the southeastern part of the country. As the maps show, the PRI's margin of victory in federal deputy elections dropped dramatically from 1985 to 1997. In 1985 the PRI won elections in twenty-three states with a margin of victory of at least 50 percent. No opposition party won

Figure 1.2.   Change in Electoral Competition: The PRI's Margin of Victory in 1985 and 1997

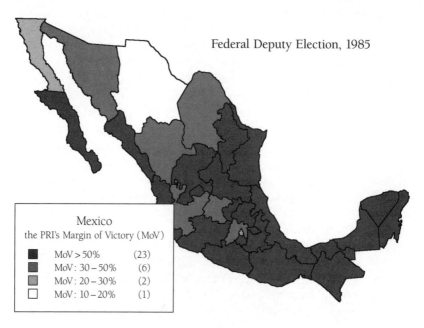

Federal Deputy Election, 1985

Mexico
the PRI's Margin of Victory (MoV)

■ MoV > 50%   (23)
■ MoV: 30 – 50%   (6)
■ MoV: 20 – 30%   (2)
□ MoV: 10 – 20%   (1)

Federal Deputy Election, 1997

Mexico
the PRI's Margin of Victory (MoV)

■ MoV: 20 – 30%   (7)
■ MoV: 10 – 20%   (10)
■ MoV: 5 – 10%   (3)
■ MoV < 5%   (3)
□ PRI < Opposition (9)

a majority of the votes in any state, and the PRI's margin of victory dipped below 20 percent only in Chihuahua, where the PRI won the federal deputy elections in 1985 with a 15 percent margin of victory. By 1997, the PRI enjoyed a margin of victory of over 20 percent in only seven states. Opposition parties won a higher percentage of the vote than the PRI in nine states. Clearly, by 1997 elections throughout Mexico were much more competitive than they had been a decade earlier.

At the same time that competitive politics was making important advances across the country, entrenched authoritarian elites in states such as Chiapas, Guerrero, and Tabasco maintained despotic control over state and local politics (Cornelius 1999; Eisenstadt 1999; Fox 1994b; Snyder 1999b). This regional disparity in the process of democratization has generated an enduring debate in the Mexican literature over the significance of subnational politics for national trends. Many scholars see local opposition victories as evidence of Mexico's progress toward greater democracy (Aziz Nassif 1994, 1996b; Guillén López 1993; Meyer 1994; Mizrahi 1995b). Others suggest that local opposition victories provide opportunities for democratic reformers to gain experience and recognition before competing for more important positions (Fox 1994b). Some have even argued that local electoral struggles have served not only to democratize local politics but also to reform national politics (Calvillo Unna 1999; Chand 2001). More pessimistic accounts stress the ability of leaders from subnational authoritarian enclaves to derail national efforts at political reform (Cornelius 1999).

In contrast to the accounts that highlight the importance of subnational politics, Bruhn (1999) suggests that national forces, not local politics, shape the process of democratization. Similarly, Vanderbush (1999) argues that opposition party control over state and local governments is largely irrelevant because power is highly concentrated at the national level and municipal and state leaders do not have sufficient authority to make meaningful changes in the political system. Crespo (1995) contends that local opposition victories actually help the PRI maintain hegemonic power by keeping the opposition at the table and working within the PRI-controlled political system. Until the opposition takes control of the presidency, these observers maintained, the PRI will continue to make all important political and economic decisions, and any opposition victories will remain merely window dressing (Bruhn 1999; Espinoza Valle 1999). Thus, these observers seem to suggest that the only important event in Mexico's transition to democracy was the election of Vicente Fox to the presidency in 2000.

This book builds upon the premise that subnational politics does have significant consequences for the national political process. Subnational politics influences national politics in Mexico in three important ways. First, municipal victories by democratic reformers can serve as springboards to state and national offices. Former opposition mayors such as Ernesto Ruffo Apel, Francisco Barrio Terrazas, and Carlos Medina Plascencia took advantage of their success at the municipal level to become governors. Similarly, Vicente Fox Quesada built upon his popularity as governor to launch a successful campaign for the presidency. Second, changes in voting behavior and partisan identification in local elections tend to carry over to national elections. Survey data suggest that once voters switch over to opposition parties in municipal elections, they are also likely to vote for opposition parties in national elections. Thus, opposition victories for municipal presidents are likely to evolve into opposition victories for national deputies, and opposition victories for governors are likely to lead to opposition victories for senators. Moreover, survey research has demonstrated that uncertainty plays an important role in Mexican voting behavior (Cinta 1999; Poiré 1999). The PRI was able to continue winning elections for many years because Mexican voters were risk averse and feared the uncertainty of life under another party. But, as Magaloni (1999) points out, voter uncertainty can be reduced by experience with opposition parties in local government. Thus, as opposition parties gain experience in state and local governance, voters are less likely to fear the uncertainty of opposition rule and more likely to vote for opposition parties. Finally, subnational politics increasingly influences national politics because the decentralization of power from the federal government to state governments is gradually increasing the policy-making authority of subnational leaders. Subnational politicians are spending an increasing proportion of total public revenues. Governors, in particular, became much more influential during the late 1990s as a result of the 1990 party convention and Zedillo's "New Federalism" (Langston 2001; Rodríguez 1997). The fact that all of the major contenders for the presidency in the 2000 elections had formerly served as governors reinforces the notion that governors have taken on a new role in the Mexican political system.

In short, the process of democratization has developed slowly and erratically since the early 1980s. Opposition victories at the subnational level have buttressed opposition movements at the national level, and national events have transformed the subnational political arena, which has been increasingly characterized by interparty competition. Together these processes have dramatically changed the political geography of Mexico. While the purpose of this book is to analyze the consequences of Mexico's transition to multiparty elections, and many scholars already have devoted much energy to explaining the causes of democratization, it is nevertheless worth summarizing some of the main causes of Mexico's transition.

In addition to the interplay between subnational and national forces described above, economic factors, international pressures, and a more active civil society contributed to democratization.

Mexico's former ruling party, the PRI, was able to dominate elections up until the 1980s to a large extent because of the tremendous economic growth and stability the party had provided throughout much of the twentieth century. The economic stability and growth resulted in a growing middle class and a better-educated and more urban population. After the 1982 economic collapse, the PRI could no longer provide economic stability and growth, and the urban, educated, middle-class sectors of society began to look for alternatives, thus establishing the foundations of the many opposition groups and democratizing movements. The currency crisis of 1994 and the economic problems that followed in its wake further consolidated public opinion against the PRI and confirmed in the minds of the public that the PRI was no longer able to deliver economic security. Thus, the civic groups and opposition movements established in the 1980s were strengthened by increasing levels of support in the aftermath of the 1994 crisis. As Denise Dresser (1996) writes, "Whereas in the past Mexicans were offered economic growth instead of democracy, now the reverse may be true. In order to compensate the population for dramatic declines in income provoked by the devaluation, the government has promised greater political opening" (159). The voting behavior literature focuses on the economic changes to explain how the PRI lost control of elections. The PRI was able to survive one economic crisis because the voters feared the uncertainty of opposition rule, but after two economic crises, the retrospective weight of many years of economic stability had worn off after more than a decade of economic crisis, and voters were willing to take their chances with something new (Magaloni 1999).

The trend toward economic liberalization also helped to break down the PRI's monopoly of power. First, through privatization and market reforms, the PRI lost access to many economic resources that had provided important sources of patronage. The restructuring of the economy weakened sectors that had been loyal to the PRI, notably organized labor, and strengthened new economic sectors that were not well organized by the ruling party, especially the export-processing industries, or *maquiladoras*. The coalitional bargain between capital and labor fell apart as the government could no longer maintain jobs and wages for organized workers and local industrialists went bankrupt in the face of international competition and decreasing subsidies (Middlebrook 1995). New economic power centers developed in regions where internationally competitive industries were located. These new industries owed their success to the market, not government subsidies and protection, and therefore were less loyal to the ruling party.

President Salinas's drive to form the North American Free Trade Agreement (NAFTA) increased international scrutiny of the Mexican political system. Opposition forces became adept in appealing to the international media to gain leverage over the ruling party. The reversals in the gubernatorial elections of 1991 in Guanajuato and San Luis Potosí, for example, have frequently been attributed to international pressure on President Salinas to clean up the electoral process before NAFTA could pass the U.S. Congress.

Opposition parties, namely the PAN and the PRD, took advantage of these political opportunities to forge new relations with the strengthened civil society and emboldened Catholic Church to develop institutional foundations and establish political support (Bruhn 1997; Chand 2001). Opposition parties began to compete successfully in some municipal elections in the early 1980s and at the state level in the 1990s. They used these victories to pressure the national government to reform electoral laws and institutions to even the playing field for opposition parties. All of these complex causal processes came together in the 1990s to forge Mexico's democratization.

Overview of the Book

Chapter 2 presents the theoretical framework that informs the research project. Drawing together insights from classic democratic theory (e.g., Black 1958; Dahl 1971; Downs 1957; Key 1949; Schattschneider 1942; Schumpeter 1942), the new institutionalist literature (e.g., Ames 1987; Carey 1996; Cox 1990; Geddes 1994; Jones 1995; Mainwaring and Shugart 1997; North 1990), and the critiques of contemporary Latin American democracy (e.g., O'Donnell 1994, 1996, 1998; Oxhorn and Ducatenzeiler 1998; Roberts 1998; Veltmeyer and Petras 2000), the chapter establishes the theoretical foundations for linking increased electoral competition and institutional change. I argue that electoral competition changes the incentives facing legislators and executives in ways that strengthen and professionalize legislative bodies and establish the basis for a more egalitarian relationship between the legislature and the executive. I further argue that competition creates incentives for elected politicians to demand greater decision-making authority from centralized authoritarian bureaucracies. Finally, I contend that competition increases the importance of electability and therefore fundamentally alters the motivations underlying the selection of candidates for elected offices.

Drawing upon in-depth case studies of three states, chapter 3 focuses on institutional changes within the state legislatures. Chapter 4 uses statistical models with data from all thirty-one states to test the hypotheses generated in chapter 3. Both the qualitative and the quantitative analyses find that states with higher levels of electoral competition have stronger and more autonomous legislatures and that the pattern of legislative change through time follows shifts in the level of electoral competition. The evidence consists of original interview and survey data collected during 1998, along with budget data on legislative expenditures.

Chapter 5 presents evidence that increasing competition alters patterns of political recruitment and the selection of candidates. Electoral competition creates incentives for the establishment of a more participatory system of candidate selection because parties are forced to choose candidates that appeal to the electorate. As a result, parties in competitive states are more likely to select candidates through open primary contests and to favor candidates with strong ties to the local community. The changes in the formal processes of candidate selection began at the local level and reflect the broader process of change unleashed by electoral competition. Using an original data set of the career paths of all governors from all the Mexican states over twenty years, this chapter demonstrates that states with competitive elections are more likely to elect governors with strong local interests instead of party loyalists sent in by the central government from Mexico City. This evidence emphasizes the new incentives for selecting more electorally appealing candidates.

Chapter 6 examines the policy implications of competition by examining how increasing electoral competition generates new incentives for elected politicians to augment their control over resources. Data on state expenditures and revenues from all of the thirty-one states demonstrate that states with more electoral competition have gained greater control over government resources. Competitive states are more likely to have control over a greater percentage of the spending in their states and to collect a higher percentage of their revenues locally, rather than depending on bureaucratic transfers from the federal government.

The conclusion explores the broader comparative significance of the Mexican experience. For the last several decades, there has been a tendency for Mexican politics to be studied in isolation from broader comparative trends and theoretical concerns. Research has been dominated by claims of Mexican exceptionalism that stress the unique experience of one-party rule. Arguably, much has been lost by this tendency. Comparative treatments of Mexico have been complicated because, until recently, political trends in Mexico have diverged substantially from other major countries in Latin America. The simultaneous process of democratization and neoliberal reform that has been taking place across Latin America during the past two decades, however, provides new opportunities to include Mexico in the broader debates of comparative politics. This book attempts to reintroduce Mexico into the broader debate over democracy in the contemporary developing world. In contrast to more traditional studies of Mexican politics, the analysis presented here is explicitly comparative and draws heavily from the insights of scholars working in a wide range of international settings. Not only can Mexico be better understood from a comparative perspective, but the Mexican case also makes it possible to address issues that have remained largely unanswered in the broader literature on democratization.

CHAPTER TWO

The Consequences
of Electoral Competition

Theoretical Perspectives

Scholars and citizens of developing and emerging market countries have expressed increasing disappointment with the results of recent democratic transitions. Their questions about the meaning and significance of democratic institutions have created a paradox for democratic theory. Classic theories of democracy have stressed the centrality of elections for generating accountability of leaders to their constituents (Black 1958; Dahl 1971; Downs 1957; Mayhew 1974; Schattschneider 1942; Schlesinger 1991; Schumpeter 1942). Research on new democracies, however, has emphasized the continuity between the old authoritarian and the new democratic governments and suggests that electoral competition has not significantly improved accountability and representation (Burawoy and Krotov 1993; Ducatenzeiler and Oxhorn 1994; Hagopian 1996; Méndez, O'Donnell, and Pinheiro 1999; O'Donnell 1993, 1994; Oxhorn and Ducatenzeiler 1998; Przeworski et al. 1999; Stokes 1997; Tarkowski 1990; Veltmeyer and Petras 2000).

What are the consequences of democratization? Does electoral competition influence the way representative institutions function? Can electoral competition be relied upon to engender meaningful representation and public policies that reflect the interests of the majority of citizens? Or, as much recent research on Latin American democracy suggests, do economic structures, authoritarian political cultures, and institutional frailties inhibit the ability of electoral competition to generate more accountable patterns of policy making?

The following analysis addresses these important questions by examining the impact of electoral competition on the functioning of representative institutions. In contrast to the research on contemporary democracies that has generated an enormous collection of new regime subtypes to describe democracies and emphasize missing components (see Collier and Levitsky 1997; Schneider 1995), this research analyzes the quality of democracy by disaggregating the concept of democracy and assessing the relationship between its procedural characteristics and its other institutional and substantive dimensions. Thus, I focus on electoral competition as a key component of democracy and analyze how increasing electoral competition influences other important aspects of democratic rule.

Dahl's (1971) conception of polyarchy provides a useful definition of democracy by outlining its minimal procedural requirements. The main elements of Dahl's procedural definition are contestation and participation. The first dimension of Dahl's polyarchy, participation or near-universal suffrage, is found in most recently democratized nations. The second dimension is contestation (also referred to as liberalization), which he defines as "the extent of permissible opposition, public contestation, or political competition" (4). While contestation may take many forms, this analysis will focus on electoral competition and its consequences, emphasizing the impact of competition on the actors, rules, and outcomes of the political game.

A focus on electoral competition shifts theory away from state-centered approaches and brings society back in by placing the electorate at the center of analysis. Electoral competition is the aggregation of individual voters' preferences. Votes for opposition parties are expressions of contestation against the current government. While contestation can take many forms, election results provide an easily quantifiable measure of contestation that can be used to make comparisons across time and space. Moreover, electoral competition is theoretically central to democratic accountability.

This research examines the long-term distribution of power across political institutions and emphasizes the role of representative institutions in mediating the relationship between electoral competition and public policy. The research on the quality of democracy in Latin America has attributed the lack of accountability in the new democracies to the concentration of power in the hands of the national executive and the related weakness of representative institutions (O'Donnell 1994, 1996; Schedler, Diamond, and Plattner 1999). This book explicitly addresses this concern by analyzing the ways in which electoral competition strengthens institutions autonomous from the national executive, thereby generating new constraints on executive power.

Building upon the conclusions of the new institutionalist literature that highlight the importance of institutions in regulating political outcomes, I attempt to bridge the theoretical divide that separates democratic theorists who stress the role of electoral competition in generating policy accountability and recent critiques of the quality of democracy in the contemporary developing world. The analysis emphasizes the role of electoral competition in generating institutional changes that alter the strategic calculus of political actors, the balance of power between contending forces, and the arena in which political decisions are made. This focus on institutional change moves beyond most of the new institutionalist literature in as much as the latter has focused mainly on the effects of institutional design, seeking to explain how varying institutional arrangements influence political outcomes. Thus, institutions are analyzed as relatively fixed constraints on political activity. Yet in most political systems, institutions are not constant but rather are being reformed on a continual basis. Therefore, my research privileges the analysis of institutional change and explores the ways in which shifting political rules alter political outcomes.

The central argument is that a shift from noncompetitive politics to competitive electoral politics creates new incentives and opportunities for political leaders that lead to long-term institutional changes. In particular, electoral competition redistributes power from executives to legislatures, from unaccountable bureaucracies to elected officials, and from party leaders to electorates, thereby creating institutionalized opportunities for the opposition to be represented and to monitor the government in order to check the power of the executive. By focusing on how electoral competition can modify the rules of the game, this analysis emphasizes the influence of institutions such as legislatures, candidate selection processes, and decision-making arenas on the relationship between elections and policy accountability. The central conclusion of the book is that increasing electoral competition strengthens representative institutions in ways that decentralize power away from the national executive and improve the separation of powers and therefore has significant consequences for accountability and the rule of law. In this chapter, I begin by reviewing competing theoretical accounts of the consequences of competitive elections and then proceed to develop an argument about the ways in which increasing electoral competition strengthens representative institutions.

What Are the Consequences of Electoral Competition? Some Competing Views

Existing research provides contending visions of the consequences of electoral competition. Classic theorizing and economic theories of voting suggest that free and fair elections are tantamount to democracy and inevitably enforce accountability and responsiveness of leaders to the electorate. Structural and political culture theories, in contrast, contend that the mere existence of free and fair elections does not guarantee responsive governance; rather, economic structures or political attitudes can create long-term obstacles to the effective consolidation of democracy.

Elections are thought to improve representation in two ways. First, through elections, citizens can promote their policy preferences by endorsing policy mandates. Second, elections allow voters to punish leaders and parties for abandoning campaign promises by drawing on retrospective assessments of performance. Empirical research in the United States has raised questions about both lines of analysis, suggesting that elections cannot enforce accountability because voters are poorly informed (Campbell et al. 1960; Converse 1964). Others have noted that multidimensional policy spaces and separation of powers make elections blunt instruments for expressing policy preferences or assigning responsibility for policy failures (e.g., Linz and Stepan 1996; Stokes 2001). In the developing world, comparative research suggests that the ability of institutionalized competition to effect change is constrained by structural conditions such as economic inequalities that limit the effectiveness of representation (Huber et al. 1997; Oxhorn and Ducatenzeiler 1998; Roberts 1998), an undemocratic political culture (Almond and Verba 1963; Wiarda 1973), a lack of social capital (de Tocqueville 1984; Putnam 1993), and weak representative institutions (O'Donnell 1996) that dilute the overall quality of democratic governance. In the following analysis I contrast the divergent expectations of structural, political culture, social capital, and institutional theories regarding the consequences of elections. I then draw on an institutionalist framework to develop an argument about the consequences of electoral competition.

Theorists dating back to James Madison have argued that elections are the essence of democracy. Madison wrote in the *Federalist Papers,* "As it is essential to liberty that the government in general should have a common interest with the people, so it is particularly essential that the branch of it under consideration [the House of Representatives] should have an immediate dependence on, and an intimate sympathy with, the people. Frequent elections are unquestionably the only policy by which this dependence and sympathy can be effectually secured" (Rossiter 1961, 327).

Madison is not alone in his contention that elections generate leadership accountability to constituents.

For theorists drawing on an economic theory of democracy (e.g., Downs 1957; Mayhew 1974; Schattschneider 1942; Schlesinger 1991; Schumpeter 1942), elections clearly have significant consequences. Market-like competition for political office through elections, they argue, will lead to responsive and accountable politicians.[1] Just as inefficient firms are forced out of the market by economic competition, unresponsive politicians are forced out of politics by electoral competition. This view is perhaps stated most succinctly by Joseph Schlesinger (1991): "Frequent elections and, today, constant polling provide nearly continuous tests of the appeal of candidates, office holders, and their policies. A party that does not respond to the electoral market will, by definition, lose to parties that do and over the long run will find itself supplanted by responsive parties" (15). Thus, electoral competition is the essence of democracy, and elections are the central mechanism for translating public opinion into policy outputs.

Other classic accounts consider electoral competition to be virtually synonymous with democracy. Shumpeter (1942) argues that "the democratic method is that institutional arrangement for arriving at political decisions in which individuals acquire the power to decide by means of a competitive struggle for the people's vote" (269). In other words, democracy is a process of selecting leaders. Schumpeter conceives of political competition in much the same way that economists think of economic competition. Economists see the benefits associated with capitalism not as preconditions for fair economic competition but rather as the result of economic competition. Similarly, Schumpeter views electoral competition as the motor of democratic freedoms: "If, on principle at least, everyone is free to compete for political leadership by presenting himself to the electorate, this will in most cases though not in all mean a considerable amount of freedom of discussion *for all*. In particular it will normally mean a considerable amount of freedom of the press" (271–72). Schattschneider (1942) similarly sees the extension of suffrage as a result of elite competition.

Later research points out that certain preconditions are in fact necessary for everyone to be able to compete freely for political leadership. Dahl (1971) includes additional requirements beyond competition for leadership positions to arrive at a workable definition of democracy. In particular, Dahl considers near-universal suffrage and basic political liberties such as freedom of the press and association as preconditions for democracy rather than outcomes of the competitive process. Without these guarantees, it is easy to stage "demonstration elections" that are devoid of any real meaning (Herman and Brodhead 1984).

According to spatial theories of voting (e.g., Black 1958; Downs 1957), voters choose from candidates along a one-dimensional ideological continuum and vote for candidates closest to their own policy preferences. Vote-maximizing candidates (or parties) in turn generate platforms to appeal to voters. In the words of Downs (1957), "Parties formulate policies in order to win elections rather than win elections in order to formulate policy" (28). Given these sets of incentives, party platforms and ultimately government policy decisions converge at the preferences of the median voter. And, in a competitive environment, governments will always formulate policies that are supported by the majority of the voters. If they do not, the opposition will win the next election with a platform that is supported by the majority of voters.[2] From this perspective, electoral competition functions like market competition to generate policy outputs preferred by the majority. Hence, elections clearly enforce governmental accountability.[3]

Prominent studies of representation in the United States are built upon the assumption that politicians and parties are responsive to citizens' demands because they fear electoral defeat. For example, Mayhew's (1974) contention that members of Congress are "single-minded seekers of reelection" focuses attention on the role of elections in generating accountability. Almost by definition, Mayhew's model affirms that "the reelection quest establishes an accountability relationship with an electorate" (6). Likewise, Cain, Ferejohn, and Fiorina (1987) state, "If representatives wish to remain representatives, their behavior will be calculated to please constituents" (3).

Erikson et al. (1993) similarly argue that electoral competition is an effective instrument for translating public opinion into public policy.[4] In contrast to the expectations of Downs, however, Erikson et al. acknowledge that policy may not coincide with public opinion in every specific instance. Rather, they find that the overall ideological tenor of a state's policy reflects the general ideological tilt of the state's electorate.

The main weakness of the economic theories of voting is their lack of structural and institutional context. In these models individual choices are constrained by other variables, and structures and institutions are rarely taken seriously. When research focuses on a single case study, as does most of the literature on elections and representation in the United States, institutions and structures are constant and therefore often fall out of the analysis unnoticed. Even in sophisticated comparative studies of the U.S. states such as Erikson et al. (1993), institutions and structures tend to be neglected because variation among the states is relatively minor compared with international variation. When these theories are considered outside of the U.S. context, the importance of other variables becomes apparent. These weaknesses highlight the need for rigorous comparative analysis that includes more diverse institutions and structures.

Scholars of democracy in Latin America have rightly been wary of "electoralism"—the mistaken idea that holding elections is equivalent to democracy (Dresser 1996; Herman and Brodhead 1984; Karl 1986). Clearly, democracy is more than simply carrying out regularly scheduled elections. The mere existence of elections does not ensure that those elections are free and fair or that the outcomes reflect the opinion of the majority. Moreover, elections can enforce accountability only at specific intervals, not continuously. Thus, effective democratic accountability requires continuous checks to curb abuse of power by elected leaders. Scholars have become intensely interested in the quality of democracy in Latin America, focusing on issues of accountability and representation (Przeworski et al. 1999). Many studies have concluded that elections alone are not enough to enforce accountability (Schedler et al. 1999; Stokes 2001); rather, other democratic institutions are vital to check the power of the executive and ensure accountability between elections (O'Donnell 1998).

In the 1970s neo-Marxist structural theory and its major offshoot, dependency theory, stressed the constraints that late dependent industrialization placed on the development of democratic political systems in Latin America and other developing regions (Cardoso and Faletto 1979; Gunder Frank 1969). Many dependency theorists believed that democracy was simply impossible in countries constrained by external dependency, but then, as dependent countries democratized in the 1980s and 1990s, structural thinking shifted. More recent structural analyses argue that while procedural democracy in the form of elections may be possible, electoral competition may not alter political outcomes in developing countries because domestic policy choices are too severely limited by global economic conditions that increase inequality and weaken the political clout of subordinate classes (Huber et al. 1997; Joseph 1999; Oxhorn and Ducatenzeiler 1998; Weffort 1998). As Roberts (1998) concludes, "There is a basic incongruence between the forms of political agency required for a project of deepening democracy and the structural and institutional environment of contemporary Latin America" (5).

Building on the insights of the structural approaches, research on the quality of democracy in Latin America highlights the failure of elections to generate accountability and improve representation (Fatton 1999; Veltmeyer and Petras 2000; von Mettenheim and Malloy 1998). Some observers have suggested that the recent transitions to democracy have not generated new patterns of policy formation or greater government responsiveness to citizens' concerns (Conaghan et al. 1990). Judicial systems have been incapable and unwilling to apply the law fairly and equally to all citizens (Méndez et al. 1999). Human rights abuses and police brutality persist (Pinheiro 1999). Furthermore, democracy has not yet successfully addressed the entrenched problems of poverty and inequality in Latin America (Chalmers et al. 1997; Petras and Leiva 1994; Tokman and O'Donnell 1998). Bait-and-switch policies among many leaders demonstrate that electoral competition alone is not sufficient to enforce policy mandates (Stokes 1997, 1999, 2001). Stokes (2001), in fact, argues that policy switches are *more* likely after highly competitive elections. In sum, significant entrenched problems persist in Latin America despite a decade of transitions from authoritarian rule.

These and related sets of conclusions about the quality of democracy in Latin America contradict the central expectations of classic democratic theorizing. The negative assessments of contemporary Latin American democracy suggest that competitive electoral processes are ineffective in generating accountable and participatory policy-making procedures due to structural obstacles. The structural theories, however, may be overly pessimistic and may overlook important variations across time and space. They also pay very little attention to the role of institutional variation in shaping the relationship between elections and policy outputs.

Political culture theory is also pessimistic about the prospects for meaningful democracy in Latin America. By emphasizing the importance of certain attitudes, especially interpersonal trust and civic engagement, rather than institutions, such as competitive elections, for successful democratic outcomes, cultural approaches overlook the dynamic consequences of institutional change. Since attitudes and cultural norms develop over long periods of time and are resistant to change, political culture theory provides little hope that authoritarian countries can democratize in a meaningful way in the short term. According to political culture theory, institutional change alone is unlikely to alter behavior because cultural factors condition how individuals respond to institutions (Almond and Verba 1963).[5]

Building on Alexis de Tocqueville's (1984) classic critique of American democracy and famous hypothesis that the "art of association" preserves common liberties, much of the recent research on political culture employs the concept of social capital (Coleman 1990; Putnam 1993). Putnam (1993) defines social capital as the stock of trust, norms of reciprocity, and networks of civic engagement in a community (167). He stresses the importance of social capital for making democracy work because, without trust, pervasive collective action dilemmas inhibit cooperation. A tradition of civic engagement and cooperation, Putnam contends, is necessary for effective institutional performance. Hence, democratic institutions require strong social capital to survive and function effectively.

Just as structural theories have difficulty explaining change, so too do political culture theories. If cultural norms are enduring and take generations, if not centuries, to change, culture cannot account for swift regime changes. The democratization of many developing countries in the 1980s and especially the extremely rapid disintegration of the communist regimes of the former Soviet Union and Eastern Europe seem inconsistent with the expectations of a political culture approach.

Structural, political culture, and social capital theories establish a limited basis for expecting major changes in political recruitment, decision-making processes, or policy outcomes in response to increasing electoral competition. The economic models of voting provide an overly optimistic and naïve account of how elections translate public opinion into policy. Institutional approaches, on the other hand, not only suggest that the growth of electoral competition will generate major changes in the political game but also are realistic about the obstacles in achieving greater accountability.

The burgeoning body of research in the "new institutionalist" tradition has persuasively demonstrated that institutions influence political outcomes in a myriad of ways and play a mediating role in the relationship between elections and policy (Ames 1987; Carey 1996; Cox 1990; Geddes 1994; Jones 1995; Linz and Stepan 1996; Mainwaring and Shugart 1997; North 1990). According to the institutional perspective, electoral competition is important in determining policy outputs, but the translation of popular demands into public policy is much more complicated than a simple Downsian model suggests. Effective accountability relies on the combination of both electoral competition and representative institutions to organize politics.

Institutional research demonstrates that individual votes are translated through an endless number of institutions before they are transformed into public policies. Electoral codes transform individual votes into electoral outcomes by determining how individual votes will be aggregated and counted. Proportional representation systems transform votes into leaders very differently than winner-take-all electoral systems (Lijphart 1984). Constitutional rules determine who has the legal right to make decisions (Sartori 1997). In a unitary system, all policy-making power belongs to the central government, whereas in a federal system, local governments may have a greater role in determining policy (Riker 1964). Other rules establish who can initiate and veto legislation, regulate how legislative debates take place, determine when and how amendments can be added, and define the conditions under which initiatives become law. Ultimately, the bureaucracy may have substantial leverage in determining how to implement the policy (Wood and Waterman 1994). In short, the relationship between electoral competition and policy outputs is mediated by a complex array of institutions.

Institutionalists are optimistic about the possibility of improving democracy. They argue that redesigning institutions can alter political outcomes (Ordeshook 1986; Schofield 1993; Tsebelis 1995). The right combination of electoral rules and constitutional powers can redistribute power from executives to legislatures (Mainwaring and Shugart 1997), strengthen party systems (Mainwaring and Scully 1995), create more autonomous judicial systems (Helmke 1998), and decentralize power to subnational governments (Willis, Garman, and Haggard 1999).

Institutional approaches provide the most useful way to analyze the consequences of electoral competition because they bridge individual and structural accounts of politics. While both the marketlike mechanism of elections and the structural constraints of global capitalism clearly influence the relationship between public opinion and public policy, neither of these approaches offers an adequate account of the consequences of electoral competition because neither takes institutions seriously. In the following sections I draw upon the insights of a wide range of institutional research to develop hypotheses for exploring the consequences of increasing electoral competition.

Institutional theories can be divided into two groups based on how enduring they see institutions as being (Hall and Taylor 1996; Hunter 1997; Koelble 1995). Static models such as historical institutionalism see institutions as largely constant, changing only during critical junctures in a process of punctuated equilibrium (Collier and Collier 1991). Others view institutions as more fluid, developing incrementally in response to changing political conditions and coalitions. From this dynamic perspective, institutions are "sticky" and act as a constraint on choice, but actors can still create and transform institutions to maximize their political influence and fulfill their policy preferences (Easter 1997; Geddes 1994, 1996). I draw upon the static models to demonstrate the vital role of representative institutions in mediating the relationship between elections and policy outputs. I build upon the logic of the dynamic models to understand how changes in the level of electoral competition influence these institutions.

Static Institutions: Representative Institutions and Accountability

Elections clearly matter for a wide array of political outcomes. In this analysis I focus on the ways in which they affect representative institutions, particularly legislatures, candidate selection processes, and subnational governments. The strengthening of these institutions is critical to the consolidation of democracy because representative institutions act as intermediaries between elections and policy outputs and check the power of executives. A growing separation of powers allows for horizontal accountability, which in turn is essential for an effective rule of law. As legislatures, governors, and state governments gain autonomy from the president, this growing separation of power provides important opportunities for greater accountability and rule of law.

Static models of institutional influence have focused on the impact of various clusters of institutions on accountability. In particular, they have emphasized the role of party systems and legislatures as intermediary variables shaping the relationship between elections and public policy. The composition of party systems has long been associated with democratic accountability, and there is an extensive body of research on party systems (e.g., Duverger 1959; Lijphart 1994; Mainwaring and Scully 1995; Sartori 1976), but with the exception of a few classic studies (Key 1949; Lockard 1959), there has been relatively little research focusing on the differences between competitive and noncompetitive party systems. Patterns of political recruitment determine who makes policy and thus who ultimately influences the types of policies made (Camp 1995c; Schlesinger 1991). Subnational governments, sometimes referred to as the "fourth branch of government," can also act as a brake on executive power, thus enforcing greater horizontal accountability (Wright 1978).

V. O. Key's (1949) classic study of southern politics in the United States emphasizes the obstacles to accountability in noncompetitive contexts and argues that effective accountability is more likely in a two-party system in which two well-organized groups of politicians constitute the "ins" and the "outs." Intraparty competition, he argues, does not generate accountability as effectively as interparty competition. According to Key, it is not necessary that the two groups have distinguishable party platforms as long as enduring groups can be held responsible for the acts of their members from one election to another. An organized group of "outs" serves to monitor and publicize the actions of the "ins," thus increasing transparency and accountability in government.[6]

Similarly, Lockard (1959) argues that multifactional one-party systems result in confusing and obscure politics that allow powerful interests to control the political process, whereas two-party systems tend to be more rational and responsible. Focusing on six states in New England, Lockard assesses the role of interparty competition in generating more responsive governance. He shows that business bears a greater proportion of the tax burden, government services for the less privileged are more generous, and legislative coalitions are more capable of overcoming minority-empowering malapportionment in competitive two-party states.[7]

Coppedge (1993) demonstrates how interparty competition changes the balance of power between patrons and clients. Comparing the competitive party system of Venezuela with the noncompetitive party system in Mexico, Coppedge finds that in Venezuela there is much less repression of labor unions and a more respectful relationship between local bosses and their clients. Coppedge argues that competition democratizes patron-client relations because clients in a competitive environment can turn to other patrons linked to different parties if their demands are not being met. Moreover, party organizations are eager to uncover examples of abuse by competing party bosses in order to enhance their own support. In the words of Coppedge (1993), "*Caciques* who have to compete use more carrots than sticks, while a broker who is the only game in town can operate with impunity" (264). Competition in rural communities and poor urban neighborhoods accounts for the relative lack of violence in patron-client relations in Venezuela as compared to Mexico.

Institutionalists have pointed to the importance of legislatures in translating public opinion into public policy. Looking at variations within the United States, Carmines (1974) examined the influence of legislatures as intermediary variables in the relationship between interparty competition and policy. Carmines provides evidence that the relationship between competition and generous social policies is more pronounced in states that have strong and effective legislatures than in states with weak legislatures.

Comparative research on the quality of democracy has also stressed the importance of strong legislatures for meaningful accountability. The unconstrained power of national executives has been widely viewed as the primary cause of the lack of accountability in the new democracies of the developing world (O'Donnell 1994; Oxhorn 1998; von Mettenheim and Malloy 1998). Conaghan et al. (1990) claim that weak legislatures and powerful executives allowed unpopular economic policies to be implemented in the Andean democracies without the support of the electorate. Much of the political economy literature similarly points to the role of unconstrained executives in pushing through unpopular reforms and thus bypassing the will of the majority (Haggard and Kaufman 1995; Heredia 1994). While many applaud the implementation of economic reform policies even when they are carried out through authoritarian means, for those interested primarily in democratic accountability, these analyses highlight the need for strong legislatures to represent the opinion of citizens in the policy-making process.[8]

A strong legislature is one that has sufficient resources and autonomy to challenge the executive and provide institutional channels for opposition forces to express their views. Comparative studies of legislatures have focused on transformative versus arena legislatures (Polsby 1975) or parliamentary versus presidential systems (Linz 1994). In this analysis the critical dimension of a legislature is its ability to perform an effective independent oversight role. As discussed in greater detail in Chapter 3, legislative strength is measured in terms of resources, autonomy, activity, and minority party rights. While a stronger legislature is not necessarily more democratic, especially if malapportionment overrepresents authoritarian elites in the assembly, a powerless legislature is clearly undesirable.

Since all of the major countries in Latin America have presidential systems, the theoretical logic of this chapter is constructed predominantly with reference to presidential systems. Nevertheless, legislative limits on executive power can take different institutional forms. In presidential systems, executives are constrained by the separation of powers and checks and balances. In a parliamentary system, the legislature has much greater institutional capacity to control and monitor the executive. First, parliaments choose the executive from within their own ranks. Second, the executive usually forms his or her cabinet with members of the legislature. And finally, the parliament can remove the executive with a vote of no confidence. The relevant issue, however, is not the formal institutional structure of legislative-executive relations but rather the practical ability of popular assemblies to check the abuses of executive prerogatives. Thus, the distinction between parliamentary and presidential systems is not a central concern here.

O'Donnell (1994) argues that the low quality of democracy in contemporary Latin America is the result of weak institutions and a lack of horizontal accountability. Horizontal accountability concerns the relationship among separate branches of government and serves to enforce the downward accountability of leaders to the electorate between elections by providing legislative and judicial constraints on executive action and instituting a system of checks and balances (O'Donnell 1993, 1998). According to O'Donnell (1998), for horizontal accountability to be effective, "there must exist state agencies that are authorized and willing to oversee, control, redress, and if need be sanction unlawful actions by other state agencies. The former agencies must have not only legal authority but also sufficient de facto autonomy vis-à-vis the latter" (119). O'Donnell (1998) contends that democracy in many Latin American countries involves delegation rather than representation because legislative and judicial institutions are weak, leaving executives largely unconstrained and able to govern by decree. As a result, many new democracies are characterized by a lack of accountability, low levels of participation, the (un)rule of law, low-intensity citizenship, and hyperpresidentialism (O'Donnell 1993, 1994, 1996, 1998).

O'Donnell's theoretical work draws a clear link between the separation of powers and the rule of law. He argues that the rule of law can be implemented only when institutions such as the legislature and the judiciary have sufficient power and autonomy to check the actions of the executive. Lorenzo Meyer (1998) similarly argues that the absence of an effective separation of powers in Mexico has inhibited the rule of law. An all-powerful presidency, noncompetitive elections, and a powerless congress have resulted in a judiciary with no independence from the executive, thereby generating unaccountability, corruption, and a police force that preys upon the weakest members of society. Meyer contends that the opposition victory in the congress in 1997 was important in establishing a separation of powers, thus breaking down the extra-institutional powers of the president that have allowed informal practices to dominate formal institutions. The election of an opposition president is clearly another step forward.

The first step to building the rule of law is getting all major actors to accept the legitimacy of the law and agree on a set of institutions for processing disagreements. As conflict between state and society increasingly takes the form of bargaining over laws and the design of institutions, the rule of law is strengthened. Once credible and impartial institutions have been established, the opposition forces can concentrate on pushing the regime to enforce the law rather than undermining the laws through extra-institutional protests. As a result, society may begin to view the law as something legitimate and meaningful. As the legislature becomes an important actor that represents voices from the opposition, it can become an arena for bargaining and thus building trust in government institutions and strengthening the rule of law.

Kurt von Mettenheim and James Malloy (1998) also highlight the importance of horizontal institutional constraints in order to develop a more participatory style of policy making. They argue:

> Given the volatility and effectiveness of direct popular appeals, a critical task for deepening electoral representation in Latin America today is to restrain the authoritarian bent of executives by diffusing and dis-

persing power among diverse institutions of liberal, democratic, and federal politics such as provincial officials, state and municipal legislatures, courts and interest groups. (7)

In short, strong legislatures, judiciaries, and subnational governments are critical for improving the quality of democracy. Stronger representative institutions, especially legislatures, subnational governments, and more open systems of candidate selection, play an important role in constraining national executives and therefore promoting greater accountability

Dynamic Institutions: Reviving Representative Institutions

While the static institutional models demonstrate the importance of representative institutions for accountability, they do not provide an explanation for the origins of institutional variation. A dynamic approach to analyzing institutions that highlights the changing incentive structures generated by democratization can overcome many limitations of static institutional analyses. In contrast to the static models that focus on how institutions shape behavior, dynamic models emphasize how rational actors construct institutions to maximize their influence over political outcomes (North 1990). The basic assumption undergirding these dynamic approaches is that self-interested politicians create institutions to further their own political careers. This approach grew out of research on the U.S. Congress (Riker 1980; Weingast and Marshall 1988) and has been most influential within the literature on U.S. politics. More recently, however, rational choice institutionalism has become prominent in comparative politics (Ames 1987; Carey 1996; Geddes 1994, 1995, 1996; Jones 1994; Przeworski 1991; Shugart and Carey 1992).[9]

Dynamic models emphasize how elite competition unleashes new demands that spread political power to a greater proportion of citizens (Schattschneider 1942) and how the logic of electoral competition allows candidates popular with the electorate to gain influence within the party, further reinforcing the control of the electorate over the political process (Schlesinger 1991). The logic of electoral competition also creates incentives for elected officials to increase their control over policy domains that affect their constituents (Hunter 1997). Therefore, in the context of increasing electoral competition, we can expect that members of the congress will seek to strengthen legislatures, elected officials will seek to strengthen their control over greater policy domains, and voters will gain greater voice in the process of political recruitment.

Dynamic institutional models provide the most fruitful means of analyzing democratization because these models can better account for institutional change. During periods of regime transition, institutions are by definition fluid and in flux. Entire constitutions and electoral systems are being redesigned. While static models see a role for institutions in shaping policy outcomes, they view institutions as intervening or independent variables. In stable situations it is reasonable to think of institutions as independent variables, but democratizing systems where institutions are in flux provide an exceptional opportunity to examine institutions as dependent variables.

There is a logic inherent in electoral competition that strengthens representative institutions during a process of democratization. In authoritarian countries, representative institutions may exist on paper, but they perform no meaningful representative functions. A shift to competitive electoral politics can breathe new life into dormant institutions that are not able to function under authoritarianism. Formal institutions seem to gain more importance relative to informal practices as electoral competition increases (Langston 2001).

Increasing electoral competition implies a broadening of the selectorate — the range of people who participate in the selection of national leaders — because, as competitive elections are used to select leaders, the number of people empowered to participate in that decision increases. In the case of a transition from one-party rule, the broadening of the selectorate takes place when voters, rather than the party hierarchy, begin to choose leaders. When leaders are chosen by a small group of party officials, the selectorate is clearly much smaller. The enlarged selectorate changes the incentive structures facing politicians and parties and changes the balance of power within parties, the government, and society as a whole. As a result, new groups gain a voice in the political process. These newly empowered forces will seek to change institutions to their advantage. Consistent with the assumptions of rational choice institutionalism, I assume that politicians are ambitious and want to move up in the political hierarchy and gain more power in the political system (Schlesinger 1966). I further assume that in order to attain their goals, ambitious politicians will respond to those with the power to promote or demote them. As electoral competition increases and the selectorate expands, the power to promote and demote begins to move out of the hands of the few and into the hands of the many (or at least the "more than a few"), so politicians can be expected to become more responsive to greater numbers of people.

In a one-party system with noncompetitive elections, the power to choose candidates generally lies with the party leadership. Politicians elected under these circumstances owe their position to party leaders, not voters, and are therefore expected to be more responsive to party leaders than to voters. When parties are not held accountable to the electorate through interparty competition, this situation generates "reciprocal accountability" (Roeder 1993; Shirk 1993). The separate branches of government, instead of acting as counterweights, remain responsive only to each other and the party leadership. Roeder identifies this pattern in communist Russia, where party leadership and party bureaucrats were accountable to each other and no one else. Shirk sees a similar pattern in China. Democratic accountability is inoperable under these circumstances. In a transition from one-party rule, the voters gain the power to veto the party leadership's selection of candidates and thus increase their ability to hold leaders accountable.

When politicians come to power on the basis of free and fair elections, they owe their job to the voters (in addition to the party leaders). Therefore, as electoral competition increases, there is a shift toward more downward accountability. Not only can opposition candidates win elections by responding to the unmet demands of the electorate, but because the ruling party becomes dependent on politicians who can win elections, ruling-party candidates can gain autonomy from and increasing influence within the party by representing the interests of the voters and demonstrating strong electoral support. Within this overall framework, there are strong theoretical reasons for anticipating consequences of electoral competition on three clusters of institutions: legislatures, candidate selection processes, and subnational governments.

Legislative Institutional Change

The predominant institutional model views legislative-executive relations as the result of constitutionally endowed powers (Mainwaring and Shugart 1997; Shugart and Carey 1992). For example, Mainwaring and Shugart claim that the nature of legislative-executive relations can be explained by the decree and veto powers of the president and the president's willingness to use these powers. In the context of regime transitions, such an approach is not very useful because variables such as constitutional powers are rapidly changing and are therefore more accurately employed as dependent variables rather than explanatory variables.

Evidence from the U.S. South and the former Soviet Union suggests that growing electoral competition is a key variable in the transformation of legislative institutions. As electoral competition increased in the U.S. South and Republican party candidates won governorships in the region, state legislatures became stronger and more active (O'Connor 1982; Rosenthal 1990). Likewise, the legislatures of the postcommunist countries underwent a profound transformation in the early 1990s as a result of the first competitive elections (Hahn 1996b; Remington 1994). The legislatures of the former Soviet Union were endowed with strong constitutional powers, yet during one-party rule they did not function as a meaningful counterweight to executive power but instead unanimously approved all legislation proposed by the party. The assembly was weak because the Communist party leadership nominated the members of the legislature and Communist party candidates were assured victory in noncompetitive elections. However, legislative-executive relations were transformed and the legislature became a significant force in Russian politics after the founding elections in 1990 (Hahn 1996b). In fact, the legislature became such a thorn in the side of the executive that Russian President Boris Yeltsin abolished the parliament and ordered tanks to fire on the parliament building in 1993.

Changes in local legislatures in Russia largely mirrored the process at the national level (Hahn 1996a; Stoner-Weiss 1996). In the case of Yaroslavl, the competitive elections of 1990 transformed local legislative behavior. After these elections the deputies elected their chairman from the democratic bloc and asserted their autonomy from the executive (Hahn 1996a; Ruble 1996). There is also evidence that democracy increased citizen contact with legislators in Russia and improved representation generally (Colton 1996).

In a noncompetitive political system both executives and legislatures are likely to owe their jobs to the same political elite. If the legislature and the executive both represent the interests of the same small group, there will be little conflict between the two branches of government and few incentives for one branch to monitor or check the power of the other. Furthermore, it is easier for executives to discipline congressional representatives in their party when the latter face no competition. This is because the representatives' power is derived from above, not from the electorate. Noncompetitive systems are typically characterized by powerful executives and a rubber-stamp congress (Agor 1971, Close 1995b; Hahn 1996b; Liebert and Cotta 1990; Remington 1994).

As elections become more competitive, the party leadership loses influence in the appointment of members of the congress. Party loyalists with no electoral appeal cannot win competitive elections. Therefore, the ruling party must choose candidates that appeal to the electorate and can successfully compete against opposition party candidates. Competition diminishes the party leadership's power in three ways: (1) it constrains their choices for candidates, (2) it increases the influence of electorally viable candidates vis-à-vis party hacks, and (3) it gives the opposition the opportunity to win seats in the congress and thus undermine the ruling party's control of the congress. Furthermore, competition creates incentives for legislators to represent voters. In countries like Mexico, where represention is based on electoral districts for the majority of seats in the legislature, electoral competition creates incentives for legislators to represent the voters in their districts. Party interests must compete with district interests for the control of the member.[10] Therefore, I expect that as elections become more democratic, elected officials will become more accountable to their constituents.

Increasing competition and its theoretical corresponding increase in responsiveness to constituents generate the conditions for greater legislative monitoring of the executive. In a competitive context, legislators and executives do not represent the interests of the same group of political elites. Rather, legislators will become more likely to represent the interests of their districts while the executive represents the interests of the country as a whole. I expect this divergence in constituencies to create new opportunities for conflict between executives and legislatures and new incentives for legislatures in competitive contexts to become active in overseeing executive behavior, proposing legislation, making amendments, and rejecting bills initiated by the executive.

Political Recruitment and Candidate Selection

Increasing electoral competition also has significant consequences for patterns of political recruitment. According to Schlesinger (1991), a highly competitive election will draw good candidates into the race, whereas a noncompetitive election will deter participation. If only one party has a chance to win the election, the politically ambitious will be attracted to the winning party. Jacobson (1992) argues that in nineteenth-century U.S. politics, "Parties faced with serious competition found it prudent to nominate attractive candidates; without this constraint — with the assurance of victory because of an overwhelming local majority — they could freely nominate incompetent hacks or worse" (19).

According to Schlesinger (1991), under competitive electoral conditions,

The market also affects the pattern of influence within market-based organizations. Because the market sends clear and unavoidable signals about performance with respect to its particular goals, individuals or units most responsible for market success can readily be identified.

> Such individuals gain influence. In a business, people who make successful sales or who are associated with a successful product will rise to power. Similarly for the political party, the winning candidates, or even those who look as though they might win, gain power. Indeed, because the most clearly defined product of the party is its candidate, there is no leeway for argument within the party, as there is in business. Influence within the party will closely follow individual success and failure in the electoral market. (15–16)

Hence, the logic of electoral competition, according to Schlesinger, gives greater power to candidates and politicians who are popular with the electorate.[11] Thus, in a context of democratization, we should expect to see popular politicians gaining influence over less popular traditional bosses within parties, since those who can win elections gain influence in their party.

Increasing electoral competition will transform the way that candidates are selected and the type of candidates selected. As the selectorate (the people empowered to select leaders) is broadened via the introduction of competitive electoral processes, the opportunities for new groups to compete for political power expand, and the incentives facing candidates, as well as those nominating candidates, change considerably. As elections become increasingly competitive, the veto power of the electorate grows stronger, and the incentives facing party leaders shift. To achieve victory in competitive elections, parties have to appoint candidates who are likely to win the support of voters. In local elections it is likely that politicians with ties to local interests will have greater electoral appeal than party loyalists sent in from the capital city. Therefore, democratization is expected to have a major impact on political recruitment patterns, leading to the election of candidates with closer ties to the local community in competitive local elections.

Competition may also lead to more democratic processes for nominating candidates, and in some cases this may include primary elections. Given the high levels of uncertainty about electoral preferences in authoritarian contexts, growing competition may create incentives for the use of primary elections. Through primary elections party leaders can better judge the electoral appeal of candidates (Geddes 1996, 20; Geddes and Zaller 1989). In the case of Mexico, electoral competition created the real threat that the PRI would not win. Candidates passed over for PRI nominations were more likely to desert the party and run on their own. Thus, the PRI was forced to find ways to select candidates that satisfied the rank-and-file members.

Changing Decision-Making Arenas

The institutional literature also suggests that increasing electoral competition will create incentives for elected officials to increase the policy domains over which they have influence. Wendy Hunter's (1997) work on the military in Brazil is useful for understanding the logic of electoral competition and its influence on institutional change. She finds that electoral competition strengthened civilian leaders vis-à-vis the military in Brazil. This happened, she argues, because military interference in politics conflicted with politicians' electoral goals and therefore compelled elected leaders to counter military influence. Specifically, the budget demands by the military cut into politicians' demands for state resources to build clientelistic networks. Moreover, if the military remained a powerful actor, elected officials were faced with a situation in which they could be voted out of office for policies that they were unable to control. Hunter further argues that competitive elections gave elected leaders greater political resources that allowed them to reduce military influence. Hence, competitive elections create new incentives and opportunities for elected leaders to maximize their control over policy making by shifting decision-making authority from authoritarian bureaucracies to democratic institutions.

Following Hunter's (1997) logic of the consequences of electoral competition for civil-military relations, we can see how electoral competition can lead to shifts in the decision-making arenas. The same dynamic of electoral politics that Hunter explains in the case of civil-military relations also takes place in the relationship between elected and bureaucratic officials in other arenas of decision making. When authoritarian bureaucracies have control over substantial policy domains, elected officials can be held responsible by voters and lose their jobs because of policy decisions over which they have no control. Such circumstances create incentives for elected officials to augment their decision-making authority at the expense of bureaucratic authority. Strong electoral support will increase the capacity of elected officials to confront authoritarian bureaucracies.

In a federal system with asymmetries in competitiveness at the local and national level, increasing electoral competitiveness at the subnational level is likely to result in increased decentralization. Demands for greater local autonomy in a federal system where local leaders are elected in more competitive processes than national leaders are one manifestation of the broader process in which increasing electoral competition creates incentives for elected officials to increase their influence by shifting decision-making authority from authoritarian bureaucracies to representative institutions. Local politicians will demand greater policy autonomy when local voters can hold them accountable for policy decisions. And local politicians gain independence from the center through their ability to win votes.

Within a federal system where leaders of subnational governments are directly elected, electoral competition is expected not only to redistribute power away from the executive to the legislative branch but also to redistribute power from the central government to state and local governments. As electoral competition takes root, the national elite is likely to lose power over local governments. Local politicians who can be held accountable by the local electorate are expected to attempt to gain control over policy spaces that affect their constituents and also to gain control over resources to enable them to carry out their policies. Again, as in the congress, the governing party will lose control over local governments because of increasing electoral constraints on ruling party candidate choice and possible opposition victories in state and local governments.

Drawing on the expectations outlined above, the chapters that follow test three main hypotheses:

> *Hypothesis I:* In the context of democratization, increasing electoral competition leads to more active, professional, and autonomous legislatures that are more capable of checking the power of the executive.
>
> *Hypothesis II:* In the context of democratization, increasing electoral competition generates more inclusive and participatory candidate selection processes that favor politicians capable of appealing to the electorate.
>
> *Hypothesis III:* In the context of democratization, increasing electoral competition at the subnational level will create incentives to shift policy formation from centralized authoritarian bureaucracies to local decision-making arenas.

The Case of Mexico:
Mexican Voters and the Prohibition on Reelection

The case of Mexico presents a unique opportunity as well as some important challenges for testing these theoretical propositions. First, the prohibition on reelection for all elected offices in Mexico means that Mexico provides a rare opportunity for testing the consequences of electoral competition because Mexico is clearly a least likely case for finding significant consequences from electoral competition. The quest for reelection is usually thought to be the driving force behind electoral accountability

(Mayhew 1974). Politicians do as their constituents would have them do because they fear electoral defeat in the next elections. In Mexico, the electoral connection exists, but it is much weaker than in a system where most elected officials seek reelection. Most Mexican politicians seek to stay in public life. Therefore, they face incentives to please their constituents to enhance their personal reputation and thus improve their chances of being elected to another post in the future. Elected officials also have incentives to remain accountable in order to further the electoral fortunes of their party. Independent candidacies are not permitted in Mexico, so there are strong reasons to stay on good terms with the party leadership. Since parties control the selection process for many elected posts, and also distribute many other jobs to loyal partisans, party members have strong incentives to please the party leadership by delivering them a safe district in the next elections. PRI governors, for example, were expected to maintain social peace in their state and win all elections in the state for the ruling party. If they were unable to do so, they would be likely to fall out of favor with the party leadership. Furthermore, following Schlesinger's (1991) logic, even without the possibility of reelection, politicians will want to please constituents to improve the electoral fortunes of their party and therefore their own position within that party. This has indeed been the case in Mexico, where governors who can win competitive state elections have strengthened their position within the PRI (Langston 2001, 508).

A second significant challenge to testing the consequences of electoral competition is that the model is based on strong assumptions about the rationality of voters. Do Mexican voters meet the expectations of voting behavior developed to describe voters in industrialized democracies? The model assumes that voters are rational, attentive to politics, and willing and able to punish parties and politicians who do not represent their interests. These assumptions about voting behavior are not unrealistic on the basis of previous survey research of Mexican voters. Domínguez and McCann's (1996) examination of voting behavior in the 1988 and 1991 elections demonstrates that Mexican voters were as attentive and politicized as voters in many industrialized Western democracies. Even though they found that retrospective economic voting was not very important, they did find that many voters employed sophisticated strategic voting methods. A large minority of voters were primarily concerned with seeing the ruling party voted out of office. Therefore, they would assess which opposition candidate was most likely to beat the PRI and would vote for that candidate, regardless of their ideological preferences. Thus, the authors found right-wing voters voting for Cárdenas and left-wing voters voting for the PAN.

The PRI did indeed perform better in many elections during the 1980s and 1990s than it should have on the basis of its economic and policy performance. The main reason for this seems to be the Mexican voters' fear of uncertainty. Since most voters had never been governed by a party other than the PRI, they were fearful that another party would not be able to rule the country (Cinta 1999; Poiré 1999). This high level of risk aversion gave the PRI extra room to maneuver and allowed them to not be accountable to the electorate. Nevertheless, by the mid-1990s, as electoral competition increased and voters gained experience with opposition party rule in states and municipalities, Mexican voters' risk aversion and fear of uncertainty became much less important (Cinta 1999; Poiré 1999). Mexican voters were clearly rational, and their behavior was governed more by retrospective voting (Poiré 1999). Hence, available evidence suggests that Mexican voters do meet the expectations of the model.

In summary, increasing electoral competition may be expected to change institutions and improve democratic accountability by changing the incentives and opportunities facing influential political actors. This perspective departs considerably from recent research on democracy in Latin America and other parts of the developing world in as much as it draws upon an institutionalist rather than cultural or structural understanding of democracy. By highlighting the importance of institutionalized opportunities for opposition forces to participate and monitor the government as well as the mediating influence of representative institutions, the theoretical approach presented here is designed to establish a more adequate basis for understanding the ways in which elections help to translate public preferences into public policy while simultaneously emphasizing the obstacles to that process. The three central sets of expectations about the consequences of electoral competitiveness revolve around changes in the process of political recruitment and policy formation. I expect that increasing electoral competitiveness will lead to stronger legislatures, more participatory patterns of candidate selection, and changes in the scope of representative institutions. In the chapters that follow, I make clear in greater detail these theoretical expectations and test them with a comparative analysis of politics in the Mexican states.

CHAPTER THREE

Legislative Change in Three States

In the spring of 1998 the state legislature of Morelos took an unprecedented step in beginning an impeachment investigation against then-governor Jorge Carrillo Olea. Carrillo was charged with human rights violations, corruption, and protecting drug traffickers (SourceMex, April 22, 1998). After the case was taken to the Supreme Court, which ruled that the state legislature had the constitutional right to impeach the governor, Carrillo was forced to resign (SourceMex, March 1, 2000). In a country where the governor traditionally has chosen the members of the state congress, and state congresses have acted as mere rubber stamps for gubernatorial initiatives, what explains this bold new activism by the state legislature in Morelos (and others across the country)?

As the case of Morelos demonstrates, legislatures can play an important role in holding executives to account. Strengthening legislatures is fundamental to the process of improving accountability and increasing the quality of democracy. One of the most significant obstacles to the development of greater accountability and more meaningful citizenship in new democracies is the lack of effective democratic representation (O'Donnell 1994). Popular assemblies have generally performed the function of democratic representation in established democracies. Moreover, legislatures play a fundamental role in checking executive power. Not only can legislatures vote down executive proposals, but they can also play a key role in guaranteeing judicial autonomy. Executive dominance

43

of the legislature gives the executive legal means of controlling the judiciary. A subservient legislature makes it easier for executives to impeach judges and control the selection process of judges. Autonomous legislatures provide important obstacles to executives attempting to shape judiciaries and public policies to reflect their personal interests. A strong and independent legislature is a vital part of a system of horizontal accountability.

Though recent research has suggested that even Latin America's "reactive" and "marginal" legislatures play an important role in policy making (Cox and Morgenstern 2001; Taylor-Robinson and Diaz 1999), historically Latin American legislatures have been very weak and often largely irrelevant to politics (Agor 1971; Close 1995b; Lions 1974). Mexico is no exception to this regional pattern. Mexico's "hyperpresidentialism" traditionally has relegated the legislative branch to a mere symbolic position in the political system (Camp 1995b; Carpizo 1978; Garrido 1989). Yet as electoral competition has increased across Mexico, the national legislature and some state legislatures have achieved new influence over the policy-making process (Thompson 2002). In the 1997 midterm elections, the ruling party lost its majority in the lower house of the national congress for the first time in seventy years. Since then, the legislature, led by a coalition of opposition leaders, has demanded a much greater role in decision making (Juárez 1998). The emerging influence of the national legislature has led to an entirely new set of rules for public policy making and legislative behavior in Mexico (Casar 1999; Lujambio 1998). Similarly, as opposition parties have been gaining strength at the state level, new sets of rules governing legislative-executive relations have emerged at the state level.

The transformation of the Mexican legislative branch raises interesting questions about democratization and political representation. What are the consequences of increasing political contestation for state legislative behavior? Are legislative institutions changing in response to growing electoral competition and challenges to the former ruling party, the PRI? Or are other forces responsible for this transformation? How are these changes playing out at the subnational level? The subsequent analysis employs a comparative study of legislatures in three Mexican states— Guanajuato, San Luis Potosí, and Hidalgo—to examine the impact of increasing electoral competition on legislative institutions.

According to modernization theory, structural variables such as societal development or complexity determine levels of institutionalization (Huntington 1965). Thus, social modernization is expected to produce legislative institutional change (Polsby 1968). More recent institutional analyses argue that constitutional arrangements and electoral rules determine the balance of power between legislatures and executives (Shugart and Mainwaring

1997; Shugart and Carey 1992). Others find that the makeup of the legislative membership explains the nature of legislative-executive relations (Cox and Morgenstern 2001). These approaches contribute to our understanding of political institutions, yet they do not provide a complete explanation of institutional change. Classic studies of democracy (Key 1949) as well as more recent comparative research (Coppedge 1993) have placed central theoretical importance on interparty competition in accounting for institutional behavior. Moreover, evidence from the transitions from one-party rule in the U.S. South, Eastern Europe, and the former Soviet Union suggests that growing electoral competition is a key variable in explaining legislative transformation (Hahn 1996b; O'Connor 1982; Remington 1994; Rosenthal 1990). By focusing on electoral competition, an understudied source of institutional change, this chapter attempts to shed new light on the relationship between democratization and institutional change. The central argument is that increasing electoral competition generates new incentives and opportunities for politicians to strengthen legislatures.

Legislative Change in Mexico

All of the Mexican state legislatures are unicameral. They are relatively small, with a mean size of just thirty-three members. As in the federal chamber of deputies, seats are allocated in a mixed system of single-member districts and proportional representation. Between 25 and 45 percent of the seats in each legislature are allocated through closed-list proportional representation, and the majority are single-member districts. Each state has a slightly different formula for allocating the proportional representation seats, and some approach a perfect proportional representation system more closely than others depending upon whether the proportional representation seats are allocated to compensate for the disproportionality of the single-member districts or to manufacture a majority for the party winning a plurality.

In general the legislatures have very meager resources. Many do not provide their members with individual offices. Most members do not have their own aides or secretaries. Many do not even have their own telephones or computers. Traditionally the local legislatures in Mexico have been largely irrelevant to the process of policy making. They have merely served as a rubber stamp to approve the governor's initiatives. In the words of Maria Guadalupe Hinajosa y Rivero, an opposition party member of the state congress in Puebla, "All of the legislative activity is distorted. The legislature does not perform the functions that it should. The governor is a feudal lord."[1] With the advent of electoral competition in some states, however, local legislatures have taken on a new importance in the Mexican political system.

Advancing democratization coupled with the increasing decentralization of power to state governments has made state legislatures a newly emerging arena for political influence (Cabrero Mendoza and Mejía Lira 1998; Rodríguez 1997; Ward and Rodríguez 1999). As competitive elections have taken root in many states, political observers have noted important changes in the behavior of the local legislatures (Alvarado 1997; Lujambio 1996b; Ward and Rodríguez 1999). Rodríguez (1997, 21) notes that governors have had a difficult time controlling local congresses in the context of strong electoral competition. Guillén López (1996) and Rodríguez and Ward (1994) find evidence of a growing separation of powers and a stronger and more autonomous local congress in Baja California in the years since the 1989 opposition gubernatorial victory. Similar patterns of increased legislative relevance characterize other state congresses where opposition parties have made significant electoral advances, including Guanajuato (Rionda 1996), Chihuahua (Aziz Nassif 1996a; Ward and Rodríguez 1999), Aguascalientes (Reyes Rodríguez 1996), and Baja California Sur (Garmendia 1996).

To date, however, there has been almost no attempt at systematic comparison of Mexican state legislatures. Furthermore, while many scholars have noted the coincidence of increased pluralism with the strengthening of legislatures, with the exception of a few excellent analyses of the national congress (e.g., Casar 1999; Weldon 1997), there has been relatively little effort to specify the causal mechanisms that underpin the relationship. The following analysis employs the logic of institutional rational choice theory to explain the changing behavior of legislators and provides comparative case study evidence and an interrupted time series regression to test systematically the relationship between electoral competition and legislative change.

Theoretical Considerations: Electoral Competition and Legislative Change

The strengthening of legislative institutions is crucial for democratic consolidation in presidential regimes because it increases what O'Donnell (1994, 1998) calls "horizontal accountability," or the capacity of the legislature to check the executive.[2] An effective system of checks and balances makes rule by presidential decree more difficult and requires that policy decisions gain the approval of the congress before becoming law. A policy-making process in which the congress is a key participant also creates more access points for opposition parties and interest groups and therefore may result in more participatory policy decisions (O'Donnell 1994, 64). In short, a strong and autonomous legislature acts as a check on the executive branch, opens up channels of popular access, and offers broader chances of representation to opposition forces.

Existing research traces the weakness of legislative institutions in Mexico back to institutional arrangements, especially to the term limits imposed upon members of congress (Lujambio 1995; Nacif-Hernández 1998). In their classic comparative study of legislatures, Loewenberg and Patterson (1979) note, "Some Latin American legislatures, like the parliament of Mexico, operate under a constitutional provision that prohibits members from serving more than one term. This provision is deliberately designed to prevent that parliament from becoming set in its ways; it also prevents parliament from being an independent force in politics" (22).

There is no immediate reelection for any elected office in Mexico, though members of both the national and state congresses can be reelected after one term out of office. It is relatively common to see legislators move back and forth between the state congresses, the national chamber of deputies, and the senate. Because of the prohibition on consecutive reelection, during PRI dominance legislators from the ruling party depended upon the executive for appointments in the bureaucracy or to be chosen as candidates for other elected positions after finishing their terms.[3] This dependence created legislative subservience to the executive at both the national and state levels. Additionally, nonconsecutive reelection restricts the ability of representatives to develop expertise. Because there is no long-term legislative career at either the national or the state level, members of congress consistently lack experience in lawmaking. González Oropeza (1994) argues that this lack of experience results in weak and irrelevant congressional committees that are incapable of proposing viable legislation.

The rules prohibiting the reelection of congressmen may explain the weakness of the Mexican national congress when compared with other countries where reelection is permitted. However, legislative institutional change and variation within Mexico suggests the importance of other variables. All of the Mexican states prohibit the reelection of legislators, yet levels of legislative influence vary considerably across the states. Furthermore, no changes have taken place in the reelection laws in recent years, yet tremendous institutional changes have taken place in many state congresses, as well as in the national congress. Other institutional variables that have been used to explain legislative-executive relations include presidential decree and veto powers (Shugart and Mainwaring 1997). Again, these variables are constant across the Mexican states and therefore cannot explain variation among the states. Similarly, institutional changes introducing (and later increasing) proportional representation in the national and state legislatures cannot account for changes in legislative behavior because they predate the transformations discussed here by more than ten years.[4] Hence, other factors beyond formal institutional arrangements must also be at work in determining the autonomy, resources, internal distribution of power, and activity of the legislatures. Modernization theory suggests that as countries become wealthier, legislatures will become more institutionalized. The in-depth comparisons presented below and the statistical results presented in chapter 4 suggest that legislative performance is not directly correlated with economic development.

While the structural and static institutional variables emphasized by previous research clearly have influence over legislative institutions, the importance of increasing electoral competition for institutional change has been overlooked. Constitutional constraints on legislative power are not the source of legislative weakness in Mexico (Casar 1999). The formal institutional structure of the Mexican Constitution provides for a system of checks and balances between the legislative, judicial, and executive branches. The constitution calls for a strong legislature and a relatively weak president. In practice, however, the formal rules of the game failed to work effectively because the conflation of the state and the ruling party that characterized the Mexican one-party system granted extensive "meta-constitutional" powers to the president (Garrido 1989; Weldon 1997). The fusion of the state and the party and the meta-constitutional powers of the president are the result of the long history of noncompetitive elections. Hence, an increase in electoral competition can be expected to break down the informal mechanisms that sustain the subservience of the legislature to the executive.

The general argument of this chapter is that in the context of democratization the increase in electoral competition implied by the shift from a one-party system to a multiparty system enhances the institutionalization of the legislative branch.[5] The research is organized around four hypotheses that test this general proposition:

Hypothesis I: Increasing electoral competition generates new incentives for legislators to develop autonomy from the executive.
Hypothesis II: Increasing electoral competition generates new incentives for legislators to demand increased resources for the legislature.

Hypothesis III: Increasing electoral competition leads to greater minority party rights and decentralization of power within the legislature.

Hypothesis IV: Increasing electoral competition results in higher levels of legislative activity.

These hypotheses are derived from the dimensions of legislative institutionalization as defined by various scholars (Hibbing 1988; Huntington 1965; Kornberg 1973; Polsby 1968; Squire 1992). According to Huntington (1965), "Institutionalization is the process by which organizations and procedures acquire value and stability" (394). Thus, an institutionalized legislature is one that is strong, stable, autonomous, and active, not weak and subservient (Polsby 1968).

According to Hypothesis I, increased electoral competition can be expected to lead to greater legislative autonomy. Autonomy from other branches of government is essential for a legislature to represent the interests of its constituents. If the legislature remains subordinate to the executive, meaningful representation is compromised when members of congress answer to the executive rather than the electorate. Increasing competition changes the incentives of both party leaders and members of congress in ways that can be expected to lead to greater legislative autonomy. In a noncompetitive system, one group of elites generally controls the selection of both the executive and the legislature. In such circumstances, both branches of government are agents of the same principal (the ruling elite), and therefore the legislature has no incentive to develop autonomy from the executive. When only one party wins elections, the ruling party's leadership also controls future career options for both the governor and the legislators, thus reinforcing the leadership's control over members. Therefore, I expect to find that similar incentives shape the decisions of both the executive and the congress in noncompetitive political contexts, resulting in substantial agreement between the two branches of government. In these cases the legislature will act mainly to rubber-stamp gubernatorial initiatives.

As the selectorate (the people empowered to choose leaders) expands through electoral competition to include voters, the incentives facing legislators change substantially. Elected officials theoretically will become more accountable to their constituents in order to further their own chances of future electoral success and strengthen the future electoral opportunities of their parties, thereby gaining favor with the party leadership. Therefore, legislators representing single-member districts facing competition will struggle to increase their power vis-à-vis the executive in order to further the interests of their districts. Following the U.S. literature on executive-legislative relations (Destler 1985; Fiorina 1981; Polsby 1986), I also expect the divergence in constituencies in systems with single-member districts between legislators and executives to create new opportunities for conflict between governors and state legislatures and new incentives for legislatures in competitive contexts to develop greater autonomy.

Party leaders also face new incentives and constraints that can be expected to contribute to greater legislative autonomy. When one party is guaranteed victory in an election, it can determine nominations on the basis of party loyalty alone. However, as electoral competition increases, demands from below for local representation reduce the leadership's ability to handpick candidates. These constraints redistribute power toward the electorate because the party must choose candidates that appeal to voters in order to win elections. Additionally, candidates that have popular electoral backing gain a degree of autonomy from the party leadership because the party needs them to win elections. Furthermore, as competition increases, opposition parties can be expected to win seats in the congress. When the ruling party loses seats, a greater share of the members of congress will not be under the control of a single party and will therefore seek to reduce the subservience of the legislature to the ruling party elite.

This process of increasing legislative autonomy is expected to be particularly pronounced in Mexico because the ruling party and the state became fused under one-party rule. Historically the president was the leader of the ruling party at the national level, while governors led the party at the state level. As leaders of the party, the executives choose the candidates for the ruling party. Without competitive elections, the ruling party candidates always win. The power of the president to appoint members of the national congress has been widely documented (Camp 1995c; Craig and Cornelius 1995; Garrido 1989; González Casanova 1970; Smith 1979). Additionally, the president has traditionally chosen the leader of the national congress (Camp 1995b, 24). To illustrate the process of candidate selection for congressional seats, Amezcua and Pardinas (1997) recount a February 1988 conversation between Carlos Salinas de Gortari, then the PRI candidate for the presidency, and Enrique González Pedrero, the governor of Tabasco:

> "Enrique, I want you to return to Tabasco to take a seat in the senate."
>
> "Carlos, I have already been a senator, and I would like to have new responsibilities . . ."
>
> "But you are talking about a regular senator, not the leader of the senate—that is what you will be."

"And how can you determine before the senate has even been elected that I will be the leader?"

"Well, you know how things work," the future president affirmed with certainty. (Amezcua and Pardinas 1997, 18, translated by author)

Available evidence suggests that these patterns of executive control are repeated in the states between the governor and the state legislature (Alcocer 1994; Graham 1971; Lujambio 1996b; Rodríguez 1997; Snyder 1999b; Vargas González 1998). Interview data also illustrate the similarities between legislative candidate selection in state governments and in the national government.[6] However, as competition increases and new electoral constraints are placed on the ability of the executives to hand-pick members of congress, the legislature will become more autonomous from the executive.

According to Hypothesis II, as electoral competition grows and the legislature increases its autonomy from the executive, the members of the legislature will have both new incentives and new opportunities to acquire more resources for the legislature. Increased resources buttress the autonomy of the legislature. A legislature needs money, staff, and facilities to develop independent sources of information. The legislature must have independent sources of information to compete effectively for power with the executive (Krehbiel 1991; Robinson 1970). A committee system is also an important resource. Without an internal division of labor, a legislature lacks the ability to effectively gather and evaluate information and hence is unable to challenge the executive (Loewenberg and Patterson 1979). In the absence of competition, resources will be of less importance to the legislature, since the members are likely to be satisfied with the information provided by the executive.

Hypothesis III predicts that as electoral competition increases, so too will the internal decentralization of power—in other words, the rights of minority parties. As competition increases, uncertainty becomes institutionalized (Przeworski 1991). Since no one knows which party will be in control of the legislature after the next elections, legislators face incentives to create a more participatory system for internal leadership. Members of the congress will decentralize power in order to protect the interests of their party in the future. When one highly disciplined party permanently controls a large majority and has no fear of losing it, the legislature is unlikely to implement reforms to increase minority party rights. However, when all parties are facing the possibility of being in the minority, members may be more likely to support measures to decentralize power and increase minority party rights in the legislature (Binder 1997).

The final hypothesis suggests that as electoral competition increases, the legislature will no longer function as a rubber stamp whose central function is to provide the appearance of democracy but will become more active and take on increasing responsibilities and influence within the political system. In a noncompetitive environment where members of congress are rewarded solely for their loyalty to the executive, members will have little incentive to meet frequently, debate legislation seriously, or propose new laws. In contrast, in a competitive environment, legislators and parties will be looking toward the next election, and both the members of congress and their parties will want to demonstrate legislative successes before the next campaign. They will also want publicity in the press for work they have done in congress. Hence, there will be incentives for the legislators to meet more frequently, debate important issues, and propose legislation.

Evidence from Three Case Studies

This chapter explores the impact of competition on legislative institutions through a comparative case study analysis of three state legislatures. As discussed in the introduction, the states of Guanajuato, Hidalgo, and San Luis Potosí were selected because all have roughly similar structural conditions, yet the patterns of political competition vary widely across the three states. Evidence from previous research suggests that the Guanajuato congress gained unprecedented influence in state politics after the PAN took control of the governor's seat in 1991 (Rionda 1996). In contrast, throughout the 1990s the congress in Hidalgo remained generally irrelevant to state politics (Gutiérrez Mejía 1990, 29–33; Vargas González 1998, 78). Survey data demonstrate that the people of Hidalgo are largely indifferent to the legislature. Only 15 percent of those surveyed just before the 1990 local legislative elections knew that members of congress were to be elected in the upcoming elections. Less than 3 percent of respondents answered that the main activity of the state legislators is to make laws, while over 50 percent answered that the members of congress "do nothing" (Vargas González 1996, 122–25).

Electoral Competition in the Three States

Competition began to emerge in Guanajuato in the late 1970s. In 1976 the PAN's candidate for municipal president of León (the industrial and commercial capital of the state) made such a strong showing that the

PRI was forced to negotiate a coalition government in the municipality. Opposition parties began to win more municipal elections in urban areas in the early 1980s (Rionda 1996, 76). Although the opposition made important inroads at the municipal level, the PRI maintained control of all statewide institutions until 1991.

The gubernatorial elections of 1991 mark a watershed in the politics of Guanajuato. The PAN candidate Vicente Fox contested the results of these elections, and his accusations of fraud were supported by the other major opposition parties. As a result of extensive civic protest against the alleged electoral fraud, President Carlos Salinas forced the PRI governor-elect Ramón Aguirre Velázquez to resign and pressured the local congress to appoint Carlos Medina Plascencia from the opposition party PAN as interim governor (Ling Altamirano 1992).[7] However, the incoming congress, which had been handpicked by Aguirre Velázquez, refused to approve the interim appointment and occupied the congress building to prevent the outgoing congress from doing so. Eventually the outgoing congress was able to meet secretly in a corner of the congress building to appoint Medina Plascencia (Rionda 1996).

The political crisis of 1991 foreshadowed the coming conflict between the new governor and the congress. The new opposition governor faced a congress controlled by representatives from the ruling party who were handpicked by the ousted governor. And, as part of the compromise of his appointment, the new governor shared power with a ruling party Secretary of Government (second in command). The installation of an opposition governor resulted in unprecedented deadlock and conflict between the congress and the governor. During its three years in office the congress did not pass the political or electoral reforms that were required before new gubernatorial elections could take place, according to the compromise in 1991. The congress did, however, take on unprecedented power in the budget process and became a real place for debate (Rionda 1996, 84–85). Before 1991 the congress had been essentially irrelevant to politics, as most gubernatorial initiatives were passed without criticism or debate by the legislature. According to Rionda (1996), "The legislation was approved in the office of the governor. The rest was just paperwork" (78).

In 1995 Vicente Fox ran again for governor and won. In 1997, Fox's party, the PAN, won a plurality in the state congress. In 2000 Juan Carlos Romero Hicks of the PAN won the gubernatorial elections, and the PAN won all twenty-two directly elected seats in the state legislature (Source-Mex, July 5, 2000). Three consecutive governors from the PAN have ruled Guanajuato, and in 1997 the PRI also lost its majority in the congress. Clearly, elections are highly competitive in Guanajuato.

The first opposition victory in San Luis Potosí took place in 1958, when Dr. Salvador Nava won the municipal elections in the capital city, becoming leader of the first opposition government in a state capital (Bezdek 1995). Nava's campaign was an attempt to bring down the influential political boss Gonzalo N. Santos. The struggles against Santos in 1958 helped to create a new political consciousness in the capital city (Calvillo Unna 1994). However, the political advances made by Nava were followed by intense repression of Nava's movement in the early 1960s and a return to PRI domination. Twenty years later Nava won the municipal elections in the capital once again.[8] The PAN and supporters of Nava continued to win in the state capital throughout the 1980s. Nava ran for governor in 1991 as a coalition candidate for the three major opposition parties (the PAN, PDM, and PRD). The election was marked by extensive postelectoral protest that, as in Guanajuato, sparked presidential intervention. In San Luis Potosí, however, the opposition refused a compromise similar to that struck in Guanajuato, so Salinas appointed another member of the PRI as interim governor. Since 1991, opposition strength has continued to grow in the state, but no opposition party has managed to win the gubernatorial elections, and the PRI maintains a majority in the congress. Thus, while there have been many visible, highly contested elections in the state of San Luis Potosí, the opposition has never been able to win control of statewide institutions.

The PRI maintained almost complete dominance over politics in the state of Hidalgo through the 1990s. Until the mid-1980s, the PRI won over 95 percent of the vote in all local elections, and until 1987 opposition parties ran candidates in less than one-quarter of the municipalities (Vargas González 1998, 61–62). By the 1990s electoral competition did increase somewhat. Opposition parties ran candidates for most offices, and the vote for the PRI began to decline. Still, only a handful of municipal elections were ceded to opposition parties, the PRI's gubernatorial candidates won at least 75 percent of the vote, and the PRI continued to win all single-member-district seats in the state congress.

As table 3.1 demonstrates, the percentage of seats in each legislature controlled by the PRI has slowly declined through time. Until the mid-1990s the decline was largely due to steady increases in the number of proportional representation seats distributed to opposition parties. No opposition party candidate won a single-member district in San Luis Potosí until 1993 or in Hidalgo until 1999. Moreover, until the late 1990s the PRI in these two states held a supermajority of more than two-thirds of the seats, enabling the ruling party to approve constitutional reforms without consulting other parties. In 1997 opposition parties made significant advances

Table 3.1. Distribution of State Legislative Seats by Party

Guanajuato

| Legislature | Years | PRI | | PAN | | Others | | Total |
		No.	%	No.	%	No.	%	
51st	1979–1982	18	75	3	12.5	3	12.5	24
52nd	1982–1985	18	75	3	12.5	3	12.5	24
53rd	1985–1988	17	70.8	4	16.7	3	12.5	24
54th	1988–1991	19	65.5	6	20.7	4	13.8	29
55th	1991–1994	20	66.67	6	20	4	13.3	30
56th	1994–1997	23	76.67	5	16.67	2	6.66	30
57th	1997–2000	12	33.33	16	44.44	8	22.22	36

Sources: 1979–1997 data from Rionda (1996, 77); 1997–2000 data from the files of staff members in the Congreso del Estado de Guanajuato.

San Luis Potosí

| Legislature | Years | PRI | | PAN | | Others | | Total |
		No.	%	No.	%	No.	%	
49th	1978–1981	11	100	0	0	0	0	11
50th	1981–1984	15	75	2	10	3	15	20
51st	1984–1987	15	75	2	10	3	15	20
52nd	1987–1990	15	75	5	25	0	0	20
53rd	1990–1993	15	75	3	15	2	10	20
54th	1993–1997	16	67	5	21	3	12	24
55th	1997–2000	14	52	10	37	3	11	27

Source: Data from the files of staff members in the Congreso del Estado de San Luis Potosi.

Hidalgo

| Legislature | Years | PRI | | PAN | | Others | | Total |
		No.	%	No.	%	No.	%	
51st	1981–1984	15	78.95	1	5.26	3	15.79	18
52nd	1984–1987	15	75	1	5	4	20	20
53rd	1987–1990	15	75	1	5	4	20	20
54th	1990–1993	15	75	1	5	4	20	20
55th	1993–1996	17	70.83	2	8.33	5	20.83	24
56th	1996–1999	18	66.67	4	14.81	5	18.52	27
57th	1999–2002	18	62.07	7	24.14	4	13.79	29

Source: Data from the files of staff members in the Congreso del Estado de Hidalgo.

Table 3.2.   District and Proportional Representation (PR) Seats in 1998 Legislatures

	Guanajuato			San Luis Potosi			Hidalgo		
	Majority District	PR Seats	Total	Majority District	PR Seats	Total	Majority District	PR Seats	Total
PAN	14	2	16	6	4	10	0	4	4
PRI	6	6	12	9	5	14	18	0	18
PRD	2	3	5	0	2	2	0	4	4
PT	0	1	1	0	1	1	0	1	1
PVEM	0	1	1	0	0	0	0	0	0
PDM	0	1	1	0	0	0	0	0	0
Total	22	14	36	15	12	27	18	9	27

in both the Guanajuato and San Luis Potosí congresses as the PRI lost its majority in Guanajuato and its supermajority in San Luis Potosí.

Table 3.2 provides a more detailed breakdown of the seats in the 1998 congresses. It shows how many seats were allocated to each party through single-member districts and proportional representation.

To capture concisely the varying levels of electoral competition in the three states, table 3.3 presents a competitiveness index for the three states. This index is the mean of the margin of victory across the legislative districts in the 1996/1997 local congressional races. The average margin of victory for a legislative seat in Guanajuato was 13.82 percent, compared to 15.03 percent in San Luis Potosí and 39.81 percent in Hidalgo. The mean margin of victory was relatively high for Guanajuato and not very different from that of San Luis Potosí because the PAN won a number of legislative races with very high margins of victory. If an alternative specification of competition (votes for the PRI minus votes for the main opposition party) is used, the difference between San Luis Potosí and Guanajuato is much greater. This alternative measurement seems to better fit the qualitative description of competitiveness in the two states provided above.

The variations in electoral competitiveness suggest that we should find the greatest levels of autonomy, resources, activity, and decentralization of internal power in Guanajuato and the lowest levels in Hidalgo, with San Luis Potosí somewhere in the middle but closer to Guanajuato than Hi-

Table 3.3. Legislative Institutional Change in Guanajuato,
San Luis Potosí, and Hidalgo

	Guanajuato	San Luis Potosí	Hidalgo
ELECTORAL COMPETITIVENESS	High	Medium	Low
Mean margin of victory	13.82	15.03	39.81
AUTONOMY	High	Medium	Low
Constitutional powers of congress	High	High	Low
Number of gubernatorial vetoes	2	0	0
Congressional staff for budget oversight	155	56	56
Congressional auditors	98	42	40
Strength of congressional oversight	High	Medium	Low
RESOURCES	High	Medium	Low
Mean internal legislative budgets, 1975–1997	6,263,000	2,995,000	2,231,000
Total staff, 1998	344	177	137
Legislative aides	37	11	5
Congressional facilities	Medium	Medium	Low
Committee strength	High	Medium	Low
MINORITY PARTY RIGHTS	High	Medium	Low
Leadership structure	Internal Regime Committee	Grand Committee	Coordinator
Multiparty control of committees	High	Medium	Low
Accessibility of information	High	Medium	Low
ACTIVITY	High	Medium	Low
Length of debate (pages)	1,525	903	N/A
Number of initiatives per year	16	10.25	3.6
Average number of radio or television interviews per year	25	19	12

dalgo. These expectations conform to initial field research observations regarding the general level of hustle and bustle in the three state congresses.

In Hidalgo, apart from Tuesdays and Thursdays during sessions, there is rarely anyone in the congress building. One telling indicator of the influence of the congress in Hidalgo is that taxicab drivers in the state capital rarely know where the congress building is. In contrast, the congresses of both San Luis Potosí and Guanajuato have a feeling of activity. Congress members are coming and going to committee meetings every day of the week. The libraries are full of aides carrying out research, and even on days when there are no sessions, the buildings are full of people working. Another startling difference between Hidalgo and the other two congresses is the attitude of PRI members of congress. When interviewed, some PRI legislators in Hidalgo seemed afraid to speak frankly. Some closed office doors before answering delicate questions about the congress and the party. One deputy answered certain questions in English so no one else would understand. Still others refused to answer questions. Many deputies in Hidalgo asked not to be cited by name. The congresses of Guanajuato and San Luis Potosí are marked by a sense of openness that is not apparent in Hidalgo.

More systematic data confirm these initial impressions. I measure the main concepts of my four hypotheses by combining Polsby's (1968) operationalization of legislative institutionalization with those of Hibbing (1988) and Squire (1992) and some additional adjustments specific to the Mexican case. Table 3.3 summarizes the main indicators used in the following empirical analysis.

Autonomy

As shown in table 3.3, autonomy is measured by the constitutional powers of the legislature, the number of vetoes the executive is forced to issue, the amount of oversight conducted by the legislature, and the assessments of congressional influence by political observers from within and outside of the congress. Constitutional powers are often considered constant and used as independent variables. Here, however, these institutional variables are employed as dependent variables. Given the ongoing and extensive reforms to state constitutions in Mexico, it seems more appropriate to view constitutional powers as the outcome of political negotiation rather than as a constraining factor that merely shapes outcomes. A more autonomous legislature can be expected to shape constitutional powers to its advantage, whereas a subservient congress cannot.

As mentioned above, the most widely used measures of legislative constitutional powers are constant across the Mexican states. There are, however, a number of minor differences in the constitutions that demonstrate varying levels of autonomy. In both Guanajuato and San Luis Potosí, the constitution explicitly states that the governor cannot veto laws affecting congressional rules and procedures. In Hidalgo the governor can veto laws dealing with the internal structure of the congress. Additionally, in Hidalgo the governor is required to present the public accounts to the congress only once a year, while in both San Luis Potosí and Guanajuato the governor is required to present the public accounts every three months, thereby giving the congress the ability to more closely monitor the governor's expenditures. These more rigorous requirements for presenting the public accounts were introduced in both San Luis Potosí and Guanajuato in 1996.

Vetoes have been extremely rare in Mexico. A veto demonstrates a loss of control by the executive over the work of the legislature. In a hand-picked congress, we would expect that the governor would never need to veto any bills because the congress would never pass any legislation that the governor had not approved. As Roderic Camp (1995b) argues, "The president may veto a bill in whole or in part, but because both chambers have always been controlled by the government party, because party nominations are influenced by the incumbent president, and because the president designates congressional leadership, little need exists for the veto power to be exercised" (25). Thus, the greater the number of vetoes the less control the executive has over the legislature and the more autonomous the legislature is.

As shown in table 3.3, there have only been two vetoes by a governor of Guanajuato in recent history, one in 1991 and another in 1998. First, in 1991 the governor vetoed a constitutional amendment requiring governors to be born in the state of Guanajuato. This amendment was directly aimed at Vicente Fox, the PAN's candidate for governor in 1991, who was born in Mexico City. The second veto took place in 1998, when Governor Fox vetoed the "Ley de Responsabilidades." The bill had been sent by Fox to the congress, but Fox vetoed the congressional version because of amendments aimed at regulating Fox's campaign for the presidency. There has never been a veto in either San Luis Potosí or in Hidalgo, suggesting that the governors in these two states have greater control over their congresses.

Although all three state constitutions call for congressional oversight of the public finances, the Guanajuato congress fulfills its oversight responsibilities to a much greater extent than the San Luis Potosí or Hidalgo congresses. The Guanajuato congress has a much larger staff for budget oversight (see table 3.3), and interviews with members of the oversight committees in all three congresses suggest that oversight is taken much more seriously in Guanajuato than in the other two states.[9] Further evidence of stronger oversight in Guanajuato is the makeup of the congressional committees responsible for budget oversight. Guanajuato is the only case of the three in which no party has the majority in the oversight committee. A member of the PRD chairs the oversight committee in Guanajuato, while the PRI maintains control over the committees in San Luis Potosí and Hidalgo. Multiparty control of oversight enhances the ability of the congress to review budgets impartially because it limits the ability of one party to overlook the abuses of its own members.

A PANista deputy who serves as the vice president of the committee that oversees public finances in San Luis Potosí contends that important steps have been taken to improve congressional oversight, but he still complains, "There is a grave problem. The comptroller is run by the oversight committee, which is controlled by the PRI. The PRI does not want to rule against its own people. We need an institution that sanctions people regardless of who they are and what party they belong to."[10] Congressional oversight of the budget in Hidalgo is extremely limited. While almost every deputy interviewed in Guanajuato mentioned fiscal oversight as one of the most important responsibilities of the congress and many deputies in San Luis Potosí also mentioned it, no deputy in Hidalgo mentioned budgetary oversight unless specifically asked about it. An opposition party deputy in Hidalgo commented, "The comptroller is completely controlled by the PRI, the system of congressional oversight is inoperable. The official party is the boss of oversight."[11]

While most political observers outside of the congresses in San Luis Potosí and Hidalgo write off the congress as basically irrelevant to politics (Gutiérrez Mejía 1990; Vargas González 1998), in Guanajuato political observers outside of the congress agree that there have been great changes in the Guanajuato congress. Santiago López Acosta, the secretary general of the Guanajuato delegation of the Federal Electoral Institute (IFE), stated, "Without a doubt the congress is more autonomous. Before [1991] they were dominated by the governor. Now they have converted themselves into an important actor. They are trying to be the control and counterweight to the governor."[12] Luis Miguel Rionda (1996) also notes the increasing autonomy of the Guanajuato congress after 1991.

Survey responses of congress members demonstrate that the legislators themselves have differing conceptions of the influence of their congresses and their relationship with the governor. As shown in table 3.4, in Guanajuato, 76 percent of legislators answered that the local congress has a lot of influence in state politics, while only 63 percent in San Luis Potosí and 57 percent in Hidalgo thought the local congress had a lot of influence.

Furthermore, when asked to rank the most important responsibilities of a member of congress, 29 percent of legislators from Hidalgo responded that supporting the governor is their most important responsibility as members of congress. No legislators in Guanajuato or San Luis Potosí ranked supporting the governor as their most important responsibility. Seventy percent of Guanajuato legislators ranked proposing laws as the most important responsibility of a congressman compared to 31 percent in San Luis Potosí and 21 percent in Hidalgo.

Table 3.4. Survey Responses of State Legislators ($N = 54$)

	Guanajuato	San Luis Potosí	Hidalgo
Local congress has a lot of influence	76%	62.5%	57%
Most important responsibility is to support governor	0%	0%	29%
Most important responsibility is to propose legislation	70%	31%	21%

Resources

Legislative resources are measured by the budgets, staffs, and facilities, along with the strength and importance of committees. The internal legislative budget is largely used to pay salaries and maintain facilities. Thus, a congress with a higher budget is able to hire more legal advisors and policy analysts and buy more equipment to enhance its ability to compete with the informational resources of the executive. Greater resources imply the possibility of greater access to independent sources of information.

Guanajuato has consistently spent more money on its legislature than San Luis Potosí, and San Luis Potosí has consistently spent more than Hidalgo. The average budget allocated to the legislature in each of the three states clearly demonstrates the difference in spending levels between the three cases. The mean budget from 1975 to 1997 was over 6 million constant (1990) new pesos for Guanajuato and less than 3 million for both San Luis Potosí and Hidalgo. These means are significantly different with 99.9 percent confidence (see table 3.3).

Not only does the Guanajuato congress have a much larger budget than San Luis Potosí and Hidalgo, but Guanajuato also has much more staff support than the other congresses. In 1998 the Guanajuato congress employed 344 people, while the San Luis Potosí congress employed only 177 and the Hidalgo congress 137. Legislative aides are especially important resources for a congress. There are 37 legislative aides working in the Guanajuato congress, compared to 11 in San Luis Potosí and just 5 in Hidalgo (see table 3.3). Moreover, in Guanajuato each party receives its own aides based on its representation in the congress. In San Luis Potosí and Hidalgo all of the legislative aides are under the control of the majority party. All of the legislative aides in San Luis Potosí work in the Legislative Research Institute. The institute is governed by a special committee of the congress, which is presided over by the president of the Grand Committee. The president of the Grand Committee proposes the names of the other members of the committee, who then oversee the institute and control its finances. Such a governing structure limits the autonomy of the institute and the resources available to opposition parties. In Hidalgo, all of the legislative aides are chosen by the coordinator of the congress, who is chosen by the governor.

In addition to substantial differences in budgets and staffing among the three legislatures, there are significant differences in the facilities of the legislatures. The facilities provided to rank-and-file members by all three congresses are extremely limited. None of the states provide individual offices, secretaries, or telephone lines to all members. Nevertheless, the facilities in Guanajuato are far superior to those in Hidalgo and San Luis Potosí. There are more telephone lines, fax machines, and computers, and a considerably larger library and archive in Guanajuato. The facilities in Hidalgo are the poorest of the three. The congressional library in Hidalgo was unable to provide any useful information, not even a copy of the state's constitution.

Interview data demonstrate that committee work has taken on increased importance in Guanajuato and San Luis Potosí. The 1997–2000 legislature in Guanajuato worked in twenty-one committees. Most committees met once a week for at least an hour, often much more. The 1997–2000 congress in San Luis Potosí worked in twenty-seven committees that generally met at least twice a month. The congress in Hidalgo had twenty-two committees. Journalists who cover the Hidalgo congress contend that the committees do nothing.[13] One deputy who serves on the finance committee claims that they meet frequently from May to June to approve the past year's budget and again from November to December to pass the next year's budget.[14] Another deputy from Hidalgo reported that the committees he belonged to had never met.[15]

Decentralized Decision-Making Procedures

The level of the decentralization of internal power is measured by the structure of internal leadership, multiparty representation on committees, and the publication and availability of information such as budgets and debates. The three cases under study vary enormously in terms of the internal structure of congressional leadership. Important changes have taken place in Guanajuato and San Luis Potosí, while Hidalgo lags far behind in allowing minority parties influence in the legislature.

While the Guanajuato state legislature became more autonomous after the 1991 appointment of PAN member Medina Plascencia, the most important changes in the internal structure of the legislature have taken place since 1997, after the PRI lost its majority in the congress. Particularly significant was the disbanding of the Grand Committee and its replacement with the Internal Regime Committee. The Grand Committee included only members of the majority party and made all important decisions regarding the work of the congress. It named all support staff, made all committee assignments, and controlled the agenda. In contrast to the hegemonic control enjoyed by the majority party in the Grand Committee, the new Internal Regime Committee includes one representative from each of the parties represented in the congress. The leadership of the Internal Regime Committee rotates among the three main parties (PRI, PAN, and PRD); each party presides over the committee for six months.[16] In 1998 for the first time in history a multiparty committee put together the agenda for the congressional session.

In an analysis of the committee system of the national congress, González Oropeza (1994) argues that one of the greatest obstacles to the institutionalization of the congress is the weakness of the committees. The committees are weak, he contends, because the Grand Committee, which functions mainly to serve the executive, dominates the committee system. Thus, the replacement of the Grand Committee with a multiparty commission is an important indicator not only of internal decentralization of power but also of the autonomy of the legislature.

The Grand Committee continues to control the San Luis Potosí congress, though important steps toward decentralizing power have been taken. The president of the Grand Committee is a member of the PRI, but the PAN has one representative on the committee. Although the opposition has representation on the Grand Committee, according to a PAN deputy, "The culture of domination by the president of the Grand Committee continues, but we are moving towards more consensus."[17]

The congress in Hidalgo has not yet decentralized power sufficiently to even have a Grand Committee. One man, the "Coordinator of the Congress," controls the Hidalgo congress. In the words of a PRI congressman, "The PRI deputies make an internal agreement with the governor to decide who will become the coordinator of the congress."[18] In other words, there is no election within the congress for the coordinator; he is chosen behind closed doors in the governor's office. According to the director of the Institute for Legislative Studies of the Hidalgo congress, "The Grand Committee was introduced in other legislatures because of pluralism. But here we have an absolute majority, so the Grand Committee is not necessary."[19] Minority parties have almost no influence in the Hidalgo congress (Vargas González 1998, 77). A further indicator of the centralized and exclusive nature of decision making in the Hidalgo congress is the extensive use of closed-door meetings by the PRI majority. Before and after most congressional sessions, the PRI members of congress meet in the coordinator's office. These meetings are not open to the public or to the other members of congress, but they seem to be where most of the important decisions are made.

Another measure of the decentralization of power is the equitable representation of minority parties in committee assignments. In Guanajuato the two most powerful committees have rotating leaderships. The PAN has an absolute majority in only four of the twenty-two committees, and the PRI has a majority in one committee. The rest of the committees in Guanajuato have no more than two out of five members from one party. In San Luis Potosí the PRI has a majority in the three most important committees. In the rest of the committees, the PRI has exactly one-half of the votes. In Hidalgo, the PRI has a majority in every committee. The chairs of the committees are also distributed among the parties more evenly in Guanajuato than in San Luis Potosí and Hidalgo.

A final measure of decentralized power is the accessibility of basic information to all the members of congress as well as the public in general. The congressional debates provide an important source of information about the congress and its members. In Guanajuato, the congress began publishing the debates in 1979 when the first opposition party members were elected. The San Luis Potosí congress only began publishing the debates in 1993. In 1999 the Hidalgo congress still did not publish debates and had no plans to do so.

State budget information is also much more accessible in Guanajuato than in the other states. In 1998 Guanajuato became the first state in the country to publish its public accounts on the Internet. Moreover, in Guanajuato, since 1995 the government has published the entire budget, detailing every expense from the salaries of every employee in the congress to the amount of money spent on office supplies. This very detailed budget is available to every member of the congress as well as every member of the public in various libraries across the state. In San Luis Potosí no fully detailed budget is available to the public. A former member of the congress complained that in the 1980s even as a member of the congress he had no access to the budget. In fact, the very general official budget has only been published in the *Periodico Official* since the late 1980s. Similarly, in Hidalgo only a very general description of the state budget is available to the public. Additionally, the Guanajuato and the San Luis

Potosí congresses publish Web pages to widely distribute information, but the Hidalgo congress does not.

Level of Activity

The final hypothesis argues that increasing electoral competition will lead to greater legislative activity. Legislative activity is measured by the length of debates, the number of initiatives proposed by members of congress, and the amount of press coverage of congressional activities. The U.S. state legislatures are often compared in terms of the full-time status of members, pay for legislators, and the length of ordinary sessions (Fiorina 1994; Patterson 1996). These indicators are relatively constant across the Mexican states. Members of congress in Mexico have always been generously compensated and, at least officially, work full time. Yet survey data and interviews demonstrate that many do not work full time in the legislature. In my 1998 survey of state legislators, only 50 percent of the members of congress reported that they spent between 75 percent and 100 percent of their professional time working on legislative matters. According to one deputy in San Luis Potosí, "'Full time' is interpreted in many different ways here in Mexico. Some people take a long time to finish their work. But if you can finish all your work quickly, then some deputies have other work outside of the congress."[20] Official data, therefore, on the full-time status and wages of members of congress are not a useful indicator of legislative activity.

The constitutionally stipulated dates for the sessions are also almost identical among the cases studied here. Each congress meets for three months in the fall and three months in the spring. But the actual number of days the congress meets is a poor measure of congressional activity because some congresses meet, take attendance, and adjourn without doing any legislative work at all, while other congresses meet for many hours. The number of pages of debate in each legislative year gives a better indication of how long sessions last and how much discussion takes place.

The length of debate in Guanajuato and San Luis Potosí is measured by the number of pages of debate recorded in the *Diario de los Debates*. The average number of pages of debate per year between 1993 and 1998 in Guanajuato was 1,525, compared to only 903 in San Luis Potosí. Since the Hidalgo congress does not record debates, there are no comparable data. The fact that the debates are not considered important enough to publish, however, suggests that there is very little debate in Hidalgo. Isauro Villanueva Aguilar, the director of Apoyo Parliamentario in Guanajuato for the past twenty years, explained that there was no *Diario de los Debates* before 1979 in Guanajuato because "before 1979, there was no debate." During legislative sessions in Hidalgo the debates that do take place tend toward the mundane, rather than dealing with important political issues. For example, during the fall of 1998 one entire session was devoted to a discussion of cellular phone use in the legislative chamber. Another entire session was spent debating whether the congress should issue a statement of sympathy for the victims of Hurricane Mitch.

The available data on legislative initiatives are limited. None of the three congresses has collected these data for more than a few years, and each collects the data in a slightly different form, so comparison is somewhat difficult. As shown in table 3.3, in Guanajuato 16 pieces of legislation were proposed by the members of congress in the congressional year 1997–98. In San Luis Potosí legislators proposed an average of 10.25 pieces of legislation per year between 1994 and 1997. In Hidalgo, members of congress proposed an average of 3.6 initiatives per year from 1996 to 1998. Clearly, legislators are presenting more initiatives in Guanajuato and San Luis Potosí than in Hidalgo. A PRD member of the Hidalgo congress commented that it was a waste of time for his party to propose legislation because the majority party would not attend to the proposals. Instead, the PRD members of congress focus on constituency service.[21]

The amount of coverage of legislative activity in the local press is an indicator of both the level of activity in the congress and the level of public interest in the work of the legislature. Interviews with local journalists suggest that there are more stories in the press about the Guanajuato congress than there were ten years ago. Rionda (1996, 88) notes that the coverage of congressional activities increased substantially after 1991. Congressmen in Guanajuato also agree that there is more publicity of legislative activity in the press today.[22] The Guanajuato local newspaper *El Nacional* prints a special section of legislative activities each week that the congress is in session.

Survey responses indicate that the members of congress in Guanajuato are interviewed by the press much more often than the legislators in the other two states. Members of congress in Guanajuato reported being interviewed on radio or television an average of twenty-five times a year, while in San Luis Potosí the average was nineteen and in Hidalgo only twelve (see table 3.3).

Evidence of Change through Time

The data presented in table 3.3 clearly demonstrate a correlation between electoral competition and legislative strength. Static spatial correlations, however, are not sufficient to demonstrate the direction of causality.

Table 3.5.   Change in Legislative Indicators in Guanajuato

	Before 1991	*After 1991*
AUTONOMY		
Gubernatorial vetoes	0	2
Congressional oversight	Very little	Much more
Staff for budget oversight	39	155
Congressional auditors	30	98
RESOURCES		
Mean budget	4,727,400	15,509,000
Total legislative staff	84	344
Legislative aides	2	37
Committee system	Inactive	Strong and active
MINORITY PARTY RIGHTS		
Leadership structure	Grand Committee	Internal Regime Committee
Multiparty control of committees	None	Proportional control
ACTIVITY		
Mean pages of debate	756	1,470

Analyzing change through time in addition to variation across cases allows for greater confidence in the direction of causality. To support the argument that increasing electoral competition causes legislative change, this section provides evidence that the electoral changes preceded the legislative changes.

I focus here on Guanajuato and San Luis Potosí because electoral competition has not increased substantially in Hidalgo and there have been very few changes in the way the congress works. The year 1991 was pivotal in the history of Guanajuato politics. In that year a member of the opposition party PAN became governor of the state. The important changes in the Guanajuato congress that distinguish it from the other two congresses have all taken place since 1991. As shown in table 3.5, most of the indicators of legislative institutionalization have changed considerably since 1991. Both vetoes in Guanajuato's recent history have taken place since 1991.

Interviews with longtime employees of the congress and members of congress who served terms before 1991 indicate that the Guanajuato congress increased its scrutiny of government expenditures substantially

Figure 3.1.   Internal Legislative Budgets

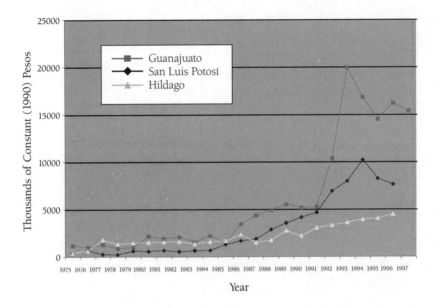

since 1991.[23] There were three times as many auditors working for the congress in 1998 as there were in 1985. The total number of people employed in the state comptroller's office increased from 39 in 1985 to 155 in 1998. For Nabor Centeno, a former congressman and legislative aide for the PAN, the biggest change in the Guanajuato congress since the early 1990s is the increased oversight of the public finances. In the previous congresses there was almost no oversight, but now, Centeno contends, the congress takes its oversight responsibilities very seriously.[24]

In the 1970s and 1980s legislative expenditures were relatively similar across the three states. Following the opposition victory in 1991, however, the expenditures in Guanajuato increased dramatically (see figure 3.1 and table 3.6).

The considerable increase in legislative spending in Guanajuato after the opposition's rise to power in 1991 is illustrated with the following interrupted time series analysis. The interrupted time series tests whether the level of spending or the rate of change in spending was significantly different after the PAN came to power. The dependent variable in the regression is the log of total legislative expenditures from 1975 to 1997 in constant

Table 3.6.   Legislative Budgets

Year	Guanajuato		San Luis Potosí		Hidalgo	
	Current Pesos*	Constant Pesos	Current Pesos	Constant Pesos	Current Pesos	Constant Pesos
1975	3	1,200	1	400	1	400
1976	3	1,000	2	667	2	667
1977	5	1,282	1	256	7	1,795
1978	4	889	1	222	6	1,333
1979	5	1,000	3	600	N/A	N/A
1980	15	2,143	4	571	N/A	N/A
1981	17	1,889	6	667	14	1,556
1982	31	2,067	8	533	24	1,600
1983	43	1,536	18	643	38	1,357
1984	97	2,205	29	659	69	1,568
1985	104	1,486	89	1,271	116	1,657
1986	412	3,433	198	1,650	278	2,317
1987	1,252	4,317	536	1,848	432	1,490
1988	N/A	N/A	1,756	2,846	1,077	1,746
1989	4,277	5,483	2,757	3,535	2,123	2,722
1990	5,139	5,139	4,114	4,114	2,167	2,167
1991	6,476	5,265	5,685	4,622	3,722	3,026
1992	14,556	10,323	9,717	6,891	4,648	3,296
1993	30,637	19,894	12,233	7,944	5,524	3,587
1994	28,055	16,799	16,955	10,153	6,514	3,901
1995	33,340	14,496	18,878	8,208	9,208	4,003
1996	48,418	16,193	22,681	7,586	13,268	4,437
1997	54,503	15,353	N/A	N/A	N/A	N/A
Mean		6,263**		2,995**		2,231**

Sources: 1975–96 data from INEGI (1986, 1991, 1994, 1998) and 1997 data from the files of staff members in the Gobierno del Estado de Guanajuato.

*Thousands of new pesos.

**$p = .01$ in one-way analysis of variance.

Table 3.7. Interrupted Time Series Regression:
The Impact of Opposition Party Control on Internal Legislative Budgets,
1975–1997 (OLS)

Independent Variables	Model 1 (N = 22)		Trimmed Model (N = 22)	
	Coefficient	Standard Error	Coefficient	Standard Error
TREND	0.116***	0.013	0.113***	0.013
DUMMY	0.888**	0.278	0.642**	0.198
TRENDUM	−0.081	0.065		
Constant	6.647***	0.135	6.677	0.135
Adjusted R²	0.934	0.932		

Source: 1975–96 data from INEGI (1986, 1991, 1994, 1998) and 1997 data from the files of staff members in the Gobierno del Estado de Guanajuato.

Note: The dependent variable is the log of the total internal budget for the legislature in constant 1990 pesos.

**p = .01; ***p = .001.

1990 pesos. To test for changes in both the mean and the slope, the regression includes a count variable from 1 to N (TREND), a dummy variable counter scored 0 for observations before the event and 1, 2, 3 . . . for observations after the event (TRENDUM), and a dummy variable scored 0 for observations before the event and 1 for observations after the event (DUMMY) (Lewis-Beck 1986).

As shown in table 3.7, the time counter variable (TREND) and the dichotomous dummy (DUMMY) are both positive and significant with 99 percent confidence. The second slope variable (TRENDUM) is not significant. These results indicate that there was a significant increase in the mean (level of spending) but not in the slope (rate of change in spending) after the PAN came to power. When the regression is re-estimated omitting the insignificant trend dummy, the results remain qualitatively unchanged.

Similar regression models for Hidalgo and San Luis Potosí show no significant change in spending when the trend is controlled, suggesting that the statistically significant increase in spending is the result of state-level causes rather than a general national trend.

Table 3.8.   Legislative Staffs

Year	Guanajuato		San Luis Potosí		Hidalgo	
	Total	Leg. Aides	Total	Leg. Aides	Total	Leg. Aides
1980	67	0	21	0		
1985	84	2	32	0		
1995	290	20				
1998	344	37	179	11	137	4

Source: Data for Guanajuato from the *Periodico Oficial del Estado de Guanajuato* (1984) and the *Proyecto del Presupuesto de Egresos del Estado de Guanajuato* (1995, 1997, 1998). Data for San Luis Potosí and Hidalgo from the files of staff members in the Congreso del Estado de San Luis Potosí and the Congreso del Estado de Hidalgo.

The Guanajuato congressional staff increased substantially in the 1990s. In 1980 there were a total of sixty-seven employees in the Guanajuato congress (including members). By 1998 the number of employees had increased more than fivefold in Guanajuato (see table 3.8).

Before 1985 there were no legislative aides at all in the Guanajuato congress.[25] The Office of Legal Advising was started in 1985 to assist with legislative research, but throughout the rest of the 1980s there were only two legislative aides.[26] For the first time in 1992 each party received a budget to hire its own staff, ending the majority party control over legislative aides.[27] There were thirty-seven legislative aides and twenty-nine advisors in the 1997–2000 congress. All of these aides have law degrees or other professional degrees.

Committees took on much greater importance in Guanajuato after 1991. Previous legislatures also worked in committees, but not as extensively as they do now. According to the director of Apoyo Parliamentario, members of congress only really began to work in committees in the mid-1990s.[28] A member of the agricultural committee noted, "The agricultural committee may have met once a year. Now [in 1998] we meet at least every two weeks, usually every week."[29] As discussed above, the important changes in the leadership structure took place in 1997 after the PRI lost its majority in the congress. Multiparty control of committees also began in the mid-1990s.

Since 1991 there has been a tremendous increase in the amount of debate in the Guanajuato congress. As shown in table 3.9, in the *Diario de los Debates,* from 1979 to 1990, there was an average of 756 pages of

Table 3.9. Congressional Activity

Years	Guanajuato Pages of Debate	San Luis Potosí Pages of Debate
1979–1980	747	
1981–1982	560	
1983–1984	680	
1985–1986	809	
1987–1988	835	
1989–1990	904	
1991–1992	1,198	
1993–1994	1,158	679
1994–1995	1,768	714
1995–1996	1,327	1,261
1996–1997	1,507	1,140
1997–1998	1,863	723
Mean 1979–1990	755.8	
Mean 1991–1998	1,470.2	

Source: Diario de los Debates, Congreso del Estado de Guanajuato, 1979–1996; Diario de los Debates, Congreso del Estado de San Luis Potosí, 1993–1997. Unpublished archives at the congressional buildings in Guanajuato and San Luis Potosí.

debate per legislative year. From 1991 to 1998 there was an average of 1,470 pages per legislative year.

Significant advances toward strengthening the legislature have also taken place in San Luis Potosí following increases in electoral competition, though these changes have not been as extensive as those in Guanajuato. The year 1991 is also an important milestone in the recent political history of San Luis Potosí. In this year civic protests against electoral fraud in the gubernatorial elections forced the PRI's governor-elect to step down. Some of the more notable changes in the San Luis Potosí congress since the electoral battles of 1991 include the legal transfer of the legislative budget from the control of the executive to the legislature, the establishment of a comptroller's office, the construction of a new congress building, and the opening of the Legislative Research Institute.

In San Luis Potosí there has been an important change in the constitutional powers of the legislature. Until the late 1980s the legislature had no separate budget. Congressional expenses such as deputy wages were paid out of the executive budget. A member of congress from the early 1980s mentioned that the legislators picked up their paychecks from the governor's office, portraying a sense that they were employees of the governor.[30] In the 1990s, the legislature began to control its own budget, and legislators no longer depend on the executive for their paychecks.

Significant changes in congressional oversight of the budget have also taken place. The state comptroller's office did not exist until 1993. In the 1980s, with only four accountants working in the entire congress, there was almost no examination of the state and municipal budgets. An opposition deputy from the early 1980s complained, "For example, in the fiftieth legislature there were seven million pesos allocated for special guests. I asked who the special guests were. The only special guests we had were on the rare days when the president of the congress actually came to work. The governor just spent the money however he wanted."[31] The state expenditures are now overseen much more closely. In 1998 the comptroller's office employed forty-two auditors.

There have also been great improvements in the congressional facilities. In 1984 the congress moved out of a corner of the Palacio del Gobierno and into its own building. In the words of Deputy José Carmen García Vázquez (a congressman in the first multiparty congress from 1981 to 1984 and in the 1997–2000 congress), "We stopped being tenants of the governor."[32] When the congress met in the Palacio del Gobierno, there was a door from the governor's office into the chamber where the congress met. According to García Vázquez, this door was used to consult the governor on every aspect of legislation and immediately send his wishes back to the congress. The new building gave the congress a much greater sense of independence.

According to the union leader for the congressional employees in San Luis Potosí, "Ten years ago there were no legislative aides, only secretaries. The secretaries did all of the work. They ran the archive and wrote the laws."[33] In 1993 the Legislative Research Institute was created to carry out legislative research and advising. By 1994 the Institute had four employees, and by 1999 it had twelve employees (Instituto de Investigaciones Legislativas 1998). The creation of the Legislative Research Institute represents a tremendous increase in the resources of the congress in San Luis Potosí. The congress's committee system is also much more active. In the 1980s the San Luis Potosí congress did not work in committees at all. According to Deputy Garcia Vázquez, in the 1980s "The governor wrote all of the legislation and just sent it to the congress to be approved. Even now there is very little debate in the full sessions. But now we work in committees and in the committees there is debate."

Clearly, in both Guanajuato and San Luis Potosí there have been many important changes in the legislatures. These legislative changes were preceded by increases in electoral competition.

When taken together, the data presented above provide substantial evidence that a shift from one-party to multiparty rule through increasing electoral competition has significant consequences for the performance of legislatures. Confirming the theoretical expectations embodied in the four hypotheses, the data show that competitive elections lead to legislative change, especially in terms of increased autonomy, resources, minority party rights, and legislative activity. The congress in Guanajuato (the most competitive state) has achieved the highest levels of strength and autonomy, whereas the congress in Hidalgo (the least competitive state) remains weak and ineffectual. The data further demonstrate that the growth of electoral competition throughout the late 1980s and 1990s in Guanajuato and San Luis Potosí preceded the institutional changes. In Hidalgo, however, very little change has taken place in either the electoral arena or the legislature.

The results of this analysis help to buttress earlier studies of the Mexican states that found a strengthening of the separation of powers in states with strong opposition parties (Lujambio 1996b; Ward and Rodríguez 1999). This study also contributes to the broader comparative study of legislative development by demonstrating that Mexico conforms to patterns of legislative transformation found in other countries in transition from one-party rule (Hahn 1996b; Remington 1994). Moreover, by focusing on legislative institutionalization, a critical component of horizontal accountability, this chapter supports the central contention of this book that increasing electoral competition can have significant influence on strengthening representative institutions, thereby increasing horizontal accountability and laying a foundation for a higher-quality democracy.

CHAPTER FOUR

Legislative Change across the Nation

Chapter 3 finds that among three states with similar structural conditions, the more competitive the state's electoral politics are, the more autonomous and active the state's legislature is. Chapter 3 further demonstrates that increases in electoral competition preceded the legislative changes in the states of Guanajuato and San Luis Potosí, suggesting that increasing electoral competition causes legislative reform. How generalizable are these findings? Are similar patterns of legislative change taking place in other states? Does the relationship between electoral competition and legislative reform hold across a larger sample of cases?

This chapter answers these questions with a quantitative analysis of electoral competition and legislative behavior across all of the states of Mexico. Because of the difficulty of gathering data across all of the states, the large-N analysis makes use of a more limited set of indicators than the case studies. The benefit of a small-N comparative case study is that it can employ thick operationalizations and provide detailed explanations of the process of reform. While a large-N analysis cannot provide such a rich description, it does allow for a greater degree of generalization, which is necessary for constructing general theories of political behavior. This chapter complements the richly textured case study data presented in chapter 3, and when taken together, these two chapters provide substantial evidence that increasing electoral competition generates new patterns of legislative behavior.

The central argument of this chapter follows the theoretical logic presented in chapter 3. In that chapter I argue that electoral competition generates new incentives and opportunities for legislators that lead to more autonomous and active legislatures with greater resources. In this chapter I test the same hypotheses developed in chapter 3, with the exception of the hypothesis relating to the rights of minority parties. Data on minority party rights are simply not available across all of the states. The three hypotheses tested here are:

> *Hypothesis I:* Increasing electoral competition generates new incentives for legislators to demand increased resources for the legislature.
> *Hypothesis II:* Increasing electoral competition results in higher levels of legislative activity.
> *Hypothesis III:* Increasing electoral competition generates new incentives for legislators to develop autonomy from the executive.

The chapter begins by presenting some general information about the local legislators in Mexico garnered from a survey of state legislators. Then I test the consequences of electoral competition on legislative resources with a cross-sectional times series regression model using the internal legislative expenditures of each state congress as the dependent variable. In the next two sections I use data from a survey of legislators in eighteen states to measure activity and autonomy. These measures are used as dependent variables in various regressions to assess the impact of electoral competition on legislative activity and autonomy. I also briefly examine some data from these surveys regarding legislators' relationships to constituents.

Local Legislatures in Mexico

Most of the data used in this chapter come from a survey applied to the members of Mexico's local congresses in 1998. The Appendix provides a copy of the survey instrument. The questionnaires were distributed by mail to all of the members of the congresses of eighteen states. Ten states were excluded from the survey because they had elections during the year the survey was conducted. As there is no consecutive reelection for members of Mexico's congresses, the entire legislature is replaced after each election. Election years, therefore, are extremely disruptive. Moreover, it is difficult to obtain useful information from deputies who have held their job for only a few weeks. Three additional states were excluded from the analysis because the congresses were unable or unwilling to pro-

Table 4.1.   States Included in Survey

Included in Survey	Excluded because of Elections in 1998	Others
Baja California Sur	Aguascalientes	Campeche
Colima	Baja California	Coahuila
Guanajuato	Chiapas	Estado de México
Guerrero	Chihuahua	
Hidalgo	Durango	
Jalisco	Oaxaca	
Michoacán	Tabasco	
Morelos	Veracruz	
Nayarit	Yucatan	
Nuevo León	Zacatecas	
Puebla		
Querétaro		
Quintana Roo		
San Luis Potosí		
Sinaloa		
Sonora		
Tamaulipas		
Tlaxcala		

vide the names and addresses of the members. Table 4.1 lists the states that were included in the analysis, the states that were excluded because of elections, and the other three states. From a total of 547 surveys distributed, 177 surveys were returned, for a response rate of 32.4 percent.[1]

Table 4.2 presents some general information from the survey about state legislators in Mexico.

The legislators are well educated. Over 80 percent have some college education. The most common careers for a legislator are law, education, accounting, and business. The members of the state legislatures tend to have relatively close ties to their states (especially when compared with governors). Sixty-four percent were educated in the states where they serve, while only 19 percent studied in Mexico City. This figure contrasts significantly with the education of governors in that only 21 percent of governors were educated in the states where they govern. (See chapter 5 and table 5.2 for some general characteristics of the governors.) Eighty-five percent of the respondents live in the districts they represent.

Table 4.2.   General Characteristics of the Local Legislators

	%	(N)
Some college education	82	(138)
Studied law	29	(48)
Studied education	10	(16)
Studied accounting	9	(15)
Studied business	7	(11)
Educated in state	64	(102)
Educated in Mexico City	19	(30)
Live in district they represent	85	(139)
Held an elected post in the past	52	(88)
Served in the local congress in the past	15	(25)
Served on the city council	27	(45)
Served as a mayor	11	(19)
Served in the national congress	11	(19)
Dedicate more than 75% of professional time to service in the congress	49	(79)

The average deputy does not have much experience in politics. Just over one-half have held an elected office. Only 15 percent have served in the local congress in the past. Twenty-seven percent have served on a city council, and 11 percent have served as a mayor. Eleven percent have served in the national congress. While local legislators are not officially permitted to hold other jobs, and all are paid generous full-time salaries, less than half of the surveyed deputies spend more than 75 percent of their professional time working on legislative activities.

The data suggest a pattern that is typical of the local legislatures in Mexico. Most of the members are educated in the state and have stronger ties to the state than to the national political elite in Mexico City. A few, however, are very closely tied to the national political elite, and they are spending a term in the "provinces" either because they have fallen out of favor with the current presidential administration or because they are simply waiting out one term from the federal congress on account of the prohibition on reelection. Until 2000, members of opposition parties were particularly likely to return to the local congresses because positions in the national bureaucracy were typically not available to politicians from parties other than the PRI.

Resources

Resources are fundamental to the functioning of an autonomous legislature. Without a sufficient budget and staff, a legislature must depend on the executive for information and allow the executive to dominate research and lawmaking. A congress with extensive resources has the possibility of acting independently of the executive, whereas a legislature with very few resources does not. Internal legislative budgets are a useful indicator of the resources available to the congress and the potential ability of the congress to develop independent sources of information. The legislative expenditures, measured by the internal budgets, are used primarily to maintain the congressional facilities and pay the staff. A larger budget enables the congress to strengthen its lawmaking capacity by hiring more legislative aides, improving the library, and buying more computer equipment.

The following analysis examines annual data on internal legislative spending, electoral competitiveness, and general socioeconomic indicators across twenty-eight of the thirty-one Mexican states from 1975 to 1996.[2] Such an extensive data set is quite rare in the literature on Mexican state politics, which has been dominated largely by individual case studies. The following analysis employs a cross-sectional time series regression to test the relationship between electoral competition and legislative resources.[3] Each of the independent variables is lagged by one year. Lagging the independent variables clarifies the direction of causality in the model and also makes sense theoretically. If the congress members are elected and take office in 1995, for example, their influence on budgets will not be felt until 1996.

The dependent variable, legislative resources, is measured by the total yearly internal legislative expenditures (in constant 1990 pesos) of each state congress. The state expenditure data are compiled and published by the Mexican government (INEGI 1986, 1991, 1994, 1998).[4] Admittedly, relying on data published by an authoritarian government can be problematic, but in contrast to statistics on social spending or GDP growth, it seems unlikely that the data on legislative expenditures would fall victim to political manipulation.

To measure the central explanatory variable (the level of electoral competition in each state through time), I replicate for the Mexican states the cross-national measure developed by Vanhanen (1990, 2000), using data from each state's legislative elections from 1975 to 1996. Vanhanen's index has two components—participation and competition. The amount of participation in the election (turnout/total population) is multiplied by

the amount of competition (100 – % votes of largest party). For this regression, Vanhanen's index is calculated using the overall level of competitiveness within each state. Aggregate statewide percentages are used
rather than district-level data because it is the overall level of competitiveness of the state that is theoretically relevant for the determination of
state budgets. The indicator is calculated using the official results from
each state's electoral institute. The data used were compiled by the Centro
de Estadística y Documentación Electoral at the Universidad Autónoma
Metropolitana—Iztapalapa in Mexico City.

Some scholars have criticized Vanhanen's index because it provides a
minimalist conceptualization of democracy, leaving out many important
components (Munck and Verkuilen 2002). These critiques do not pose
significant problems for this analysis because the attempt here is to dis-
aggregate democracy and focus on its basic procedural dimensions. Vanhanen's index is useful because it is a standard measure that is available
for cross-national comparison, and unlike other standard indices of democracy, it is replicable for the Mexican states. All of the statistical analyses performed here were also carried out using a variety of other measures
of electoral competition, including the two separate components of Vanhanen's index, the margin of victory, and the percentage vote for the PRI.
All of these measures are closely correlated, and the results do not vary substantially when different measurements are used. Ultimately, Vanhanen's
index is preferable because it stresses the comparability of the study rather
than the specific Mexican context of declining PRI rule.

Clearly, electoral fraud has taken place in some state elections during
the period from 1975 to 1996. In cases where fraud has been committed,
official electoral results provided by the states' electoral institutes reflect
the fraudulent vote count rather than the actual votes. It would be impossible to gather statistics on the actual vote count. Even if it were possible to obtain the actual vote count, the possibly fraudulent official statistics are more useful for the purposes of this analysis than the actual
results. Unlike studies of voting behavior, where the true results matter,
this analysis is trying to measure the level of openness in the political system in terms of the amount of allowable opposition and contestation.
Therefore, the true vote count is less important than the amount of opposition that is permitted by the regime. The official electoral results provide
a reliable measure of allowable contestation. Imagine, for example, that an
opposition party actually won an election, but the ruling party controlled
the polling stations and the electoral institute to such an extent that it was
able to manipulate the ballots and claim victory. In such a case it would
be more accurate to record the election as a win for the ruling party and

hence a less competitive election than to use the actual electoral results, which would consider the election highly competitive. For these reasons, I use the official electoral results.

In addition to an independent variable for electoral competitiveness, the regression equation also includes control variables for the state GDP (INEGI 1996, 2000), state GDP per capita (INEGI 1996, 2000; Nacional Financiera 1995, 13–15), the number of legislators in each congress (Crespo 1996), the presence of a divided government, the level of urbanization in the state (Nacional Financiera 1995, 13–15), and the total population (Nacional Financiera 1995, 13-15). Modernization theory suggests that more "modern" (i.e., wealthier and more urban) areas will have more institutionalized legislatures (Huntington 1965). Therefore, I expect that a state with a greater GDP and GDP per capita and a higher level of urbanization will have a more institutionalized legislature and will therefore spend more on the legislature. I also expect that a congress with a large number of members will have a higher legislative budget simply to pay the extra members' salaries. Furthermore, the divided government dummy is expected to be positively related to legislative spending because prior research has posited a central theoretical role for divided government in legislative development (Lujambio 1996a). In fact, Lujambio argues that the central explanatory variable in the legislative institutionalization of the Mexican states is divided government. Similarly, Cox and Morgenstern (2001) see the percentage of the congress supporting the executive as a key variable. The control for total population is also expected to be positive because a larger state will tend to have more money to spend on a legislature.

Table 4.3 shows the results of the cross-sectional time series regression using a GEE estimation (corrected for first-order autocorrelation) of the impact of electoral competition on internal legislative budgets.

In support of Hypothesis I, the electoral competitiveness index is positive and just barely misses standard levels of significance ($p = 0.056$); thus, the coefficient is significant with 94 percent confidence. Hence, states with higher levels of electoral competition have greater legislative spending. The divided government variable is also positive and highly significant, confirming the importance of the makeup of the congress in influencing congressional development. Surprisingly, both GDP and GDP per capita are insignificant, suggesting that a state with a big economy does not provide significantly more resources to its legislature. Also unexpectedly, when other important variables are held constant, the number of members of each congress has a negative impact on legislative expenditures.[5] The level of urbanization is positive and significant. As expected, the total population

Table 4.3.   Cross-Sectional Time Series GEE Regression: The Impact
of Interparty Competition on Internal Legislative Budgets, 1975–1996
(Corrected for First-Order Autocorrelation)

	Dep. Var. = Internal Legislative Budgets
Vanhanen's index	53.566
	(1.91)
Divided government dummy	1,331.664
	(2.59)**
GDP	0.000
	(0.17)
GDP per capita	0.0003
	(0.02)
Number of legislators	-157.590
	(2.23)*
Urbanization	5,357.702
	(2.55)*
Total population	1.754
	(5.43)**
Constant	1,518.220
	(0.60)
Observations	466
Number of group (state)	28

Note: Absolute value of z statistics is in parentheses.
*$p < .05$; **$p < .01$.

is positive and significant. Thus, the more urban and large the state's population, the greater the internal legislative budget is.

The estimation results suggest that increasing electoral competition
has important consequences for the resources allocated to the legislature,
even after divided government is controlled. Furthermore, the insignifi-
cance of the control variables for GDP and GDP per capita suggest that
contrary to the expectations of modernization theory, the level of economic development does not have an important impact on legislative
resources. The statistical results of the cross-sectional time series analysis fit well with the more qualitative findings of chapter 3, which uses a
much broader range of indicators to establish the relationship between

electoral competitiveness and legislative resources in just three states. Evidence that the pattern found in the case studies holds across twenty-eight states and twenty-two years provides much greater confidence in the generalizability of the conclusions of chapter 3.

The regression analysis of legislative budgets focuses on the macro-level relationship between electoral competitiveness and legislative change. The theoretical logic underpinning the central hypotheses, however, focuses on individual behavior as well as macro-level institutional changes. The survey data presented in the following sections illuminate the micro-level changes in the behavior of individual members of congress that undergird the macro-level relationship found here.

Activity

In this section I analyze the impact of electoral competition on legislative activity. Does the legislature actually do anything, or does it merely serve as a rubber stamp for executive proposals? The level of legislative activity is an important component of legislative development. The data used to analyze both legislative activity and autonomy come from the survey described above. The unit of analysis in these models is the individual legislator. This contrasts with the previous cross-sectional time series model, in which the unit of analysis is the state.

Implicit in the theoretical propositions outlined in chapter 3 are both micro-level changes in the behavior of individual members of congress as a result of the incentives they face and macro-level changes in the institutional behavior of the legislature as a whole in response to changes in the state-level political context. Therefore, this chapter looks at both individual district-level changes in electoral competitiveness and changes in aggregate electoral competitiveness at the state level. Micro-level electoral competitiveness is measured in terms of the actual level of competition each legislator faced in his or her district when elected. Macro-level competitiveness is measured by the overall level of competitiveness in the state. Thus, even in a largely noncompetitive state, there are usually some competitive districts where legislators are elected in close races. These members are expected to act differently from their colleagues in the same state who were elected in noncompetitive districts with large margins of victory. Theory suggests that both the general electoral environment in the state and the individual level of competitiveness faced by legislators matter. It is expected that district-level electoral patterns will influence the behavior of the individual members of congress, whereas the general state level of electoral competition will be most important for understanding macro-level institutional changes in the legislatures.

Three questions from the survey provide measures of legislative activity and constitute the dependent variables in the following analysis. The first dependent variable is a ratio variable and is therefore estimated with ordinary least squares regression (OLS). The last two dependent variables are ordinal variables, which create problems for estimation with OLS (Greene 1993)[6] and are therefore estimated with ordered probit.

The first dependent variable (LAWSDEP) is a measure of the law-making activities of the congresses. Theoretically, the main purpose of a legislature is to make laws. In the Mexican states, however, the legislature is not the only institution with the constitutional power to propose new laws. Most of the state constitutions also allow the executive, the judicial branch, and the municipal governments to propose laws. Traditionally the executive has written and proposed most of the laws, and the legislature has merely acted as a rubber stamp to approve them. As the legislature becomes a more relevant institution, it is expected that the legislators will begin to take a greater role in producing legislation.

To measure the extent of the legislatures' lawmaking activities, each deputy was asked, "Approximately what percentage of the laws passed in your state were initiated by a deputy?"[7] The individual responses of each legislator are used at the dependent variable. The responses vary from 0 to 100 percent of the initiatives. Obviously, there is a "correct" answer to this question, and the actual data of legislative initiatives could be used instead of survey data. Most state legislatures, however, do not keep records of this type of information, making collection of real data impossible. Moreover, the vast majority of laws passed by local congresses are largely irrelevant politically, dealing with issues such as the transfer of land titles. Hence, the percentages of actual bills introduced by legislators may not be as useful an indicator as the perceptions of the legislators about the percentage of bills introduced by members of the congress.

The dependent variable is regressed against two measures of electoral competition. The first indicator, Vanhanen's index, is the same competitiveness index used in the previous regression of legislative expenditures. It is calculated using aggregate state-level data. Because the following analysis employs individual-level data, a second indicator of individual-level electoral competitiveness that is calculated with district-level data is also used. The district-level indicator is the margin of victory in the local congressional election of each legislator; thus, each legislator's responses on the survey are matched up with the election results from his or her district. The margin of victory is calculated by subtracting the percentage vote for the runner-up party from the percentage vote for the winning party. The district-level indicator is calculated separately for each deputy using the electoral results for the congressional district in which the surveyed member was elected. This indicator assesses the individual-level causes of legislative behavior by examining the electoral incentives that face each legislator. As in the national electoral system, all of the Mexican states have a mixed electoral system in which 25 to 45 percent of the state congressional seats are distributed via proportional representation. The aggregate state margin of victory is used for survey respondents with seats distributed through proportional representation, since their district is essentially the entire state. Vanhanen's index is expected to be positively related to legislative initiatives, while the margin of victory is expected to be negatively related to legislative initiatives because the higher the margin of victory, the lower the electoral competition.

Since the district-level indicator measures the electoral conditions under which each legislator is elected, it is expected to be most effective in predicting the behavior of individual legislators. The state-level indicator is an aggregate measure of the general level of competitiveness in the state and is therefore expected to be more successful in predicting the institutional behavior of the congress as a whole rather than the behavior of individual members. In fact, however, both indicators are quite powerful in explaining both individual and aggregate behavior. This seems to be because the two measures are quite highly correlated.

Since the legislative initiatives variable is measuring the legislator's perception of the institutional behavior of the congress rather than the individual-level behavior of members, aggregate rather than individual-level control variables are used. The independent variables are the same as those used in table 4.3. State GDP (INEGI 1996, 2000), state GDP per capita (INEGI 1996, 2000; Nacional Financiera 1995, 13–15), the number of legislators in each congress (Crespo 1996), the presence of a divided government, the level of urbanization in the state (Nacional Financiera 1995, 13–15), and the total population (Nacional Financiera 1995, 13–15) are included as controls.

Table 4.4 presents the results of the OLS regression using the reported percentage of initiatives proposed by deputies as the dependent variable.

Both of the competitiveness indicators are statistically significant with 99 percent confidence. As expected, Vanhanen's index is positive and the margin of victory is negative, indicating that the greater the level of electoral competitiveness, the higher the percentage of legislative initiatives originating with legislators (as perceived by the legislators themselves). Again, the divided government dummy is positive and significant,

Table 4.4. The Impact of Interparty Competition on Legislative
Initiatives (OLS)

	Dep. Var. = LAWSDIP	
Vanhanen's index	1.384	
	(2.61)**	
District margin of victory		−0.373
		(3.20)**
Divided government dummy	16.343	16.250
	(3.66)**	(3.66)**
GDP	0.004	0.003
	(5.68)**	(4.97)**
GDP per capita	−3.296	−2.564
	(2.03)*	(1.66)
Number of legislators	−0.443	−0.116
	(1.02)	(0.27)
Urbanization	40.292	36.493
	(2.20)*	(1.94)
Total population	−0.020	−0.017
	(4.50)**	(4.15)**
Constant	11.592	23.101
	(0.48)	(0.91)
Observations	136	130
R^2	0.38	0.40

Note: Absolute value of t statistics in parentheses.
*$p < .05$; **$p < .01$.

suggesting that the legislatures are more active where the legislature is not
controlled by the same party as the executive. The state GDP is positive
and highly significant in both of the estimations, suggesting that the larger
the economy of the state, the more active the legislature is. Strangely, after
total GDP is controlled, GDP per capita is negative. Population is also
negative and significant in both of the equations. Thus, the higher the
standard of living in the state and the more populous the state, the less
active the legislature is. The number of legislators is insignificant in both
equations. The overall fit of the model is respectable, with R^2s of 0.38
and 0.40.

The second dependent variable (SPEAKCOM) is a measure of the activity and importance of the congressional committees. Each deputy was

asked, "How often do you speak in a committee meeting during a typical month of a legislative session?"[8] The answers were coded 1 = never, 2 = one or two times, 3 = between three and ten times, 4 = more than ten times. The higher the value of the SPEAKCOM variable, the greater the discussion and activity of the legislative committee system. The third dependent variable (RADIOTV) indirectly measures congressional activity through media coverage of the congress. The amount of coverage of congressional activities in the media indicates how relevant the legislature is by measuring public interest in the legislature's activities. Each deputy answered the question "How many times have you been interviewed for a radio or television program in the past year?"[9] The answers were coded 1 = one to five times, 2 = five to ten times, 3 = ten to twenty times, 4 = twenty to fifty times, and 5 = more than fifty times.

Both the aggregate state-level Vanhanen's index and the district-level margin of victory are used to measure electoral competition. The dependent variables SPEAKCOM and RADIOTV measure individual-level behavior rather than institutional behavior: how often each legislator speaks in committee and how often each is interviewed by radio and television programs. Therefore, I expect that the district competitiveness indicator will be a better predictor of these two variables than the aggregate measure. The control variables are also individual-level variables rather than statewide variables. The level of education of each deputy is included because it is expected that legislators with more education will be more active than those with less education. Members who are trained as lawyers are also expected to be more active than others, as are those who have held elected positions in the past. Therefore, dummy variables for lawyers and past elective experience are also included as controls.

Table 4.5 presents the results of the ordered probit analysis of SPEAK-COM and RADIOTV.

In model 1, Vanhanen's index is positive, as expected, but not significant. The district-level margin of victory is negative, as expected, and statistically significant with 95 percent confidence. These results indicate that the smaller the margin of victory by which a legislator wins his or her election, the more often he or she will speak in committee meetings. Thus, legislators elected in more competitive elections are more likely to be active in committee meetings. Education level is also a powerful predictor of participation in committees. Congress members with more education speak in committee more often than those with less education. Training as a lawyer and past experience in elected office do not seem to matter.

Again in the RADIOTV regressions, Vanhanen's index is positive and the district-level margin of victory is negative, as expected, though neither

Table 4.5.   The Impact of Interparty Competition on Legislative
Activity (Ordered Probit)

	Model 1: Dep. Var. = SPEAKCOM		Model 2: Dep. Var. = RADIOTV	
Vanhanen's index	0.024		0.019	
	(1.09)		(0.95)	
District margin of victory		−0.013		−0.008
		(2.42)*		(1.64)
Education level	0.345	0.416	0.237	0.222
	(3.13)**	(3.51)**	(2.46)*	(2.19)*
Elected position	−0.015	0.030	−0.144	−0.021
	(0.08)	(0.15)	(0.87)	(0.12)
Lawyer	0.105	0.039	−0.013	0.087
	(0.49)	(0.18)	(0.07)	(0.45)
Observations	161	147	167	153
Pseudo-R^2	0.04	0.07	0.02	0.02
Log-likelihood	−148.78	−131.12	−256.37	−233.07

Note: Absolute value of z statistics in parentheses.
*$p < .05$; **$p < .01$.

of the competitiveness indicators is statistically significant at conventional
levels of confidence. The district-level indicator, however, is statistically
significant with 90 percent confidence. Again, education is positive and significant, but the other control variables are not significant. The pseudo-
R^2, a measure of goodness of fit in ordered probit models, is very low in
all of the estimations. Admittedly, the independent variables are not explaining very much of the variance. Nevertheless, as I am just testing statistical relationships and not trying to make predictions from this model,
the low pseudo-R^2 is not of great concern.

     In sum, the positive statistical relationship between electoral competi-
tiveness and legislative activity found in the survey data provides further
evidence that competitive elections matter for legislative behavior. The specific electoral context facing an individual legislator has a significant impact on the way the legislator behaves. These results provide micro-level
evidence of the relationship between competition and legislative development and support the findings from the case studies in chapter 3.

Autonomy

Congressional autonomy from the executive is a fundamental aspect of developing a viable system of checks and balances. The legislature must be able to act autonomously from the executive if it is to serve its function as an agency of horizontal accountability. In this section I examine the relationship between legislative autonomy and electoral competition.

To assess the relative independence of the congress, I examine legislators' perceptions of their responsibilities and their relative time commitments to various activities. In particular I use the survey data described above and focus on questions that measure the relative importance that legislators place on oversight, lawmaking, and supporting the governor. The three variables used to measure congressional autonomy come from one question in which the legislators were asked to rank nine legislative activities according to how much time they dedicated to each. Among the activities the members were asked to rank were "Oversee the activities of other government agencies" (OVER), "Propose laws" (LAWS), and "Support the governor" (SupGov).[10] As argued in chapter 3, strong oversight is an indicator of legislative autonomy. The ranking of "Propose laws" when compared with "Support the governor" is also a good indicator of legislative autonomy. In a more autonomous congress, we would expect that legislators would spend more time proposing laws than supporting the governor.

Each of the dependent variables is an ordinal variable, so each model is estimated with ordered probit. I use the same two indicators of electoral competition as in the previous regressions: the state-level Vanhanen's index and the district-level margin of victory. These two measures are inversely related: the higher the margin of victory, the lower the electoral competition. Since the dependent variable measures the individual behavior of legislators, the district-level indicator is theoretically more relevant and is therefore expected to be a better predictor for these models. Legislators elected in competitive elections are expected to be more concerned with fulfilling the legislative responsibilities of oversight than legislators elected in noncompetitive districts. Therefore, the coefficient of the margin of victory variable in the equation using OVER as the dependent variable is expected to be negative, indicating that the higher the margin of victory by which the legislator was elected, the less time he or she spends on oversight. Similarly, the coefficient for Vanhanen's index is expected to be positive.

Legislators elected in noncompetitive elections are more likely to have been appointed by party leaders and the governor and are therefore more likely to be concerned with pleasing the governor than with making laws. Hence, the coefficient of the margin of victory in the regressions of LAWS is expected to negative, and in the regression of SupGov it is expected to be positive. Vanhanen's index is expected to be positive in the regression of LAWS and negative in SupGov. The aggregate level of competitiveness in the state is less directly associated with the individual behavior of legislators. Therefore, Vanhanen's index is expected to have a weaker influence in these models than the district margin of victory.

The other independent variables used in these equations are education level, past political experience, legal training, and a dummy variable that takes on a value of 1 if the governor and the deputy are from the same party and 0 if the governor and the deputy are from different parties. I expect that education, past political experience, and legal training will be positively related to the measures of lawmaking and oversight and negatively related to the measure of subservience to the governor. It seems likely that more educated and experienced legislators will be more independent and autonomous. The final independent variable controls for the party affiliation of the governor and the legislator. I anticipate that a legislator from the same party as the governor will be more likely to support the governor and less likely to oversee the behavior of the governor. Therefore, I expect the coefficients of the same party dummy to be negative when regressed on OVER and positive when regressed on SupGov.

Table 4.6 presents the results of the ordered probit estimations of legislative autonomy.

Model 1 estimates the impact of electoral competition on the amount of time each legislator dedicates to oversight. Vanhanen's index is positive but not statistically significant. The district-level margin of victory is negative, as expected, and statistically significant with 95 percent confidence. None of the control variables is statistically significant. Contrary to the original expectations, more educated legislators are no more likely to spend time overseeing other government agencies than less educated deputies. Past political experience in elected offices and training as a lawyer also have no significant impact on the oversight activities of individual congress members. Likewise, the same party dummy is insignificant in both regressions.

The dependent variable in model 2 measures the amount of time each legislator dedicates to proposing laws. As anticipated, Vanhanen's index is positive and the district margin of victory is negative. Both the state and the district competitiveness indicators are statistically significant with 99 percent confidence. Therefore, both legislators in generally competitive states and legislators elected in competitive district elections spend more

Table 4.6. The Impact of Interparty Competition on Legislative Autonomy (Ordered Probit)

	Model 1: Dep. Var. = (10 − OVER)		Model 2: Dep. Var. = (10 − LAWS)		Model 3: Dep. Var. = (10 − SupGov)	
Vanhanen's index	0.003 (0.15)		0.058 (2.78)**		−0.003 (0.13)	
District margin of victory		−0.010 (2.15)*		−0.013 (2.69)**		0.014 (2.77)**
Education level	0.009 (0.09)	−0.030 (0.30)	0.078 (0.76)	0.038 (0.35)	0.064 (0.60)	0.043 (0.38)
Elected position	0.050 (0.30)	0.071 (0.41)	0.099 (0.57)	0.020 (0.11)	0.029 (0.16)	−0.023 (0.12)
Lawyer	−0.118 (0.63)	−0.107 (0.56)	−0.119 (0.62)	−0.119 (0.59)	0.063 (0.32)	0.117 (0.57)
Same party	−0.237 (1.41)	−0.211 (1.20)	−0.002 (0.01)	0.032 (0.17)	0.861 (4.56)**	0.795 (4.04)**
Observations	161	147	159	146	151	139
Pseudo-R^2	0.004	0.01	0.01	0.01	0.04	0.05
Log-likelihood	−331.04	−300.34	−307.84	−277.84	−275.29	−249.15

Note: Absolute value of z statistics in parentheses.
*$p < .05$; **$p < .01$.

time proposing laws than deputies from less competitive states and districts. Again in model 2, none of the control variables are significant.

Model 3 estimates the impact of electoral competition on the relative importance each legislator places on supporting the governor. The coefficient of Vanhanen's index is negative but not statistically significant. The coefficient for the district margin of victory is positive and statistically significant. Therefore, the data suggest that the level of competition each individual legislator faces influences the legislator's relationship with the governor. Legislators representing competitive districts are less likely to spend the bulk of their time supporting the governor, whereas legislators elected with large margins of victory are more likely to spend time supporting the governor. The only control variable that is statistically significant is the same party dummy. The coefficient is positive, indicating that deputies from the same party as the governor are likely to dedicate more time to supporting the governor than deputies from other parties.

The individual-level survey data illuminate the micro-level foundations of legislative autonomy in competitive contexts. Legislators from competitive districts are more likely to spend time on oversight, suggesting that deputies who were elected to congress in competitive elections face greater incentives to take oversight seriously than those who ran in noncompetitive elections. When the results of model 2 and model 3 are compared, it seems clear that electoral competitiveness also creates incentives for legislators to spend more time making laws and less time supporting the governor, thereby enhancing the independence of the congress.

Constituency Relations

In addition to the questions on legislative development and institutionalization, which are the main focus of this book, the survey of the legislators asked a battery of questions about legislators' relationship with their constituency. Understanding this relationship is important because in the end it is the relationship between a government and its citizens that matters most to democracy.

Unfortunately, however, it is difficult, both theoretically and empirically, to disentangle the differences between constituency service and patronage. On the one hand, increased electoral competition should result in stronger ties between legislators and their constituents because legislators will attempt to both improve their own chances for reelection (or election to another post when reelection is not permitted) and to improve their position within their party by securing the party's future victory in the district. On the other hand, in Mexico many traditional ruling party legislators are either leaders in a corporatist organization such as the CTM and the CNC or members of prominent cacique families.[11] A strong relationship between a legislator and his or her district may be the result of the traditional clientelistic bargain in which caciques distribute material benefits in exchange for votes. As competition increases, this relationship may break down if opposition parties attempt to reorient elections around policy platforms and good governance rather than patronage. This has certainly been the case with the PAN in Mexico. The PAN has struggled to devise new strategies of mobilization while rejecting traditional exchanges of patronage for political support (Mizrahi 1998, 108). The result of the PAN's rejection of clientelism has often been an apparent detach-

Table 4.7. The Impact of Interparty Competition on Constituent Relations (Ordered Probit)

	Model 1: Dep. Var. = PUBAUD	Model 2: Dep. Var. = MEETING	Model 3: Dep. Var. = SPEECH	Model 4: Dep. Var. = SERVICE	Model 5: Dep. Var. = GODF	Model 6: Dep. Var. = RETURN
District margin of victory	0.009 (1.81)	0.004 (0.84)	0.007 (1.50)	0.005 (0.93)	0.013 (2.27)*	0.008 (1.52)
Education level	0.078 (0.73)	0.236 (2.22)*	0.255 (2.36)*	0.200 (1.79)	0.213 (1.55)	0.154 (1.33)
Elected position	0.128 (0.70)	0.151 (0.81)	0.115 (0.62)	−0.036 (0.19)	0.176 (0.80)	0.332 (1.62)
Lawyer	−0.067 (0.33)	0.029 (0.14)	0.047 (0.22)	−0.076 (0.35)	0.115 (0.47)	0.186 (0.80)
Observations	140	142	135	144	136	132
Pseudo-R^2	0.01	0.02	0.02	0.01	0.04	0.02
Log-likelihood	−187.37	−169.23	−167.27	−142.93	−103.46	−142.77

Note: Absolute value of z statistics in parentheses.
*$p < .05$; **$p < .01$.

ment of the PAN from a mass base. In interviews with local deputies, members from the PAN tended to stress their policies and their record of effective administration, whereas members from PRI were more likely to point to their success in distributing material benefits. Given these problems, it is not too surprising that the survey data show no clear association between electoral competition and constituency service.

Table 4.7 presents the results of various measures of constituent relations. The models test the impact of electoral competitiveness on the frequency with which legislators have public audiences with their constituents (PUBAUD), attend meetings in their districts (MEETING), give speeches in their districts (SPEECH), provide services for a voter (SERVICE), go to Mexico City to solicit support for their district (GODF), and return to their districts (RETURN).[12] The only regression in which the margin of victory is significant is the GODF model. Members from competitive districts are less likely to go to Mexico City to solicit support for their districts from the federal government. The intention of this question was to tap the legislator's connectedness to the national political elite, as opposed to the state political elite. Deputies from less competitive areas were better connected to the PRI-dominated federal government than were their counterparts in more competitive districts.

This chapter used multivariate statistical techniques to test the conclusions of chapter 3 across a larger set of cases. It presented aggregate state data in a cross-sectional time series analysis to demonstrate a positive relationship between electoral competition and legislative resources. The chapter then provided individual-level data from a survey of local congress members. The survey data demonstrated that the competitiveness of the elections in which each legislator was elected had a significant impact on the legislator's behavior. In particular, legislators elected with small margins of victory were more likely to speak in committee meetings and be interviewed on the television or the radio. They also spent more time overseeing other government agencies and making laws and less time supporting the governor. Thus, the data support the general conclusion that increasing electoral competition generates a more active and autonomous legislature with more resources.

More highly educated and experienced legislators were expected to be more active and autonomous. The data suggest that more highly educated deputies tend to be more active but not more autonomous. Therefore, we can expect that if future members of the local congresses are more educated, the legislatures will be more active but not necessarily more autonomous from the governor.

The most important finding of this chapter is the consistent positive relationship between electoral competition and the measures of legislative resources, activity, and autonomy. These results buttress those found in chapter 3 and have important implications for the future of Mexican politics. It seems likely that as competition continues to take root and grow across Mexico, the legislative branch will increase its influence in the states of Mexico. Legislative development, in turn, is expected to improve horizontal accountability and thereby have important consequences for the quality of democracy.

CHAPTER FIVE

The Recruitment of Governors

In states across Mexico where hotly contested elections are determining who governs, the profile of governors is changing in important ways. For example, in a debate between the two candidates for the governorship of the state of Nuevo León in 1997, the PRI candidate José Natividad González Parás stated, "I love Nuevo León a lot. I studied here. I did not go to Mexico City to a prestigious and expensive school to study because I had confidence in the institutions of my state" (*El Norte,* April 25, 1997, 4B, cited in Diaz 2000). In a country where governors have traditionally been selected by the president, and legal training in the National University (Universidad Nacional Autónoma de México [UNAM]) has virtually been a requirement to become a part of the political elite, why would a gubernatorial candidate stress the fact that he had not attended a prestigious university in Mexico City?

More generally, what is driving the change in patterns of political recruitment in the Mexican states? Does the introduction of competitive elections as the primary means of selecting leaders affect the type of people who actually gain leadership positions? Or does the transition from authoritarian to democratic politics simply use a different process to recycle the same traditional elites into powerful positions? The study of political recruitment answers the question "Who governs?" Answering this question is critical for developing an understanding of how any political system functions. How leaders are chosen and who those leaders are have significant consequences for representation. Political recruitment links state and society by determining who constitutes the state and how people move from society to the state (Czudnowski 1975). Shifts in patterns of political recruitment are important indicators of change in a polity. Moreover, if increasing political competition results in new leaders who emerge from society and represent local interests, rather than the interests of the established political class, then, just like independent legislatures, these new leaders can provide an important check on the power of the national executive. Thus, changes in patterns of political recruitment for governors that favor local interests can have important consequences for horizontal accountability, especially in a context such as the Mexican states, where traditionally presidents have exerted tremendous influence over governors. In sum, more inclusive patterns of political recruitment can result in important shifts of power away from party elites and into the hands of voters.

In this chapter I examine the impact of electoral competitiveness on the recruitment of governors and candidate selection processes in Mexico. The central argument is that as electoral politics becomes more competitive, the incentives and opportunities of politicians and party leaders change in ways that can be expected to lead to more inclusive processes of candidate selection and different types of people arriving at leadership positions. More specifically, I expect that growing political competition in the Mexican states will lead to governors with strong political ties to the states they govern rather than strong ties to the national political elite.

Alternative Approaches to the Study of Political Recruitment

Each major theoretical approach to the study of comparative politics provides a different explanation for why patterns of political recruitment vary across countries and change through time. Modernization theory suggests that as society becomes more economically and socially complex, patterns of recruitment become more universalistic and merit based (Rejai 1969). Clubok, Wilensky, and Berghorn (1969), for example, argue that political modernization leads to ideological acceptance of citizen equality, which results in a more open recruitment system, characterized by the decreasing presence of traditional families in leadership positions. They find that the influence of traditional families in the U.S. Congress has declined through time. Likewise, Peter Smith (1979) argues that the middle classes increasingly have gained control over government positions in Mexico as a result of gradual socioeconomic development.

In contrast to the optimistic view of the modernization theorists, political culture theory argues that patterns of political recruitment are largely determined by the unique cultural characteristics of each polity, which are relatively resistant to change from the forces of modernization. Thus, a shift from authoritarian rule to democracy may not significantly alter patterns of political recruitment if cultural values are not also changed. In the words of Roderic Camp (1995c), "Contrary to modernization arguments, traditional patterns of behavior are often flexible, ingrained, and somewhat impervious to institutional changes" (10). Cultural theorists tend to predict (and find) stability rather than change. In contradiction to Smith's (1979) findings that the composition of the Mexican leadership has changed substantially over the course of the twentieth century, Camp (1995c) argues that "although elite criteria have altered somewhat over a century, in many respects they remain unchanged" (9). According to Camp, political recruitment in Mexico is largely controlled by clientelism and personalist networks known as *camarillas*. The political culture theorists stress the importance of informal rules and cultural practices rather than formal institutions or economic structures. In fact, Camp (1995c, 28–29) argues that increased competitiveness in a political system does not obstruct informal networking cliques, though he does acknowledge that it may create more paths for politicians seeking leadership positions.

Similar to political culture theory in their pessimistic outlook, some structural theories argue that class systems and economic structures constrain the capacity of institutions and political events to change patterns of political recruitment. Traditional oligarchs are extremely flexible and capable of adapting to changing economic and political conditions in order to maintain their economic and political dominance. Therefore, traditional families are likely to maintain important influence over leadership positions regardless of economic or political transformation. If, as Wasserman (1993) contends, the prerevolutionary elite were able to maintain significant influence in the state of Chihuahua after the Mexican Revolution, truly a most unlikely context for a traditional oligarchy to survive, it seems unlikely that most (less dramatic) institutional changes will be able to dislodge an oligarchy. Similarly, Hagopian (1996) argues that the traditional elite in the state of Minas Gerais, Brazil, was able to remain intact throughout the twentieth century, surviving multiple regime changes and extensive economic transformation. At the extreme, this argument suggests that nothing ever changes in politics and that the same traditional elite have always occupied and will continue to occupy the state to promote their economic interests.

While each of these theories contributes to a broader understanding of political recruitment by emphasizing important explanatory variables, the most useful theoretical approach for understanding the changing patterns of leadership selection is an institutional rational choice model. Modernization theory can explain change but not stability, and political culture and neo-Marxist structural theories can explain stability but not change. Theories that stress the way institutions shape the incentives and opportunities of individual actors can provide a more accurate and nuanced account of how and why patterns of political recruitment remain stable in some circumstances and change in others.

The institutional approach to the study of political recruitment can be traced back to Joseph Schlesinger's (1966) seminal work on political ambition. Schlesinger argues that the career paths of politicians are determined by the opportunities they have for advancement and the calculations they make as individuals. Similarly, Black (1972) argues that institutional variables influence the rational calculations of politicians and determine their career paths.

Building upon these classic works of political recruitment, I argue that the shift from noncompetitive elections to competitive electoral processes significantly changes the process of political recruitment. When candidates have to compete in competitive elections to gain political office, different kinds of experiences become more valuable, and different types of people gain power. In noncompetitive contexts, party leaders are free to select candidates for elections on the basis of loyalty and service to the national party without concern for the electoral appeal of the candidate. Competitive elections constrain the choices of party leaders when selecting candidates. In elections where candidates are likely to face stiff competition from opposition parties, electability becomes a great concern, and parties must select candidates to appeal to voters in order to win elections.

A key aspect of electability is the relationship between the candidate and the electorate. In Mexico, traditionally governors have been selected because of their loyalty to the president, not their ties to the local constituency. As electoral competition increases, it is expected that successful gubernatorial candidates will have closer ties to the local electorate than to the national political elite. Thus, it is likely that they will have built their careers in the state rather than in the national government.

Not only are the types of candidates expected to change, but also the process through which candidates are selected. Since public opinion cannot be freely expressed in authoritarian regimes, authoritarian leaders rarely have a good understanding of public opinion (Geddes 1996; Geddes and Zaller 1989). Primary elections are a useful tool for finding out which candidates appeal to the electorate. As elections become more competitive, parties may turn toward primary elections to select candidates. Other inclusive methods of selecting candidates may also be used.

To explore these theoretical propositions more thoroughly, I examine the impact of increasing electoral competition on patterns of political recruitment of governors in Mexico. This chapter tests two central hypotheses:

> *Hypothesis I:* As elections become more competitive, party leaders are more likely to turn to more inclusive methods to select candidates.
>
> *Hypothesis II:* The more competitive the state, the more likely it is that successful gubernatorial candidates will have closer ties to the local electorate than to the national political elite.

I test these hypotheses on the basis of qualitative case study data and regression analysis, using data from all the governors of all the states from 1970 to 1998.

Primary Elections

The use of primary elections is an important indicator of more inclusive processes of candidate selection. The PRI has traditionally selected its candidates through closed internal negotiations. The closed system of candidate selection is one of the key differences between Mexico's authoritarian one-party system and other one-party systems that are generally considered democratic (Sartori 1976). Democratic selection of ruling party candidates has changed the nature of the Mexican political system in profound ways. Meyer (1989, 343) argues that allowing PRI members to choose candidates would undermine the metaconstitutional powers of the president, reverse the chain of command from top down to bottom up, free officials from central control, and help create a separation of powers. At one time internal democratization of the PRI was thought to be necessary for the broader democratization of Mexico (Meyer 1989), but now it seems as though the democratic selection of PRI candidates may be the only way for the PRI to survive in a new electorally competitive Mexico.

The PRI has experimented periodically with primary elections since 1965. In July 1965, the PRI's national chairman, Carlos A. Madrazo, attempted to implement free elections for local party militants to select party leaders and a primary system for the selection of municipal presidents and city council members. Traditionally, governors had chosen municipal candidates. The first primary for municipal candidates took place in Baja California without any major problems. Then in Sinaloa, Governor Leopoldo Sánchez Celis ensured the victory of his own candidates with fraudulent primaries. Madrazo overturned the victories, but the governor ran his candidates as independents and won. Due to resistance from local PRI bosses such as the governor of Sinaloa, Madrazo was forced to resign as the national chairman of the PRI in November of 1965, and the reforms for more democratic selection of PRI candidates were abandoned (Bailey 1988, 107–11).

During the term of De la Madrid, the PRI again attempted to increase local voices in the selection of candidates (Cornelius 1987, 24). De la Madrid's reform for "direct consultation with the grassroots" began in 1983 in the municipality of Salina Cruz, Oaxaca. A direct vote by the members of the local PRI selected the party leadership from among the various factions that were struggling for power in the municipality. Then in 1984 in Nayarit the direct consultation was again tried. The results were promising and the idea was adopted by the Twelfth Party Assembly. But then in the state of Hidalgo in 1984, primaries for municipal candidates were marred by fraud and resulted in extensive protest (Vargas González 1991). The new reform for consultation with the bases was then only applied intermittently, and eventually the president of the PRI, Adolfo Lugo Verduzco, announced in 1985 that although the PRI continued its commitment to the process of direct consultation, the consultations would be attempted flexibly, according to the specific conditions in each state. Furthermore, Lugo stated that unity and internal discipline were indispensable and that the process of consultation would proceed gradually (Bailey 1988, 116–19).

Morris (1995) argues that the primaries brought on disunity within the PRI and led to defections to other parties, thereby weakening rather than strengthening the PRI. Chand (2001), in contrast, demonstrates that more inclusive processes of candidate selection in Chihuahua helped the PRI to win after electoral defeats by the PAN. After the PRI's rule in the state was challenged by extensive civic protests against electoral fraud following the 1986 gubernatorial elections, the ruling party democratized candidate selection for the 1989 local elections. According to Chand, growing electoral competition had spurred the adoption of democratic methods of candidate selection. Chand (2001) argues, "PRI candidates [imposed from Mexico City] were at a major disadvantage when running against PAN candidates, who had been democratically elected by a convention of rank-and-file PAN members and often acted as lightening rods of regional resentment against the central government" (246–47). The PRI's democratically selected candidates did well in the 1989 local elections, and Chihuahua became a model for other states, prompting further movements for internal democratization of the PRI.

The Fourteenth Party Assembly of the PRI in 1990 again called for the democratization of candidate selection and required potential candidates to have support at the local level. The new emphasis on local support weakened labor and peasant nominations and increased the number of popular sector and local business nominations. The new reform, however, continued to allow candidates to be appointed by the central party leadership whenever it was deemed good for the party, and often the new statutes were simply ignored by President Salinas (Langston 2001; Morris 1995, 93). In fact, the democratic selection of candidates was almost always overridden in favor of the handpicked candidates. Morris (1995) estimates that in 1991, 90 percent of the candidates were selected by the national party leadership. For example in 1991, the two most serious contenders against Sócrates Rizzo in the gubernatorial primaries in Nuevo Leon were pressured not to run.

Again in the state elections of 1992, grassroots input was minimal. Salinas ended the party reforms altogether by overturning the new statutes in the next party assembly. According to Morris (1995, 94–95) this was because of conflict over candidate selection in a number of states. In 1991 in Yuriria, Guanajuato, for example, PRI members upset about the candidate selection process set fire to the local PRI office. In Colima President Salinas forced two popular local politicians not to compete in the gubernatorial primaries so that his favored candidate, Socorro Díaz, from Mexico City could win the primaries. Díaz, however, lost the primary when the two candidates who had been forced out threw their support to another candidate. Diaz then publicly accused the PRI of rigging the election against her. Langston (2001, 495–96) argues that Salinas overturned the newly inclusive candidate selection statutes in order to maintain his control over the party.

In 1995 President Zedillo ordered the leader of the CEN (National Executive Committee) of the PRI to develop democratic rules for the nominations of governors. At the party assembly of 1996, the governors were much more influential than they had been before and were able to push through reforms that significantly restricted the ability of the president to choose his successor. They wrote new rules that required presidential candidates to have electoral and party experience. This was an attempt to disqualify many members of Zedillo's cabinet from being selected as the PRI's presidential candidate (Langston 2001, 504–5). Unlike Salinas, Zedillo was unable to simply ignore the reforms.

In the state elections of 1998, the importance of candidate selection again came to the foreground. In 1998 the PRI held open gubernatorial primaries in the state of Chihuahua (SourceMex, July 8, 1998). The elections in Chihuahua were of particular importance to the PRI because the opposition party PAN had governed the state since 1992. Fearing that Artemio Iglesias, an old-style political boss who controlled the PRI's political machinery in the state, would gain the nomination but then lose the general election, the president of the national PRI, Mariano Palacios Alcocer, declared that the PRI would select its candidate through an open primary in which all voters, regardless of party affiliation, could vote. Patricio Martínez, a relative newcomer to politics, won the primary and went on to win the general election, proving that the PRI can survive in democratic elections (De Cordoba 1998).

On the same day that Patricio Martínez won back Chihuahua for the PRI, Ricardo Monreal, the candidate for the center-left opposition party PRD, won the gubernatorial elections in the state of Zacatecas, taking control of the first statehouse for the PRD. Monreal, a former member of the PRI, deserted the ruling party when he was denied its gubernatorial nomination in a traditional backroom deal (De Cordoba 1998). Zacatecas had long been a stronghold for the PRI. In the federal congressional elections of 1997, the PRI won the state by an almost 24-point margin. (Interestingly, the only two states in which the PRI had a higher margin of victory in the 1997 elections—Baja California Sur and Nayarit—also both elected PRD governors in 1999.) The PRI's loss in Zacatecas to the PRD, therefore, was a serious blow to the ruling party.

The experience in Chihuahua and Zacatecas in 1998 provided an important lesson for the PRI. Since then the ruling party has increasingly relied upon primary elections to select governors. Primary elections were also carried out in Sinaloa, Tamaulipas, Puebla, and Tlaxcala in 1998 (De Cordoba 1998), and the PRI held primary elections in many states to select gubernatorial candidates in 1999. Of course, the most important primary elections took place in November 1999, when for the first time ever the PRI used an open primary to select its presidential candidate for the 2000 elections (Preston 1999). As electoral competition has spread across Mexico, the PRI has increasingly turned toward democratic primaries to select its candidates. Growing electoral competition also allowed lower-level party members to gain influence within the PRI and design more inclusive rules for selecting the party's candidates (Langston 2001).

Political Recruitment of Governors

While many studies of political recruitment have focused on the power of traditional families (Clubock et al. 1969; Hagopian 1996; Wasserman 1993), in postrevolutionary Mexico political power has been concentrated in the hands of the ruling party leadership ("the revolutionary family") rather than a traditional oligarchy. The power to select candidates has been highly centralized in the hands of the president (Camp 1995c; Garrido 1989; Smith 1979). Therefore, the most important shifts in patterns of political recruitment in the Mexican states are from control by national party elites to control by state and local leaders. To examine changing patterns of political recruitment in the states, I focus on the most important political actor in state politics, the governor. Though Mexico has a formally federal system, historically the states and their governors have been almost entirely dependent upon the central government. Not only does the central government control the public finances of the states, but the president also has the informal power to appoint and remove governors.

The Selection of Governors

According to the Mexican constitution, governors are elected by direct election. Nevertheless, scholars of Mexican politics have long asserted that in practice the president handpicks governors. Ruling party candidates generally have been designated by the national leadership rather than selected through primary elections (Camp 1977; Garrido 1989), though, as discussed above, primary elections have been used increasingly to select gubernatorial candidates since the late 1990s. The president, as leader of the ruling party, usually names the PRI's gubernatorial candidate, and from its foundation in 1929 up until 1989, the ruling party won every gubernatorial election in the country (Hansen 1971, 110–11; Rodríguez 1997, 26).

While most observers tend to agree that the president chooses the governors, it is difficult to find empirical data to substantiate this popular view of the gubernatorial selection process. Martínez Assad and Arreola Ayala (1987) compiled data from various political narratives of the gubernatorial selection process to demonstrate that governors are typically appointed by the president. While they acknowledge that the testimonials of disaffected political elites may not be completely reliable, the similarities of the accounts by many different individuals tend to enhance each particular story. Braulio Maldonado, the former governor of Baja California (1953–1959) contends,

> I occupied the first constitutional governorship of the state of Baja California through the same mechanism that is used in Mexico today to arrive and occupy the so-called posts of popular election. I was selected and designated by the president of the Republic, who in those days was my distinguished friend don Adolfo Ruiz Cortines. And all of the functionaries, large and small, that occupy posts of popular election have been designated in this way in our country, from 1928 to today. This is an axiomatic truth. (Quoted in Martínez Assad and Arreola Ayala 1987, 116, translated by author)

Similarly, Martínez Assad and Arreola Ayala quote an account of the selection of Carlos Armando Biebrich as candidate for governor of Sonora in 1973. President Luis Echeverría reportedly had the following conversation with his Secretary of Government:

> "Tell Biebrich to prepare, he is going to Sonora as a candidate. . . ."
> "Mr. President, there is a serious problem — Biebrich is not old enough."
> "No, Mr. Secretary, that is not a problem. Go talk with the governor and tell him to change the state constitution." (Quoted in Martínez Assad and Arreola Ayala 1987, 117, translated by author)

Amezcua and Pardinas (1997) also provide substantial interview data supporting the view that the president controls gubernatorial candidate selection. For example, they quote Luis Martínez Villacaña, De la Madrid's Secretary of Agrarian Reform, describing his selection as the PRI's candidate for governor of Michoacán. President De la Madrid reportedly said to him: "Listen, Luis, the president of the party told me that you were the right man for Michoacán, and I decided that it should be you, but I want you to think about it because I would lose a very good Secretary of Agrarian Reform" (quoted in Amezcua and Pardinas 1997, 32, translated by author).

In contrast to these anecdotal accounts of gubernatorial appointment, Díaz-Cayeros (1997) argues that the president cannot simply appoint his most preferred candidate as governor but must negotiate with state-level power brokers. The president relies on the support of these local leaders, Díaz-Cayeros contends, because they mobilize votes and provide necessary political support for the candidate. The president's choice is thereby constrained by the local-level veto players. Camp (1977, 33) similarly acknowledges that the president sometimes has to compromise with powerful interests in the state.

Nevertheless, the typical career path for governors is an education at UNAM followed by a career in the national bureaucracy. Governors often have little or no connection to the states they govern (Snyder 1999b). In a comparison of the career paths of winning and losing gubernatorial precandidates, Camp (1977) found that the most important experience for a winning gubernatorial precandidate was a high position in the federal government.[1] A position in the federal government was important, Camp maintained, because the politician was more likely to be known by the president and the national political leadership and to have more access to the national leaders. Writing in the late 1970s, Camp further contended that national political experience would become increasingly important in the future.

The Removal of Governors

During one-party rule, not only did the president have significant control over the selection of gubernatorial candidates, but he also had the informal power to dismiss governors and replace them with interim governors (Rodríguez 1997). Sometimes governors were removed from office because of conflicts with the president. In other instances, governors were removed to be promoted to more prestigious positions in the federal government. Table 5.1 shows that Mexico's presidents have used that power with varying frequency in modern times, replacing a total of sixty-eight governors between 1934 and 1994.

If the president wished to remove a governor from office, typically he would ask the governor to resign or take a leave of absence. Most governors were well aware that they had no real alternative to resignation. If they went quietly, there was a chance that they could reap some consolation prize for their cooperation and perhaps make a political comeback in the future. If, however, the governor refused to step down, the president could remove him or her involuntarily through Article 76 of the constitution, which gave the president the power to dismiss governors through his control of the senate. In the words of Jeffrey Weldon (1997), "This [Article 76] is the club behind the door that the president rarely needs to use. Governors can recognize that leaving voluntarily is better than being forced out by the Senate" (254). Senatorial approval was never problematic because

Table 5.1. The Number of Governors Removed by Each President

President	Number of Governors Removed
Lázaro Cárdenas, 1934–1940	17
Manuel Ávila Camacho, 1940–1946	5
Miguel Alemán, 1946–1952	9
Adolfo Ruiz Cortines, 1952–1958	5
Adolfo López Mateos, 1958–1964	3
Gustavo Díaz Ordaz, 1964–1970	1
Luis Echeverría Alvarez, 1970–1976	6
José López Portillo, 1976–1982	2
Miguel de la Madrid, 1982–1988	4
Carlos Salinas de Gortari, 1988–1994	16

Source: Martínez Assad and Arreola Ayala (1987, 109) and Rodríguez (1997, 25).

the senate remained under the control of the president with a large majority for the ruling party until the election of Vicente Fox in 2000 (Garrido 1989; González Oropeza 1987).

Since governors cannot be reelected, they are further constrained by the president because they are likely to seek a career in the federal government when their term as governor is over (Snyder 1999b). To land a good job in the federal government, they must be on good terms with the president. Through these informal mechanisms of presidential power, sustained by the noncompetitive nature of the Mexican political system, presidents maintained significant control over governors and the politics of state governments. According to Luis Javier Garrido (1989), "State governors are subject to the president's orders, as party chief, since they owe their tenure in office, not to the electorate, but to the president's unwritten powers. Through their allegiance to the party, governors surrender the autonomy of their states to the federal government or, more precisely, to the president" (425).

In general, the governor is thought to be safe if he or she can maintain general tranquility in the state, deliver the state's vote for the PRI, and avoid direct conflict with the president (Rodríguez 1997). Amezcua and Pardinas (1997) show that the majority of governors forced out of office by Salinas had failed to deliver the vote for the ruling party in their states. An interview with the disgraced governor of Quintana Roo, Mario Villanueva, supports this view of the governor's responsibility. Expressing his feeling of betrayal by the ruling party leadership after he was charged with drug trafficking, Villanueva states, "I did my part, I made all the party's candidates win. I gave them money. I ran campaigns for them. I controlled the state" (SourceMex, March 1, 2000).

The Consequences of Interparty Competition for Gubernatorial Candidate Selection

The increase of electoral competition has tremendous consequences for the way gubernatorial candidates are selected and for the type of candidates selected. Many analysts of Mexican presidentialism have argued that the overwhelming power of the president is derived not from direct constitutional powers but from the informal institutional mechanisms of the one-party system in which the party and the government are fused (Díaz-Cayeros 1997; Garrido 1989; Weldon 1997). Garrido (1989) argues that respect for the popular vote would eventually result in a democratic plural party system that would strip the president of his metaconstitutional powers. According to Weldon (1997, 255), Mexican presidentialism depends upon PRI control of congress, high levels of party discipline within the PRI, and the continuation of the president as leader of the party. If any of these conditions are not met, Weldon claims, the Mexican president's metaconstitutional powers cannot be sustained. While Weldon's three conditions are obviously highly related to levels of electoral competition, Weldon does not articulate a direct link between interparty competition and the breakdown of presidentialism as Garrido does. Díaz-Cayeros (1997) sees rising opposition electoral power as the central explanation of the breakdown of the traditional process of gubernatorial candidate selection. He states, "The dynamic of entry and the triumph of opposition parties in local elections during the last decade have provoked a new pattern of gubernatorial nomination within the PRI. The party now tries to field candidates with real prospects of winning in fair and clean elections" (16).

Lapses in presidential control over governors during the 1990s seem to confirm that President Zedillo did not have the same power that his predecessors had. The most dramatic example of the presidency's declining power was Zedillo's conflict with Tabasco governor Roberto Madrazo. In 1995, after substantial postelectoral conflict and allegations of electoral fraud in the gubernatorial elections, Zedillo negotiated with the PRD for the Tabasco governor to resign. Governor Madrazo refused to step down, and Zedillo was unable to force him out of office. Weldon (1997) ascribes these events to the personal characteristics of President Zedillo. Eisenstadt (1999) similarly attributes the breakdown in the ruling party discipline to Zedillo's lack of political acumen and the growing power of local political bosses. In contrast to these two accounts, I see the breakdown in presidential power in Tabasco as part of the broader process of democratization that is destroying the informal mechanisms of power that have sustained Mexican presidentialism. The breakdown of one-party control of national politics has the paradoxical effect of allowing authoritarian enclaves to flourish in some corners of the country while at the same time democracy is taking root in other regions.

Empirical Evidence

To illustrate the different career paths of governors, I return to Guanajuato, one of the states examined in the case studies of chapter 3. I compare the careers of the four governors who ruled Guanajuato from 1985 to 1999. The changing pattern of governors' career trajectories in Guanajuato is very similar to changes in San Luis Potosí. In both cases the governors who took office in the mid-1980s had the profile of a presidential appointee nominated in backroom negotiations. After extensive civic protest and allegations of electoral fraud in 1991 in both Guanajuato and San Luis Potosí, candidates with more local career trajectories came to power. Even in Hidalgo, the governor elected in 1993 had a more locally oriented career, though he was closely tied to the former governor and the traditional local bosses who had controlled Hidalgo politics for many years.

Rafael Corrales Ayala, the governor of Guanajuato from 1985 to 1991, provides a good example of a governor with a nationally oriented political career. Corrales Ayala was born in the capital city of the state of Guanajuato, but he left the state to attend the National Law School at UNAM in Mexico City. He later taught classes and was an administrator at the National Law School. His career was centered entirely in Mexico City. Among his most important positions were Secretary General of the National Executive Committee of the PRI, Assistant Attorney General of Mexico, and Secretary General of the Department of Tourism (Camp 1995a). He also served three terms as federal deputy from Guanajuato. Federal deputies are usually appointed by the president, so service in the national congress tends to demonstrate strong ties to the national leadership rather than a meaningful relationship with a local constituency.

The PRI's candidate for governor of Guanajuato in 1991 had also spent most of his life in Mexico City. Ramon Aguirre Velázquez was born in San Felipe, Guanajuato, but he left his hometown when he was young to attend preparatory school and university in Mexico City. He studied public administration at UNAM and began working at the Secretary of the Treasury at the invitation of a university professor. He became Undersecretary for Expenditures in the Echeverría administration and was elected federal deputy from Guanajuato in 1979. He declined his seat in congress to work in the Secretary of Programming and Budgeting. As Undersecretary of Budgeting he worked closely with both Miguel de la Madrid and Carlos Salinas de Gortari (Amezcua and Pardinas 1997). He served as the mayor of Mexico City from 1982 to 1988. After spending most of his life in Mexico City, actually serving as the regent of the Federal District, and having never held an elected office in the state of Guanajuato or served in the state government, he was chosen as the PRI's candidate for governor. Aguirre claims there was no internal competition—he was simply notified in a phone call from the president's office that he would be the PRI's candidate (Amezcua and Pardinas 1997, 104–5).

Aguirre Velázquez never took office as governor of Guanajuato because he was forced to resign after extensive civic protests and allegations of electoral fraud. President Salinas appointed Carlos Medina Plascencia from the PAN, not Vicente Fox, the ostensible winner, to serve as interim governor. In contrast to Corrales Ayala and Aguirre Veláquez, Medina Plascencia had never served in the federal government and had developed his career in León, Guanajuato. Medina Plascencia was a businessman and only became involved in politics in 1982, when López Portillo nationalized the banks. Medina Plascencia was educated at the Monterrey Institute of Technology and was a professor at the Institute's branch in León. Before being appointed governor, he had been a member of the León City Council and mayor of León (Camp 1995a).

In 1995 Vicente Fox, also a member of the center-right opposition party PAN, was elected governor of Guanajuato. Fox had a very similar career profile to Medina Plascencia. He had attended secondary and preparatory school in León, attended the Universidad Iberoamericana in Mexico City and then returned to León to develop a career in business. He was the CEO of Coca Cola Mexico and then started his own business, becoming general director of the Grupo Fox, a business conglomeration of the export-oriented agro-industry and shoe industry in León. He was also the vice president of the Industrial Association of Guanajuato and the secretary of finances for the PAN in the state of Guanajuato. In 1988 he was elected in a single-member district as federal deputy from León (Valencia García 1998, 118).

These descriptions provide a sense of how different the candidates' careers were in Guanajuato after the 1991 elections. Alone, however, they do not provide very convincing evidence of a general relationship between elections and political recruitment. To systematically test the influence of competitive elections on patterns of gubernatorial recruitment, I created a database with every governor of every state in Mexico from 1970 to 1998.

The database has 184 observations and includes biographical data from each governor merged with electoral data from gubernatorial and federal congressional elections. The biographical data come from various sources, including Roderic Camp's *Mexican Political Biographies, 1935–1993* (1995a), various editions of the *Diccionario biográfico del gobierno mexicano* (Presidencia de la Republica 1987, 1989, 1992, 1993), and SourceMex. The gubernatorial election data are taken from *Mexico social* (Banamex 1996), the Centro de Estadística y Documentación Electoral of the Universidad Autónoma Metropolitana—Ixtapalapa, and SourceMex. The 1970 to 1994 federal congressional election results are from Castellanos Hernández (1997). The 1997 results are from the Web page of the Instituto Federal Electoral (www.ife.org.mx).

Table 5.2 presents some of the general characteristics of the governors.

Most governors were born in the states they govern, but only about one-fifth of the governors attended universities in the states they governed, compared to 65 percent educated in Mexico City. Almost half of all governors studied law, though economics, business, and engineering were also quite common careers for governors. The large percentage of governors with law degrees is consistent with Camp's work on elite recruitment, in which he stresses the importance of the National Law School in Mexico City for recruiting political elites (Camp 1977, 1995c, 1999).

Very few governors had held state-level elective office prior to being elected. Only 17 percent had served as a member of the state congress, and 22 percent had been mayors in the states they governed. Experience in the federal government was much more common for governors than experience in state or local politics. Fifty-seven percent of governors served in the National Chamber of Deputies and 44 percent were in the Senate. Governors tended to have career profiles very similar to those of the national political elite that form the national congress and national bureaucracy. Most governors were educated in law in Mexico City, and they had served in elective posts in the federal government more frequently than in local or state politics.

Over 60 percent of the governors were closely associated with one of the major branches of the Mexican corporatist system. Twenty-eight percent of the governors had close ties to the National Peasants' Confederation (CNC), 24 percent were affiliated with the National Confederation of Popular Organizations (CNOP), and 9 percent were affiliated with the Confederation of Mexican Workers (CTM). In strong contrast to earlier generations of postrevolutionary governors, only a very few governors from 1970 to 1998 had served in the military.

Table 5.2. General Characteristics of the Governors

	%	(N)
Born in the states they governed	86	(142)
Educated at a university in the states they governed	21	(33)
Educated at a university in Mexico City	65	(102)
Studied law	48	(80)
Studied economics	9	(15)
Studied business	8	(14)
Studied engineering	8	(14)
Served as a mayor in the states they governed	22	(37)
Served in the local congress in the states they governed	17	(29)
Served in the federal chamber of deputies	57	(96)
Served in the senate	44	(76)
Affiliated with the CNC	28	(30)
Affiliated with the CTM	9	(11)
Affiliated with the CNOP	24	(26)
Served in the military	6	(8)

This section employs regression analysis to test the impact of electoral competition on the local orientation of gubernatorial career paths. I have constructed two indicators of "localness" to serve as dependent variables. The first dependent variable (LOCAL) is an index of local orientation calculated by adding one point for governors who attended university in the states they governed, one point for each term served in the state congress, and one point for each term as mayor in the state. Thus, the higher the index, the more experience the governor had in the state. Location of university attendance is included because of the importance of universities in the recruitment process (Camp 1995c). Just as the national university was traditionally the most important institution for recruitment into national politics, the state universities are the most important institutions for recruitment into state politics. Membership in the federal congress is not included in the index because federal deputies and senators are generally chosen by the president (Garrido 1989), so membership in the national congress is a better indicator of close ties with the president than close ties to the local political scene. I expect that the variable LOCAL will be greater in states with higher levels of electoral competition, demonstrating that governors in competitive states are more likely to have greater local experience.

The second dependent variable (FEDLOC) measures the local versus national orientation of the governors' careers. If all of the important positions held by the governor (including private sector work as well as government work) were in the state governed, the variable took on a value of 5. If all of the important positions in a governor's career were outside the state, then the variable was scored 1. If governors' careers were about equally divided between the state and the Federal District, the variable took on a value of 3. Governors who had mixed careers but fell closer to one side than the other were scored 2 and 4. Table 5.3 presents the distribution of the values of the two dependent variables and demonstrates that experience in Mexico City is much more common among governors than local experience.

Both of these dependent variables are regressed on the same set of independent variables. The main explanatory variable, state electoral competitiveness, is measured with the competitiveness component of Vanhanen's index (100 − % votes of largest party) (Vanhanen 1990, 2000).[2] I expect the competitiveness measure to be positively related to the two indicators of localness, indicating that the more competitive the elections, the more locally oriented the winning candidate. Vanhanen's index is calculated separately for each governor, using the overall percentages won by each major party in the governor's state in the federal congressional elections immediately preceding the gubernatorial elections. The electoral statistics from the federal congressional races are used to capture the level of electoral competitiveness perceived by the national party leaders when nominating gubernatorial candidates rather than the actual level of competitiveness in the gubernatorial elections. Since local legislative elections typically take place on the same day as the gubernatorial elections, in most cases the federal congressional elections were the most recent elections prior to the gubernatorial elections and therefore provided the best measure of the state's competitiveness as perceived by the party leadership. Using the election results from the actual elections of each governor creates problems for establishing the direction of causality, since obviously the gubernatorial elections take place after the candidate is selected.[3]

Measures for state GDP per capita (INEGI 1996, 3), state geographic distance from Mexico City (Palacios Roji Garcia 1998), level of urbanization (Nacional Financiera 1995, 13–15), total population (Nacional Fi-

Table 5.3.   Distribution of Values for Dependent Variables

Value of LOCAL	Frequency	Percentage
0 = least local	99	63.46
1	33	21.15
2	17	10.90
3 = most local	7	4.49
Total	156	100.00

Value of FEDLOC	Frequency	Percentage
1 = least local	54	32.53
2	17	10.24
3	42	25.30
4	25	15.06
5 = most local	28	16.87
Total	166	100.00

nanciera 1995, 13–15), and total GDP (INEGI 1996, 3) in each state are also included as control variables. According to the predictions of modernization theory, more economically advanced states should have more inclusive processes of candidate selection. Therefore, I expect the GDP per capita to be positively related to the two dependent variables. The logic of modernization theory also suggests that the level of urbanization should be positively related to more inclusive patterns of political recruitment. The distance variable is included because it is expected that elites from states close to Mexico City will be more likely to attend university and hold jobs in the Federal District, whereas elites from states far away may be more likely to stay in their home states to develop their political careers for simple geographic reasons. The variable is measured by the miles between Mexico City and each state capital (Palacios Roji García and Palacios Roji García 1998). Total population and total GDP are included because it is expected that the larger the state in terms of population and economy, the more opportunities there will be to develop a career in the state, and therefore the more likely politicians will be to stay in the state rather than work in Mexico City.

Because of the ordinal nature of the dependent variables, both of the equations are estimated with an ordered probit regression. Table 5.4 presents the results of the regressions.

Table 5.4. The Impact of Interparty Competition on Governors' Local Orientation (Ordered Probit)

	Model 1 Dep. Var. = LOCAL	Model 2 Dep. Var. = FEDLOC
Vanhanen's index	0.022	0.015
	(2.48)*	(1.92)
Distance	−0.0003	0.0004
	(1.17)	(1.99)*
Urbanization	0.149	0.287
	(0.16)	(0.36)
GDP	0.000	0.000
	(0.35)	(0.89)
Population	−0.0002	0.000
	(0.76)	(0.50)
GDP per capita	−0.007	0.040
	(0.19)	(1.16)
Observations	156	166
Pseudo-R^2	0.03	0.03
Log-likelihood	−151.46	−245.76

Note: Absolute value of z statistics in parentheses.
* $p < .05$; ** $p < .01$.

As expected, the competition variable is positive when regressed against the dependent variables. In the LOCAL regression Vanhanen's index is statistically significant with 95 percent confidence. In the second model, the competiveness index just barely misses the traditional 95 percent level of confidence with a $p = 0.055$. Thus, the relationship is significant with 94 percent confidence. The data demonstrate that the more competitive the federal congressional elections leading up to the governors' race, the more likely it is that the winning candidate has had a locally oriented career.

Neither the GDP per capita nor the urbanization variable is statistically significant in either of the regressions, indicating that the local orientation of governors' careers is not related to the level of modernization in the state. The distance variable is insignificant in the first regression but significant and positive in the second regression. Thus, the farther away the home state of the governor is from Mexico City, the less likely

Table 5.5.   The Impact of Interparty Competition on Governors' Local Orientation (Ordered Probit), PAN Governors Excluded

	Model 1 Dep. Var. = LOCAL	Model 2 Dep. Var. = FEDLOC
Vanhanen's index	0.021	0.012
	(2.32)*	(1.48)
Distance	0.000	0.0003
	(1.33)	(1.70)
Urbanization	0.136	0.263
	(0.14)	(0.33)
GDP	0.000	0.000
	(0.26)	(0.89)
Population	0.000	0.000
	(0.66)	(0.51)
GDP per capita	−0.003	0.042
	(0.09)	(1.22)
Observations	152	162
Pseudo-R^2	0.03	0.03
Log-likelihood	−146.08	−240.68

Note: Absolute value of z statistics in parentheses.
* $p < .05$; ** $p < .01$.

the governor is to have developed his or her career in the Federal District. The total population and the total GDP measures are insignificant in both equations, indicating that the size of the state is not important in determining the career paths of governors.

The pattern of local career trajectories is particularly typical of PAN politicians. It is possible that the relatively few PAN governors are driving the results of the regressions presented above. To test for this possibility, Table 5.5 presents the results of the same models with the PAN cases dropped.

Both of the coefficients for the electoral competition variable are positive, as expected, and the coefficient remains highly significant in the LOCAL regression but loses significance in the FEDLOC regression. Hence, while the inclusion of the PANista governors strengthens the results, the basic relationship is present even among governors from the PRI.

Democratization in the form of increasing electoral competitiveness has a tangible influence on patterns of political recruitment. The data presented on the history of primary elections and the career paths of governors are consistent with the two central hypotheses of this chapter. Hypothesis I predicts that as elections become more competitive, the ruling party will rely increasingly on more inclusive methods to select their candidates. In 1998, for example, the PRI used an open primary to select its gubernatorial candidate in the highly competitive state of Chihuahua but employed the traditional *dedazo* to choose its candidate in Zacatecas, a state traditionally dominated by the PRI. Their success with the primary in Chihuahua and the failure of the appointed gubernatorial candidate in Zacatecas resulted in further reliance on primary elections within the PRI. The second hypothesis posits that states with more competitive elections will be more likely to nominate and elect governors with greater experience in local politics rather than candidates sent in from Mexico City. Case study data combined with a statistical analysis of data from all of the governors from 1970 to 1998 suggest that states with more competitive elections are more likely to elect candidates with careers rooted in the state than candidates who parachute in from Mexico City.

The theoretical approaches of political culture and neo-Marxist structuralism predict stability. The changes in candidate selection in Mexico over the past twenty years suggest that political culture and the class system have not prevented institutional changes in the electoral arena from generating substantive results in the process of political recruitment. GDP per capita and urbanization, important measures of socioeconomic development and modernization, were not significant in the regression equations, suggesting that modernization theory may not be very useful in explaining patterns of political recruitment. The empirical evidence suggests that the hypotheses derived from an institutional perspective are more plausible. In particular, the data support the argument that increasingly competitive elections generate new incentives and opportunities for candidates and party leaders that result in more inclusive patterns of candidate selection and successful candidates with closer ties to local constituencies.

The increasingly local orientation of Mexico's governors has important consequences for horizontal accountability. In the past, the governors were subservient to the president. Therefore, local interests were disregarded in favor of national interests. Moreover, state governments played no significant role in checking the power of the national executive. As governors become increasingly oriented toward pleasing a local constituency and more independent of the established national political class, they can begin to serve as meaningful counterweights to the national executive. Moreover, changes in the candidate selection process result in important shifts of power away from party leaders and toward voters. In sum, growing political competition at the state level has generated new patterns of political recruitment for governors. This, in turn, has paved the way for more independent state governments that can more readily check the power of the national executive.

CHAPTER SIX

Changing
Decision-Making
Arenas

As electoral competition has taken root at the state and municipal level in many areas across Mexico, democratically elected mayors and governors have begun to demand more autonomy from the central government and more control over local fiscal policy. As a result, the federal government has increasingly ceded more power and resources to those governments. For example, in the spring of 1995, Mayor Francisco Villarreal Torres of Ciudad Juárez set up municipal tollbooths to compete with the federal tollbooths and collect fees for crossing the international bridge that connects Ciudad Juárez to El Paso, Texas. Four days later the army removed the municipal tollbooths and arrested the mayor (SourceMex, April 26, 1995). A few months later, President Zedillo announced his plan for a "New Federalism" to increase the share of government revenue that was transferred to state and local governments. Zedillo also announced a plan to raise the portion of the international bridge fees allocated to border cities and states from 10 to 25 percent (SourceMex, August 9, 1995).

In another example of subnational leaders demanding greater autonomy from the federal government, Patricio Martínez, the governor of the state of Chihuahua who had just won back the state for the Revolutionary Institutional Party (PRI) after six years of National Action Party (PAN) rule, took on the federal authorities in the spring of 1999. This time the dispute had to do with the licensing of illegally imported cars. Martínez planned to register and tax almost two million illegal cars in the state of Chihuahua, keeping the revenues for the state coffers. The federal government claimed that the registering and taxing of cars fell under federal jurisdiction and threatened to cut off federal transfers to the state if the policy was enacted (De Cordoba and Friedland 1999; SourceMex, May 26, 1999). In response to the conflict, President Zedillo issued a decree to legalize 750,000 illegally imported pickup trucks, and the opposition-controlled national chamber of deputies approved a bill to legalize two million illegally imported cars (SourceMex, May 3, 2000).

Why would Patricio Martínez, the electoral hero of the PRI, want greater autonomy from the leaders of his own party who controlled the federal government? More generally, what causes decentralization, and what determines how decision-making authority is allocated within a political system? Does increasing political competition influence the arenas in which policy is produced or the institutional actors who have control over particular policy spheres? Or do institutional arrangements and other forces such as economic necessity and political expediency determine where policy decisions are made? These questions have important implications for the study of democracy in Latin America because decentralizing power to subnational leaders creates new checks on presidential power. State governments in a federal system can be thought of as the fourth branch of government because they can act in a myriad of ways to constrain the power of the national executive (Wright 1978). Horizontal accountability is enhanced by taking power out of the hands of the national executive and putting it into the hands of state leaders.

The central argument of this chapter is that increasing electoral competition will shift policy-making control from unaccountable bureaucratic actors to elected officials. This happens, I argue, because politicians selected in competitive elections face incentives to extend their influence over greater policy domains in order to meet the demands of their constituents. Strong electoral support, in turn, bolsters the ability of elected politicians to gain greater control over policy making. Prior research has focused on the impact of democratization on the distribution of decision-making authority between military and civilian leaders (Hunter 1997). Others have been concerned with the role of insulated and politically unaccountable technocrats in economic policy making (Centeno 1994; Conaghan et al. 1990). In light of the international financial community's recent interest in promoting decentralization (Inter-American Development Bank 1997; Organisation for Economic Co-operation and Development 1998; Peterson 1997), a new focus of political research has been the distribution of power between national and subnational governments (Rodríguez 1997; Willis et al. 1999). The implementation of decentralization policies that shift policy-making power from national to subnational governments clearly has been the most visible and highly promoted example of changing policy-making arenas in recent years.

I focus on decentralization policies as a subset of changing decision-making arenas because of the asymmetries in political competition between subnational political environments and the national government in the case of Mexico. In Mexico during the 1990s many states and municipal governments were more competitive than the national government. This asymmetry in levels of political competition resulted in increasing autonomy for those states and municipalities with greater electoral competition than the federal government. Noncompetitive states, meanwhile, did not gain as much autonomy as the competitive states. This divergence occurred because subnational governments with high levels of electoral competition were more likely to seek policy autonomy from the central government than their counterparts in subnational governments with low levels of electoral competition. I test this argument against the expectations of other explanations of decentralization with a statistical analysis of patterns of local fiscal autonomy in the Mexican states. By focusing on subnational politics and the interests of subnational leaders, I emphasize the bottom-up dynamics of decentralization rather than the top-down dynamics that have dominated the decentralization literature.

The study of decentralization in Mexico allows us to shed light on important issues regarding the consequences of electoral competition and subnational politics. Given the tremendous variation in levels of political competition and the highly heterogeneous nature of the process of democratization across subnational units in Mexico, the allocation of greater power and resources to subnational governments has important consequences (both positive and negative) for the quality of democracy in the nation as a whole. Just as the process of democratization has been uneven across the Mexican states, so too has the process of decentralization, with some states gaining extensive control over multiple policy arenas and others remaining under the control of the federal government (Cabrero Mendoza 1998; Díaz-Cayeros 1995). Thus, increasing electoral competition at the state level leads to greater policy autonomy for those states that are more competitive. More democratic subnational governments take more policy responsibility from the less democratic national government, thereby improving the quality of democracy in the nation as a whole.

The following chapter explores the relationship between democratization and decentralization. In the first section I review alternative explanations for the causes of decentralization. Next, I present the theoretical logic that guides this chapter. Then I provide statistical evidence to test the significance of electoral competition and other institutional and structural variables in explaining variance in the levels of fiscal autonomy among the Mexican states.

Explaining Shifts in Policy-Making Arenas: Previous Research

To explain decentralization and growing local autonomy, scholars have pointed to variables as diverse as shifts in the political economy (Morris 1992), the rational calculations of vote-maximizing national leaders (O'Neill 2000), legitimacy crises (Grindle 2000; Rodríguez 1997), and static institutions such as electoral timing and candidate selection processes (Linz and Stepan 1992; Willis et al. 1999).

Some structural accounts emphasize the links between decentralization and the shift in economic orientation from import substitution industrialization (ISI) to neoliberalism. Morris (1992), for example, argues that as production for the domestic market declines in favor of production for the international market, industries find new advantages to locating near borders and transportation hubs rather than in the capital city. An open economy allows industries largely located in the periphery, such as agriculture and mining, to compete in the world economy without the discriminating taxes and exchange rates that hampered their growth during ISI. Furthermore, since ISI policies centralized power, resources, and government subsidies in and near the capital cities at the cost of the peripheral areas, reductions in government spending under neoliberalism had more severe consequences in the center than in the periphery. As a result, people and production moved from the center to the periphery (Fox 1992). The redistribution of people and production then fuels demands for local autonomy and leads to political decentralization.

Others have argued that there is an elective affinity between the globalization of the world economy and decentralization because producers require increased flexibility and efficiency to compete successfully in the world market. Therefore, regional economic actors will demand political decentralization in order to increase the efficiency of public sector service delivery, and central governments concerned with economic development will respond to the demands of the regional economic interests (Doner and Hershberg 1996).

A related set of rationales focuses on the inefficiencies associated with the overconcentration and diseconomies of scale involved in Latin America's megacities. In Mexico City, for example, urban problems such as over-crowding, pollution, and dwindling supplies of drinking water provide substantial incentives for industrial and demographic decentralization (Aguilar-Barajas and Spence 1988; Stansfield 1992). Regional economic development projects that decentralize production may help to relieve some of the problems of congestion in the capital cities and in turn lead to some form of political decentralization.

Much of the rational choice literature on decentralization builds upon economic models of fiscal federalism that provide theoretical justifications for the benefits of decentralization but few explanations of why individual politicians would choose to implement these policies. In general this research tends to be prescriptive rather than explanatory (see, e.g., Bird 1993; Inter-American Development Bank 1997; Oates 1972; Organisation for Economic Cooperation and Development 1998; Tiebout 1956).

While the prescriptive rational choice theories of decentralization imply that decentralization will happen naturally because it is the most efficient way to allocate public resources, decentralization presents a fundamental anomaly for explanatory rational choice models: Why would power-maximizing national politicians voluntarily cede power and resources to subnational governments? To explain this apparent anomaly, some rational choice theorists have argued that national leaders may implement decentralization policies when their party is likely to lose national elections in the near future but has strong electoral prospects in subnational elections (O'Neill 2000). Employing a softer, more nuanced sense of rationality, others have explained decentralization as a response to crisis and as a means of maintaining the stability and legitimacy of the political system (Grindle 2000).

For the case of Mexico, Rodríguez (1993, 1997) argues that the economic crisis of the early 1980s led to declining legitimacy for the PRI and forced the party leadership to decentralize some policy-making power to state and local governments in order to placate demands for democracy, regain legitimacy, and hold onto power. She further argues that the PRI ceded control of nonvital functions in order to maintain control of the most important state powers. Rodríguez's explanation of decentralization stresses the top-down dynamics of the process. She asserts that the prospects for decentralization ultimately reside with the willingness of the ruling elite to relinquish power. She states, "The central government, after all, decides why, where, what, and how to decentralize" (Rodríguez 1997, 8). More substantial decentralization did not take place, Rodríguez (1997) contends, because "the willingness to decentralize political power still did not exist" (141).

Other work on decentralization in Mexico has also placed primary emphasis on the interests of the national ruling party. Kathleen Bruhn (1999) argues that the PRI allowed the opposition some control at the local and state level in order to distract their attention and undermine their ability to compete for control at the national level. Foweraker (1993) and Stansfield (1992) make a related argument about the decentralization of the education system in Mexico. They contend that education policy was decentralized to undermine the power of the national teachers' union. Decentralization has also been portrayed as an attempt to shift blame away from central authorities and maintain legitimacy for the government during a period of economic crisis and shrinking federal budgets (González Block 1991; Grindle 1996; Trejo and Jones 1998).

Molinar Horcasitas and Weldon (1994) present the most systematic evidence of how decentralization has served the interests of the PRI. In an examination of the determinants of funding for PRONASOL, a poverty alleviation project that funneled resources through subnational actors, they find that political considerations played an important role in the allocation of resources. They demonstrate that the decentralization policy embodied in PRONASOL was driven not only by technical or economic motivations but also by a political logic designed to regain electoral support for the ruling party. Molinar Horcasitas and Weldon's data suggest that at least in the short term the project was successful in generating electoral support for the PRI.

Institutional approaches to decentralization have emphasized variables such as the timing and sequence of elections and the rules of candidate selection. Linz and Stepan's (1992, 1996) central thesis is that the sequence of elections during democratization determines whether political identities are constructed around regional or national interests. If the first competitive elections in a democratizing country are national elections, as was the case in Spain in 1977, then national political parties are likely to form and generate political identities based on nationwide interests. Conversely, if the founding elections of a new democratic regime are subnational elections, politicians are likely to focus on subnational issues, and parties representing local interests are likely to emerge. A party system formed around local interests and local political identities is much more likely to generate demands for local autonomy.

Similarly, Willis et al. (1999) focus on static institutions that influence the structure of the party system and the sensitivity of national politicians to subnational interests. They argue that the timing of national and subnational elections and the party rules of nomination are the main explanatory variables for decentralization. When national legislators are elected at the same time as governors and mayors, national politics will be more sensitive to local political interests than if national legislators are elected at the same time as the president. This is the case, they argue, because legislators elected at the same time as local leaders arrive in office on the coattails of governors and mayors. If however, national legislators are elected at the same time as the president, then they arrive in office on presidential coattails, thus diminishing the sensitivity of national politics to subnational actors. Alternatively, Turner (1998) argues that subnational politicians elected at the same time as national leaders tend to be less autonomous because they are elected on the coattails of the national politicians. Nonconcurrent national and subnational elections, he posits, encourage decentralization because local issues rather than national issues dominate subnational elections. Garman, Haggard, and Willis (2001) further posit that decentralization is more likely when candidate nominations are controlled by local elites rather than national party leaders and in open-list proportional representation systems rather than closed-list systems.[1] In essence, they argue that countries with institutions favoring decentralized party systems are likely to have greater levels of political decentralization than countries where the electoral institutions favor centralized parties.

Employing a more dynamic conception of institutions, Stoner-Weiss (1997) attributes the growing demands for local autonomy in the Russian regional governments to the introduction of competitive elections. Democratization of regional politics led to decentralization because the democratically elected leaders became accountable to the voters and therefore demanded new powers to meet the needs of the public. Electoral competition generates new incentives for elected politicians to increase their control over policy because when elected leaders can be held accountable by voters for policy decisions that they do not control, they will struggle for greater autonomy and decision-making authority. Stoner-Weiss asserts, "Multi-candidate, competitive elections in the Russian heartland created an impetus for increased regional power over policy. Not unreasonably, if local politicians were to be held accountable to their constituents, then they insisted on having more control over policy" (56–57). Competitive elections at the subnational level have generated greater demands for local autonomy in other countries such as Venezuela (Kraemer 1999).

Electoral Competition and Decentralization in Mexico

A combination of both the structural and the dynamic institutional approaches provides the most convincing explanation of political decentralization in Mexico. In Mexico the shift to an open economy led to a boom along the northern border, thereby decentralizing industrial production (Gwynne 1992; Wong-Gonzales 1992). This transfer of industrial production to the periphery resulted in higher standards of living at the border in comparison with the rest of the country. As a result, the northern states' demands for better public services put strains on the centralized political system. New social actors emerged as a result of the economic development. Among these new actors were small and medium-sized entrepreneurs who joined forces with the PAN to challenge the ruling party in the electoral arena to demand better public services and more effective government administration (Chand 2001; Mizrahi 1994, 1995c). The resulting increase in electoral competition in these states then spurred new demands for local autonomy. The Mexican states that are more democratic have tended to be those states that are most connected to the international economy. As local businesses begin to compete in the international market, they become more concerned with the efficient provision of public goods. As a result they sponsor opposition parties and spur increased electoral competition, which in turn generates incentives for elected politicians to demand greater control over areas that affect their constituents.

To date, most of the research on decentralization has stressed the interests and actions of national elites and ignored the interests and actions of subnational actors. While these top-down approaches shed important light on the process of decentralization, the uneven nature of local political autonomy in Mexico suggests that bottom-up pressures have also been important in decisions to reallocate control to the subnational governments. An approach that focuses solely on the interests and whims of the national elite misses a substantial piece of the explanation.

Increasing electoral competition at the state level in Mexico has generated new incentives and opportunities for state-level politicians to develop autonomy from the central government. Since the leaders of noncompetitive states generally owe their position to the national party leadership who nominated them as ruling party candidates, they have little incentive to struggle for autonomy from the central government. Local leaders' only real constituency in noncompetitive states is the national party leadership. Therefore, their interests lie in doing as they are instructed by party leaders. In contrast, political leaders in electorally competitive states derive their power from their electoral appeal at the subnational level. Hence, they will have strong incentives to gain control over the policy domains that concern the voters in their states. For this reason I expect states with competitive elections to develop greater fiscal autonomy from the central government than states dominated by noncompetitive elections.

This approach differs from some institutional approaches in that it focuses on intranational variation in patterns of decentralization rather than international variation. An examination of the heterogeneous pattern of decentralization within one country draws attention to the different interests and incentives of subnational politicians. Willis et al. (1999) assume that the incentives of subnational politicians are constant and that the process of decentralization is even across subnational units. They contend that all subnational politicians favor increased local fiscal autonomy. They also assume that candidate selection processes vary among countries but not within countries. Yet a brief comparison of the candidate selection processes of the PRI, PRD, and PAN in Mexico demonstrates substantial intracountry variation along this variable. The differences in decentralization, Willis et al. argue, are the result of static institutions that vary across nations (but not within nations) to determine the balance of power between subnational- and national-level politicians. In contrast, I argue that the political context of each subnational unit determines the incentives that face subnational leaders and thereby influences the level of autonomy of each state from the central government.

My approach also differs from many accounts of Mexican politics that stress the importance of opposition governments. Some observers of Mexican politics have placed central explanatory importance on the role of opposition party victories in generating different political outcomes (Rodríguez and Ward 1992, 1994, 1995a). Many suggest that electoral competition matters only insofar as it allows opposition party members to win elections. My model, in contrast, sees the dynamic of electoral competition, not necessarily opposition victory, as the key explanatory variable. Elected officials in competitive areas are expected to act differently from those in noncompetitive areas, regardless of their party.

The Mexican political system is formally federal, with three layers of government: the national, state, and municipal levels. Each state has its own constitution and an elected governor and legislature. Municipalities also elect an executive and a legislative council. While on paper Mexico has all of the formal institutions of a strong federal system, in reality it has functioned as a highly centralized regime in which power and resources have been tightly controlled by the president and national executive branch. The president has traditionally exerted informal powers to control governors. Governors have been essentially appointed by the national executive through the president's control over the nomination process within the ruling party, and since the president also has been able to dismiss governors through his control of the senate, the governors have served at the pleasure of the president.

Until the 1990s, most state governments demonstrated almost no independence from central authorities. Throughout the 1990s, however, some states began to exert substantial autonomy. What is driving this change in intergovernmental relations? Before 1989, state elections were relatively uncompetitive, and the PRI ruled all thirty-one states. During the 1990s, electoral competition began to emerge slowly in a number of states. Increasingly competitive elections at the state level breathed new life into the previously dormant federal institutions of the Mexican government. In states with noncompetitive elections where the PRI was guaranteed victory, the state's political leadership owed its position to the national party elite that selected them as candidates. Under these circumstances, the state leadership's strongest incentives were to do as the national leaders told them. Leaders of noncompetitive states are not expected to try to augment state resources or develop autonomous policy domains. Rather, they are most likely to be content taking orders from the central government. Moreover, most of the governors of noncompetitive states come from the national bureaucracy and return to the national bureaucracy once their term is over.

As electoral competition increases at the state level, leaders are expected to develop greater concern for the interests of the voters in the state. Since the national party can no longer guarantee their election (in the case of members of the PRI), and they can be held accountable by the voters for bad policy decisions, they will face incentives to gain control over greater policy domains and struggle for autonomy from the central government in order to be able to implement policies to enhance their political careers rather than simply take orders from the central government. One of the most important outcomes of growing electoral competition in the states has been the increasing importance of governors in national politics (Langston 2001; Rodríguez 1997). Governors flexed their muscles at the PRI's national assembly in 1996, pushing for reforms that ultimately opened the way for three governors to compete in the PRI's first presidential primary (Langston 2001).[2]

Even though reelection is prohibited for all offices in Mexico, there are strong incentives for governors of competitive states to be accountable to voters. The vast majority of governors in Mexico remain in politics and often seek other elected offices. All three major party candidates for the presidential elections in 2000 had served as governors. Those that are seeking political appointments in government bureaucracies after their gubernatorial terms must be in good standing with their party. Traditionally, the most important test for PRI governors was whether they were able to assure victory for the PRI in all elections in their state during their term. Assuring victory for the PRI may be difficult in competitive states, and the ruling party has been punished at the polls for the actions of unpopular

PRI governors. Therefore, there are clear incentives for a governor in a competitive state to remain attentive to the demands of the voters. Opposition governors also face incentives to be responsive to citizens in order to further their own political careers and to increase the potential of their party to win future elections.

One of the most important means of developing greater control over public policy is to control greater sources of income. Without independent sources of income, local policy autonomy can be easily contained by the central government's control over budget transfers. Raising more revenue locally allows local politicians much greater autonomy over resources and ultimately over policy outputs. For local governments to perform effectively and ensure their autonomy, they must be able to raise revenues independent of the central government (Oates 1993). The tax- and fee-raising capacity of local governments, therefore, is a key indicator of their autonomy. While it may seem counterintuitive to talk about increasing taxes as an indicator of increased responsiveness to citizens' demands, it does make sense in the context of Mexican local government. Local governments historically have collected almost no revenue and therefore have had no possibility of developing policy autonomy. Thus, increasing local revenues is essential for developing greater policy autonomy and meeting the demands of citizens. The following empirical analysis examines both revenue and expenditure decentralization. It examines total public goods provision in the Mexican states as well as the capacity to generate revenue locally in each state.

Empirical Evidence

In this section I use data from all of the thirty-one Mexican states over nine years in a cross-sectional time series regression analysis to test the influence of electoral timing, an export-oriented economy, and electoral competition on patterns of local fiscal autonomy. I focus on state fiscal policy to test systematically the relationship between electoral competition and the fiscal autonomy of subnational governments. For the dependent variables I use a measure of local public goods provision and a measure of local fiscal autonomy. The budget data used in this section are published by the Mexican government (INEGI 1991, 1994, 1998). The database includes local public goods expenditures, locally generated tax revenue, locally collected government fees (*derechos*), federal transfers (*participaciones*), and total income of each state from 1988 to 1996. The regression analysis does not make use of data from before 1988 because electoral competition only began to emerge in the states in the late 1980s.

To test the relationship between electoral competition and local fiscal autonomy, I use a data set that contains both cross-sectional and time series observations. As with the cross-sectional time series model in chapter 4, this model is also estimated using a GEE approach. The first dependent variable measures each state's per capita public goods expenditures (in constant 1990 pesos). When per capita federal transfers are controlled, this provides a good indicator of local public goods provision.[3] The second dependent variable measures revenue decentralization using per capita revenue generated within the state (including taxes, fees, and products in constant 1990 pesos). The greater the per capita state income derived from local revenue sources, the greater the local fiscal autonomy.

Independent variables are used to assess the impact of electoral competition, the timing of elections, and export production on local fiscal autonomy. Control variables for per capita federal transfers, total state GDP, state GDP per capita, urbanization, and state population are also included (INEGI 1996, 52; Nacional Financiera 1995, 13–15). As in the other chapters, Vanhanen's index is used to measure electoral competition.

Drawing on the central hypothesis of Willis et al. (1999), the model includes an independent variable for the timing of national and subnational elections. In Mexico national deputies are elected every three years. Every six years the deputies are elected at the same time as the president. Of the thirty-one states, eleven states elect governors and municipal presidents at the same time as the national elections (Banamex 1996, 636–37). Following the logic of Willis et al., it is expected that these states will be more autonomous than states that do not have concurrent subnational and national elections. The timing variable takes on a value of 1 for states that elect governors and municipal presidents at the same time as the national deputies. The variable takes on a value of 0 for the states that hold their gubernatorial and municipal elections at other times.

To test the expectations of the structural theories that emphasize the importance of an export-oriented economy for local autonomy, the model includes a variable measuring the importance of export production in each state. This variable is the per capita wages and salaries in the *maquila* export industry each year in each state (Nacional Financiera 1998, 498–99).[4] The logic of the structural theories suggests that states with strong export sectors have greater autonomy over their fiscal policy and therefore generate more revenue locally instead of depending upon federal transfers. Thus, the variable for export wages is expected to be positively related to locally generated revenues.[5]

The first model examines the impact of electoral competitiveness, electoral sequencing, and export wages on per capita public goods expenditures, holding federal transfers constant. Vanhanen's index is positive and statistically significant. Thus, the more competitive the state, the greater the local public goods provision.

In contrast to the expectations of the static institutional approach to decentralization, the timing of elections has no significant impact on local public goods provision. When the level of electoral competitiveness is held constant, states that conduct their subnational elections at the same time as the national legislative elections provide no statistically different level of public goods than those states that hold their elections at other times. The coefficient for export wages is also insignificant. As expected, the coefficient for per capita federal transfers is positive and significant. The controls for GDP and GDP per capita are both positive but just miss the 95 percent confidence level. The urbanization variable is negative and just misses standard levels of significance. The control for state population is not significant. Table 6.1 presents the results of the regression.

The second model estimates the significance of the independent variables on per capita locally generated revenue. Again, Vanhanen's index is positive and highly significant. The electoral timing dummy is insignificant. The export sector variable is positive and just misses standard levels of significance ($p = 0.06$). Thus, there is some evidence that states with strong export sectors raise more revenue locally and are less dependent on transfers from the federal government. The variable for per capita federal transfers is positive and significant. GDP and GDP per capita are positive and significant. Urbanization and total population are insignificant.

The statistical data presented in models 1 and 2 seem to provide strong evidence that the level of electoral competition has a significant positive influence on local fiscal autonomy. Yet some may argue that this statistical relationship is a result of the fact that the PRI dominated the federal government and punished states that voted heavily for the opposition by denying them federal funds. If this is the case, then the higher percentage of local revenue in electorally competitive states may be merely a statistical artifact of the reduced federal transfers. The data presented here suggest that this is not the case because the statistical models hold federal transfers constant.

Model 3 tests the contention that more competitive states are discriminated against in federal transfers. The model uses per capita federal transfers as the dependent variable. Electoral competition is insignificant in this equation. Moreover, when this same equation is estimated using the vote for the PRI instead of Vanhanen's index, the PRI vote is also insignificant. Vanhanen's index, though insignificant, is actually positive, suggesting that federal transfers may actually go up in more competitive

Table 6.1.   Cross-Sectional Time Series GEE Regression: The Impact of Electoral Competition on State Fiscal Policy (Corrected for First-Order Autocorrelation)

	Model 1: Dep. Var. = Public Goods Expenditures per Capita	Model 2: Dep. Var. = Locally Generated Revenue per Capita	Model 3: Dep. Var. = Federal Transfers per Capita
Vanhanen's	13.857	0.447	0.871
index	(3.92)**	(2.92)**	(0.82)
Electoral	5.372	−2.152	61.012
timing	(0.08)	(0.45)	(1.84)
Export wages	0.129	0.020	0.007
per capita	(0.77)	(1.79)	(0.10)
Federal transfers	0.923	0.030	
per capita	(4.53)**	(2.96)**	
GDP	0.000	0.000001	0.000
	(1.84)	(2.16)*	(0.26)
GDP per capita	0.022	0.002	0.007
	(1.77)	(2.18)*	(1.45)
Urbanization	−518.230	−0.429	−59.976
	(1.89)	(0.02)	(0.48)
Population	−0.078	−0.004	−0.016
	(1.56)	(1.34)	(0.80)
Constant	300.864	−9.247	240.000
	(1.46)	(0.70)	(2.64)**
Observations	279	279	279
Number of	31	31	31
group (state)			

Note: Absolute value of z statistics in parentheses.

* $p < .05$; ** $p < .01\%$.

states. This is consistent with evidence from Chand (2001, 246), Molinar Horcasitas and Weldon (1994), and Bruhn (1996, 157–58) that the federal government strategically targeted more federal funds to states that are opposition strongholds in order to undermine opposition support.[6]

The theoretical explanation proposed here stresses the importance of electoral competition rather than opposition victory. It is possible that the statistical results presented in table 6.1 are being driven by a

Table 6.2. Cross-Sectional Time Series GEE Regression: The Impact of Electoral Competition on State Fiscal Policy (Corrected for First-Order Autocorrelation), Opposition-Governed States Excluded

	Model 1: Dep. Var. = Public Goods Expenditures per Capita	Model 2: Dep. Var. = Locally Generated Revenue per Capita	Model 3: Dep. Var. = Federal Transfers per Capita
Vanhanen's	14.892	0.437	0.790
index	(4.09)**	(2.89)**	(0.70)
Electoral	33.287	−2.094	75.618
timing	(0.55)	(0.39)	(2.14)*
Export wages	0.111	0.022	0.089
per capita	(0.51)	(1.30)	(0.76)
Federal transfers	0.830	0.028	
per capita	(4.26)**	(2.82)**	
GDP	0.0002	0.000001	0.000
	(2.60)**	(2.07)*	(0.18)
GDP per capita	0.020	0.002	0.007
	(1.85)	(2.53)*	(1.38)
Urbanization	−666.227	−3.729	−86.900
	(2.70)**	(0.19)	(0.66)
Population	−0.098	−0.004	−0.012
	(2.14)*	(1.21)	(0.59)
Constant	416.417	−9.171	250.745
	(2.25)*	(0.65)	(2.65)**
Observations	252	252	252
Number of group (state)	29	29	29

Note: Absolute value of z statistics in parentheses.
* $p < .05$; ** $p < .01\%$.

few outliers of opposition government, which would indicate that opposition government, not electoral competition, is the key explanatory variable. To test for this possibility, I reestimated the results from table 6.1 with all of the observations of opposition rule dropped from the data set. These results, presented in table 6.2, show that electoral competition is positive and significant even when the states ruled by opposition parties are dropped.

PRI governments in competitive states are more likely to have greater fiscal autonomy than PRI governments in uncompetitive states. In some ways the results are even stronger when the opposition states are omitted. In model 1, GDP, urbanization, and population all become statistically significant. In model 3 the electoral timing variable is positive and significant, suggesting that states that have local elections at the same time as national elections receive more federal transfers.

In sum, the data provide evidence that more electorally competitive states have greater fiscal independence from the central government and provide more public goods to their citizens. Additionally, there is some evidence to suggest that more export-oriented states have greater fiscal independence. The variable for concurrent subnational and national elections is not significant in any of the models of expenditure or revenue decentralization. The data are consistent with the hypothesis that electoral competition creates incentives for elected politicians to acquire new influence over expanded policy-making arenas. The data also lend some support to the structural models that suggest that states with more export-oriented economies will have more autonomy from the central government. Finally, the analysis suggests that electoral timing is not important in determining local fiscal autonomy.

This chapter examines the influence of increasing electoral competition on local autonomy, one aspect of a broader process of changing decision-making arenas. Building on the institutional literature, I develop a dynamic institutional explanation of decentralization to shed new light on the relationship between democratization and decentralization. The chapter tests static models that emphasize electoral rules against a dynamic model that emphasizes the changing incentives generated by a shifting political context. In an examination of the bottom-up dynamics of decentralization, the data suggest that in the case of Mexico increasing electoral competition is much more important for explaining relative local fiscal autonomy than the timing of elections. The strong results of the empirical analysis provide support for a model emphasizing the dynamics of institutional change rather than the static approaches that have dominated the institutional literature. The model also provides some evidence that an export-oriented economy creates incentives for local politicians to demand autonomy from the central government.

This analysis departs from the dominant studies of decentralization by focusing on intranational rather than international variation. The findings highlight the importance of intranational variation and suggest the dangers involved in assuming that levels of local autonomy and democratization are constant across subnational units. The results of the empirical analysis also support the contention that the interests of subnational actors vary according to the political context they face.[7]

In sum, this chapter has provided further evidence of the ways in which increasing political competition strengthens horizontal accountability. By shifting power from centralized authoritarian bureaucrats to democratic local governments, increasing electoral competition has had important consequences for the process of policy making and has also created new centers of power that are capable of checking the dominance of the national executive.

CHAPTER SEVEN

Conclusion

This book has argued that growing electoral competition strengthens democratic accountability by shifting power from executives to legislatures, from party leaders to voters, and from national elites to local constituencies. The growth of opposition challenges to one-party rule in the Mexican states has strengthened legislative bodies, altered patterns of political recruitment, and changed the locus of decision making. Statistical data show that the level of electoral competition is a strong and consistent predictor of legislative behavior, political recruitment, and decentralization even when traditional explanatory variables, such as social and economic modernization and static institutions, are held constant. Electoral competition has breathed new life into previously moribund legislative and federal institutions. The volume of legislative activity, press attention, and oversight has increased dramatically in response to growing electoral competition. Likewise, competition has produced major changes in the process of political recruitment, leading to innovations in methods of candidate selection that have resulted in candidates who have stronger ties to the local communities they represent. Finally, electoral competition has resulted in a significant erosion of centralized bureaucratic power as political competition for office at the state level has generated new demands for local autonomy and greater independence in state fiscal policy. All three sets of changes have important consequences for representation and accountability because they take power out of the hands of the national executive and open up new channels of access for citizens to shape policy and influence the choice of candidates.

137

In addition to providing new insights into Mexico's transition to democracy, these findings have important implications for general theories of comparative politics, especially the study of democratization, institutional change, decentralization, and subnational governance. First, the
findings of this study take us beyond existing research on democratization
and democratic consolidation by addressing key questions about the consequences of democracy for political recruitment, institutional change, and
decision-making arenas. Previous research has concentrated either on
explaining the causes of democratic transition or on evaluating the incom-
pleteness of democratic consolidation, with central emphasis upon the
problem of the lack of accountability. This study addressed the latter in
three distinct ways, having focused explicitly on how and why increasing
electoral competition strengthens checks on centralized power and executive authority and multiplies citizen access to and influence over politics. Moreover, the study points to the usefulness of disaggregating the
concept of democracy. Examining how the substantive and procedural
components of democracy are interrelated allows researchers to answer
fundamental questions about the quality of democracy without falling into
the morass of defining and differentiating various types of regimes.

Second, this study transcends the traditional approach to institutions
by establishing a logic for understanding the electoral basis of institutional change, thus focusing on the causes of institutional change rather
than the consequences. Most research treats institutions as constants and
focuses on explaining how institutions shape political outcomes. In the
current context of democratic reform in Latin America, however, constitutions and electoral codes are being redesigned and rewritten continu-
ally, and few studies have attempted to explain these changes.[1] In the
Mexican states, the formal rules of the game have often provided a very
limited guide to actual institutional practice. Legislatures are endowed
with substantial constitutional powers, but they rarely initiate legislation
and typically approve all of the governor's bills without debate, thus allowing the governor to dominate state policy making. State governments
are similarly provided extensive autonomy from the central government
by the constitution, but in reality they have historically been subservient
to the national party leadership. Competition has infused new life into old
institutions and also generated institutional changes. Shifts in the political
balance of power have led to efforts to protect newly gained positions
through electoral, institutional, constitutional, and other sets of reforms.
Whereas the institutional literature emphasizes the ways in which static
institutions such as proportional representation and district size shape
the nature of partisan competition, the findings of this research instead

highlight the ways in which partisan competition has generated institutional changes. This study thus reverses the dominant lines of causation in the institutional literature to emphasize the fact that institutions are the product of political self-interest and the game of politics. They are not immutable constraints on political actors, nor are they the result of decisions made by enlightened princes. An approach to institutions that stresses the dynamic logic of political change provides significant advantages over static conceptions of institutions.

Third, I have drawn attention to the importance of subnational variation in the process of democratization and institution building. Often, institutional reform and democratization at the national level conceal substantial and significant variation at the subnational level. In Mexico, some states, such as Hidalgo, continue to function as one-party authoritarian systems. Other states, such as Chihuahua, have vigorous two-party competition. And still other subnational arenas, such as the Federal District, have three viable parties contesting local elections. A country with a multiparty national legislature may be formed from a majority of uncompetitive local districts if there are regionally based parties. Evidence from chapter 4 suggests that legislators from uncompetitive districts act differently from those who represent competitive districts. Aggregate levels of competition between parties may not be as important as the level of competition in individual districts for understanding the nature of political systems.

Generalizations based on national-level conditions miss this variation and may lead to inaccurate categorizations of regime type. Not only can this lead to erroneous conclusions in studies of regime change, but it also has substantial consequences for the discipline of political science more generally. Regime type has served as a central explanatory variable in many areas of political research. The consequences of regime type on public policy outcomes have long been a central concern for comparative politics (see Remmer 1978, 1985–86, 1990). The political economy literature maintains an ongoing debate over the importance of regime type for economic policy decisions (Haggard and Kaufman 1995; Remmer 1986, 1990; Smith and Acuña 1994; Stallings and Kaufman 1989). Studies of human rights have found regime type to be an important determinant of state sponsored violence (Mitchell and McCormick 1988; Poe and Tate 1994). Likewise, liberal theories of international relations posit a central explanatory role for regime type in explaining international conflict behavior (Russett 1993).

The research presented here has shown that subnational politics can diverge substantially from national trends. In countries such as Brazil, where state and local governments spend more than 60 percent of the total public funds (Willis et al. 1999, 13), this divergence can have substantial consequences for national outcomes. If classifications of regime type were calculated using a weighted average of political competition among subnational and national governments based on relative shares of public expenditures, Mexico might be more democratic than Brazil. Standard measures of regime type that do not factor in subnational variation may be making serious mistakes in classifying and comparing regimes, thereby undermining entire research programs that rely on these cross-national indicators. Moreover, this problem continues to grow as decentralization policies are implemented and subnational governments gain increasing autonomy. In many countries, subnational governments are not only controlling significant proportions of government revenues and expenditures but also controlling electoral institutions and polling stations, police forces, and judicial systems, as well as contracting debt internationally. In some cases, subnational governments are even maintaining their own currencies and developing independent economic and political relationships with other nations (French 1996; Woodruff 1999). Thus, the lack of serious attention to subnational variation is not merely an inconsequential oversight but rather a fundamental issue that needs to be addressed by all political researchers exploring the consequences of regime type.

Fourth, by providing important new information about local legislators and governors, this study has demonstrated the important consequences of local democracy for effective policy making and established a basis for understanding the potential consequences of decentralization. Most existing research on decentralization overlooks the actual institutional capacity of subnational governments and therefore provides an incomplete analysis of the likely outcome of decentralization. This study, by contrast, has systematically explored the variety of governance in thirty-one subnational units. The findings presented above suggest that decentralization is likely to lead to more efficient and participatory policy making only when power is decentralized to subnational governments in which leaders are selected through competitive electoral processes. If resources are decentralized to governments in noncompetitive contexts, then it is likely that the resources will end up in the hands of local authoritarian elites, and policy outcomes may actually become less consistent with the interests of the population. Political competition seems to be a key variable in determining how the policy-making process functions at the subnational level and thus how successful decentralization attempts will be.

Finally, this research has important implications for the study of democratization in Mexico. Growing electoral competition and the strengthening of representative institutions at the subnational level have important consequences for the broader process of democratization in Mexico.

Since the end of the revolution, the president of Mexico has handpicked his successor in a process know as the *dedazo,* or finger pointing. This tradition was finally broken in 1999, when the PRI selected its presidential candidate in an open primary election for the first time in the party's history. In the late 1990s, the PRI also lost control of the national chamber of deputies, confronting the president with an opposition-controlled legislature and fundamentally altering the process of decision making at the national level. In the year 2000, an opposition candidate was elected president. These changes reflect the growth of electoral competition at all levels of government. The evidence presented in this book provides a guide to what kinds of changes can be expected at the national level as a result of Vicente Fox's election. Democratization not only has resulted in more independent legislatures, more participatory patterns of political recruitment, and greater democratic control over public policy at the state level but also has had substantial consequences for the national political environment. Growing competition at the subnational level has percolated up into the national arena, profoundly altering the established contours of Mexican politics. Not only is the PRI blocked from imposing its policies and favorite candidates on the states, but it also has been forced to reinvent itself to compete more effectively in national elections.

As a result of growing electoral competition and opposition party strength at the subnational level, democratic enclaves began to emerge in Mexico in the 1980s (Rodríguez and Ward 1995b). In these democratic enclaves, opposition parties helped to guarantee the basic rights of citizenship, enforce universal suffrage, and eliminate electoral fraud. As these enclaves grew to incorporate most of the urban areas across the country, researchers began to focus instead on the remaining authoritarian enclaves (Cornelius 1999; Fox 1994a, 1994b). The growth of democratic enclaves and the gradual shrinking of authoritarian spaces have had significant influence on the national process of democratization in Mexico. Democratic control of local politics influences national politics by reducing electoral fraud and changing voting behavior and partisan identification. Moreover, local-level democracy provides opportunities for opposition leaders to gain experience and expertise, thus reducing voters' uncertainty and risk aversion regarding opposition parties. Local democracy generates local policy innovations that have influenced national democratic reforms.

One of the greatest obstacles to democracy in Mexico has been the extensive use of electoral fraud by the governing party. While electoral manipulation can take place at the highest levels of government (with the infamous computer failure during the 1988 presidential elections being a prime example), the most pervasive forms of fraud take place at local polling stations where individual citizens cast their ballots. The PRI has traditionally relied upon the support of local authoritarian bosses in non-competitive districts to deliver the vote through fraud, coercion, and manipulation. Unaccountable government officials and police forces in non-competitive areas enforce the control of local bosses over the electoral process. Votes won in these authoritarian enclaves can tip the balance in close elections (see Fox 1994a, 1994b). The growing strength of an opposition party creates important obstacles to traditional machine politics and fraud. Effective competition at the subnational level allows opposition parties to monitor elections and contain coercion and fraud at local polling stations.

Gradual changes in voting behavior and partisan identification at the municipal level also tend to carry over to state and national elections. The PAN's success in local government in the city of León, Guanajuato, for example, has created an electoral base for the PAN in state and federal elections. Since the late 1980s, the PAN has consistently won León's electoral districts in state and national elections (Rionda 1997; Shirk 1999; Valencia García 1998). Other cities that have elected local PAN governments also tend to vote heavily for the PAN in state and federal elections (Alonso and Tamayo 1997; Guillén López 1995; Orozco 1997). Hence, once opposition parties make inroads at the municipal level, they create opportunities for electing state and national legislators from opposition parties and strengthen electoral bases for opposition parties in gubernatorial and presidential campaigns. In this way, the consequences of local electoral competition have percolated up from the municipal arena to the state and national level, culminating in the 1997 election of an opposition majority in the national chamber of deputies and the 2000 election of opposition party member Vicente Fox as president.

Local-level democracy has also provided a place for democratic leaders to gain experience and make a name for themselves, allowing them to move up in the party ranks and compete in statewide and national elections. Many of the most important national opposition leaders began their political careers in local government. The first three opposition governors (Ernesto Ruffo Appel in Baja California, Carlos Medina Plascencia in Guanajuato, and Francisco Barrio Terrazas in Chihuahua) came to power after successful mayoral administrations. Vicente Fox built upon his success as governor of Guanajuato to win the presidency in the 2000 elections. Local government is providing a training ground for opposition party leaders and preparing them for future positions in higher levels of government. Successful opposition administrations at the local level have also helped to reduce voters' fears of the uncertainty of opposition rule.

The growth of electoral competition in the subnational arena is also generating institutional innovations that are changing the relationship between citizens and their government. Opposition governments have introduced, tested, and streamlined new forms of more accountable governance, proving to the ruling party and to citizens that things can be done differently. One of the most important examples of institutional innovation at the subnational level that has influenced national politics is the introduction of photographic voter identity cards by the Ruffo government in Baja California (Espinoza Valle 1999). After Ruffo proved that it could be done, Salinas introduced voter identity cards at the national level, taking an important step forward for procedural democracy. The new electoral codes introduced in Baja California, Chihuahua, and San Luis Potosí also provide important examples of state-level reforms that have motivated similar changes at the national level (Aziz Nassif 1996b; Calvillo Unna 1999; Espinoza Valle 1999). Additionally, under the leadership of Vicente Fox, Guanajuato became to the first state in the country to publish the public accounts on the Internet so that citizens could monitor how their tax money was being spent. Again, the pressures for the growth of transparency have expanded beyond that state into the national political arena.

The new participatory style of governance introduced by opposition governments created new expectations for government at all levels. PAN-controlled municipal governments across the country initiated "Citizen Wednesdays," where on a first-come-first-served basis citizens are invited to meet with the municipal leaders to express their opinions (Cabrero Mendoza 1995; Vanderbush 1999). Many opposition governments have also been successful in reducing corruption, improving service provision, and generally making local government more efficient (Rodríguez and Ward 1992, 1994; Vanderbush 1999; Ziccardi 1995). As the expectations of citizens have changed, the PRI has been forced to reform itself at the local level and take seriously issues such as corruption, accountability, and efficiency in order to compete with strong opposition candidates. PRI reforms at the local level designed to help challenge local opposition parties have led to higher standards for government across the country. For example, the introduction of primary elections to choose local candidates created new expectations that all candidates should be chosen in democratic processes.

Finally, increasing decentralization is strengthening the influence of subnational governments. During the past decade, the states in Mexico have taken on a much greater role in the distribution of health care and education (Grindle 1996; Rodriguez 1997). The states also have increased significantly their share of public expenditures (Cabrero Mendoza 1998). As municipalities and states take on greater responsibility for public policy, opposition governments at the state and local level are having even more opportunities to implement innovative policies and reform the government.

The process of democratization in Mexico is the result of an inter-action between the assertion of subnational autonomy in democratic en-claves and the imposition of central authority in authoritarian enclaves. In more democratic states, opposition parties have pushed through impor-tant democratic reforms, thereby ratcheting up the minimum expecta-tions of the citizens. The national government has responded by intro-ducing similar reforms at the national level and then imposing these reforms on the more authoritarian states. The reform of electoral laws and institutions provides the most vivid example of this process (see Becerra et al. 1996; Crespo 1996).

Electoral competition also has implications for the responsiveness of public policy to the demands of the electorate. In a presidential system, competition strengthens the checks and balances that are necessary to control the influence of the president. The research on democratic con-solidation has pointed to the overwhelming centralization of power in the hands of the executive and the related weakness of representative institu-tions as the main cause for the lack of accountability in the new democ-racies (O'Donnell 1994; Oxhorn 1998; von Mettenheim and Malloy 1998). Strengthened legislatures, more participatory patterns of political recruit-ment, and greater democratic control of decision-making arenas influence democratic accountability by shifting power away from executives toward legislative bodies, local constituents, and subnational governments. These changes are important for democratic accountability because they create new opportunities for monitoring and overseeing executives. The devel-opment of institutions autonomous from the executive creates influential positions available to opposition forces. These newly empowered actors have incentives and opportunities to monitor and publicize nonrespon-sive behavior, and it is likely that increased monitoring will induce politi-cians to act more responsively.

While the specific indicators used in this analysis and the particular details of the institutions may be unique to Mexico, the general conclu-sions regarding the importance of subnational politics for understanding and classifying regime types, the utility of disaggregating democracy, and the value of a dynamic approach to institutions apply far beyond the bor-ders of Mexico. Because state governments in Mexico are being studied, many important variables are held constant; this facilitates analysis but may also limit generalizability. All of the states operate within a larger fed-eral, presidential system with a mixed proportional representation and single-member-district electoral system. All of the states also underwent a transition to democracy characterized by the breakdown of rule by one highly centralized and disciplined dominant party. Because these important variables are held constant, the precise mechanisms by which electoral competition strengthens representative institutions may be unique to Mexico. For example, the changes in political recruitment that focus on growing local autonomy may be unique to Mexico because of its tradition of extreme presidentialism and centralization. Changes in political recruitment in other polities may take on different forms. Nevertheless, comparative evidence suggests that electoral competition has strengthened representative institutions in many other contexts. For example, competitive elections strengthened judiciaries in provincial Argentina (Bill 2000), strengthened provincial legislatures in Russia and the U.S. South (Hahn 1996b; Rosenthal 1990), and weakened authoritarian bureaucracies in Brazil (Hunter 1997). Still, the generalizability of this study may be limited in so far as some of the beneficial institutional consequences outlined for the case of Mexico may have some significant disadvantages in other countries. Also, the rather odd electoral system in Mexico may make some of the outcomes of electoral competition unique to Mexico.

The institutional changes resulting from electoral competition discussed in this book are clearly beneficial in the Mexican context but may not improve the quality of democracy in all circumstances. In the case of Mexico during authoritarian one-party rule, power was highly concentrated in the hands of the president. One observer referred to the Mexican president as a virtual dictator that was elected every six years (Brandenberg 1964). The president was able to exercise unconstrained power because of his control over the ruling party and the high levels of discipline within the party. As electoral competition increased and party discipline declined in Mexico, there were new obstacles to the president's ability to dominate politics. As a result, electoral competition generated stronger legislatures, more open processes of political recruitment, and more local autonomy, thereby enhancing horizontal accountability and improving democratic quality. In other contexts the breakdown of party discipline may not have such beneficial consequences. In Brazil, for example, one of the greatest obstacles to higher-quality democracy is the inchoate party system (Mainwaring 1999; Weyland 1996). The overly weak and fragmented party system in Brazil has compromised the ability of parties to promote accountable governance. Once the deinstitutionalization of Mexico's authoritarian party system is complete, it remains to be seen whether Mexico will be able to institutionalize a democratic party system or will instead follow Brazil's path. In a case like Brazil, further breakdowns in party discipline are unlikely to improve democratic accountability.

Similarly, increased local fiscal autonomy may not always be good. In the context of Mexico, where fiscal policy is highly centralized, some decentralization to more competitive states is advantageous. But too much fiscal autonomy for subnational governments has proven disastrous for Argentina's economy (Remmer and Wibbels 2000). While decentralization does not necessarily improve the quality of democracy, the pattern outlined in chapter 6 does. A top-down policy of decentralization may redistribute power to local governments that are less competitive and less responsive to local constituents than the central government. States' rights advocates in the U.S. South whose real objective was to maintain segregationist policies provide a good example. Similarly, in Mexico decentralizing power to the government of a state like Hidalgo is unlikely to improve the quality of governance there. The process of decentralization outlined in chapter 6, however, does seem likely to improve democratic quality because fiscal autonomy is most likely to be decentralized to the most competitive states and least likely to be decentralized to the uncompetitive states. If the process is being fueled by electoral competition at the state level, then those states that gain more autonomy are the most competitive states.

Even in terms of legislative development, some may argue that stronger legislatures are not necessarily more democratic. This may be particularly relevant in countries where malapportionment results in legislatures that are dominated by authoritarian elites from rural areas (Snyder and Samuels 2001). While a rubber-stamp congress is clearly not beneficial for democracy, an obstinate, uncooperative congress can also cause problems for governability (Linz 1994; Linz and Valenzuela 1994). Since the election of Vicente Fox in 2000, Mexico's national congress has blocked almost every important reform proposed by the president. Some Mexicans are becoming impatient with the fighting between the congress and the president and the slow progress of political reform. On the other hand, scholars of divided government in the United States have argued that American voters intentionally vote for divided government because they do not trust either party to rule on its own and prefer the moderate agenda that emerges from constant compromise in a divided government (Alesina and Rosenthal 1995).

Moreover, some scholars are wary of the entire idea of horizontal accountability, suggesting that increases in horizontal accountability may not actually improve democratic accountability (Schmitter 1999). According to this view, too many veto points may create even greater obstacles to democratic accountability than a dominant executive. Furthermore, horizontal accountability may empower state agencies that are not elected or democratically accountable, thus constraining the power of a democratically elected president. Again, however, in the case of Mexico's transition from hyperpresidentialism and one-party rule, greater checks on the executive's prerogatives are clearly beneficial.

The basic structure of the electoral system, a set of variables that has been widely viewed as an important determinant of political outcomes, dropped out of the preceding analysis because the electoral system is largely constant across the Mexican states. These electoral variables may take on greater importance when the consequences of electoral competition are examined outside of the Mexican context. While the prohibition on consecutive reelection in Mexico suggests that Mexico is a least likely case for finding significant consequences from electoral competition, the large number of single-member districts in the legislature may generate a stronger electoral connection in Mexico than in countries with no single-member districts.

Many scholars have found comparisons between Venezuela and Mexico to be particularly useful because of the similar degree of party discipline and the high levels of penetration of interest groups by the ruling parties (Coppedge 1993; Crisp 1997; Davis 1989). Such a comparison begs the question of why electoral competition in Venezuela did not do more to bring about greater accountability. The answer may lie in the differences in the electoral systems. The theoretical logic developed in this thesis builds upon the central idea that there is an electoral connection between a politician and a local constituency. In Mexico, this is the case for over half of the legislators in the country, who are elected in single-member districts. Up until the constitutional reforms of 1993 in Venezuela, however, there was no real connection between the lawmakers and a local constituency. Members of both houses of the national congress were elected on one ballot with no names, just party labels. The closed-list proportional representation system was even further removed from the voters because the selection of candidates was dominated by the national party, and the local party organizations had very little influence over the candidates or the rankings in the party lists (Crisp 1997). Others have noted that in Brazil, where legislators are elected via open-list proportional representation, lack of accountability has also been a problem (Mainwaring 1999).

These cases provide an important reminder that electoral rules mediate the relationship between electoral competition and democratic accountability. The argument developed here must be tempered by the degree to which electoral rules provide an electoral connection between elected leaders and voters. The connection is strongest in countries where all members of the legislature are selected in single-member districts, as in the United States (Mayhew 1974). The connection is weakest when all legislative seats are distributed through closed-list proportional representation, as in Venezuela prior to the 1993 reforms. Mixed systems and open-list proportional representation systems fall somewhere between the extremes of the United States and Venezuela. Hence, some of the details of the argument may be unique to Mexico, but the general conclusions are more widely applicable to many newly democratized countries.

The major concern that has surfaced in the wake of democratization in Latin America is the issue of democratic accountability. Emphasis has been placed on the insufficiency of competitive elections to guarantee responsiveness to the electorate. While there may be institutions under which electoral competition alone is insufficient to generate accountability, this study shows that when the electoral system is held constant, competition systematically alters the incentives facing politicians in ways that strengthen representative institutions and enhance political accountability.

Moreover, this study suggests that the research on democratization needs to be refocused. More systematic analysis should be done to assess the consequences of democratization. This book has provided evidence that democratization influences legislative behavior, political recruitment patterns, and fiscal policy. Important avenues for future research include the examination of the impact of increasing electoral competition on other key institutions such as judiciaries, law enforcement, and electoral institutions. To assess further the consequences of electoral competition for democratic accountability, future comparative research might also provide more detailed analysis of the relationship between policy outputs and public opinion in competitive and noncompetitive contexts.[2]

Finally, the data presented above emphasize the importance of subnational politics in influencing national political outcomes. Comparative political scientists have long neglected the study of subnational political phenomena. One of the most important implications of this book is that measures of regime type based on national-level indicators may be poorly reflecting the true nature of regimes. Thus, entire bodies of research that use regime type as a central variable may be undermined by widely used measures of regime type that do not take subnational variation into account.

Instrument for Survey of State Legislators

1. ¿En qué partido milita Ud.? _____

2. ¿Siempre ha militado por el mismo partido?
   Sí
   No   ¿En qué otro partido? _____

3. ¿En qué año nació Ud.? _____

4. ¿De dónde es Ud.? Ciudad _____ Estado _____

5. Cuando el congreso no sesiona ¿donde vive Ud.? _____

6. ¿Cuál es su nivel de educación?
   1. Primaria
   2. Secundaria
   3. Bachillerato
   4. Profesional
   5. Póstgrado

7. ¿Qué profesión estudió Ud.? _____

8. ¿Dónde asistió a la universidad? (O preparatoria/secundaria)
   Cuidad _____ Estado _____
   ¿Es pública   o privada   ?

9. ¿Pertenece Ud. a alguna organización laboral, empresarial, profesional, o religiosa?
   Nombre de la organización: _____
   No pertenece

10. ¿De qué tendencia política se considera Ud.?
    1. Extrema derecha
    2. Derecha
    3. Centro-derecha
    4. Centro
    5. Centro-izquierda
    6. Izquierda
    7. Extrema izquierda

11. ¿Ha sido diputado(a) local anteriormente?
    Sí   ¿En qué distrito? _____
    No

12. ¿Ha tenido otros cargos públicos de elección?
    No
    Sí   ¿Cuáles? _____   _____
                         _____   _____

13. ¿Ha. tenido un puesto en el gobierno federal que lo haya desempeñado en el D. F.?

No

Sí

14. ¿Cuántos años ha vivido en el D. F.? _____

15. Durante el año pasado ¿qué porcentaje aproximado de su tiempo profesional pasó Ud. en asuntos legislativos (incluyendo respuestas a pedidos de sus electores)?

   1. Menos de 25 por ciento

   2. Entre 25 y 50 por ciento

   3. Entre 50 y 75 por ciento

   4. Entre 75 y 100 por ciento

16. Usando una escala de 0 a 7, en la que 0 es ningún interés y 7 es mucho interés ¿cuánto interés tiene usted en ser candidato por:

	Ningún Interés					Mucho Interés		
Diputado(a) local (otra vez)?	0	1	2	3	4	5	6	7
Presidente(a) Municipal?	0	1	2	3	4	5	6	7
Gobernador(a) del estado?	0	1	2	3	4	5	6	7
Diputado(a) federal?	0	1	2	3	4	5	6	7
Senador(a) federal?	0	1	2	3	4	5	6	7
Presidente(a) de la Republica?	0	1	2	3	4	5	6	7

17. ¿Cuál es el problema más importante que tiene su estado?

_____

_____

18. ¿Cuántos asesores hay en el congreso de su estado? _____

19. ¿Cuántas comisiones hay en el congreso de su estado? _____

20. ¿Cuántas veces se reunen las comisiones al mes? _____

21. ¿Tiene Ud. una oficina de atención ciudadana en su distrito para recibir sus electores?

Sí

No

22. ¿Cuántas veces ha sido entrevistado para algún periódico durante el año pasado? _____

23. ¿Cuántas veces ha sido entrevistado para un programa de radio o de televisión durante el año pasado? _____

24. ¿Cuántas cartas y llamadas recibe Ud. de sus electores durante un mes normal? _____

25. ¿Cuántos electores recibe Ud. en citas personales durante un mes normal?

_____

26. Desde su punto de vista ¿cuánta influencia política tienen las siguientes personas u organizaciones en la política de su estado?

	Mucha Influencia	Alguna Influencia	Poca Influencia	Ninguna Influencia
Los Ayuntamientos Municipales				
El Congreso Local				
El Gobernador del Estado				
El Presidente de la República				
El Congreso Federal				

27. ¿Con cuánta frecuencia hace usted los siguientes acciones durante un mes normal?

	Nunca	Una o Dos Veces	Entre 3 y 10 Veces	Más que 10 Veces
Tener audiencias públicas en su distrito				
Asistir a reuniones en su distrito				
Dar discursos en su distrito				
Intervenir para proveer un servicio para un elector				
Ir al D. F. para solicitar apoyos para su distrito				

28. ¿Con cuánta frecuencia hace usted los siguientes acciones durante un mes típico de una sesión legislativa?

	Nunca	Una o Dos Veces	Entre 3 y 10 Veces	Más que 10 Veces
Hacer uso de la palabra en el pleno				
Hacer uso de la palabra en comisión				
Negociar con otros diputados el apoyo para sus proyectos				
Regresar a su distrito				
Introducir legislación				

29. ¿Qué porcentaje aproximado de las leyes aprobadas en su estado vienen de iniciativa

de algún diputado(a)? _____
del Gobernador? _____
del Supremo Tribunal de Justicia? _____
de los Ayuntamientos Municipales? _____

30. Usando una escala en que 1 es muy probable y 10 es no probable ¿con cuánta probabilidad vota Ud. por una política a la que personalmente se opone, pero la mayoría de sus electores apoyan?

Muy Probable   No Probable
1   2   3   4   5   6   7   8   9   10

31. Usando una escala en que 1 es muy probable y 10 es no probable ¿con cuánta probabilidad vota Ud. por una política a la que personalmente se opone, pero su partido apoya?

Muy Probable   No Probable
1   2   3   4   5   6   7   8   9   10

32. ¿Cree usted que la educación es mejor manejada por: (Marque sólo uno)
    1. el gobierno federal?
    2. el gobierno estatal?
    3. el gobierno municipal?
    4. iniciativa privada?

33. ¿Cuáles son las responsabilidades más importantes en su rol de diputado(a)? Anote de 1 a 9; 1 es la actividad en que Ud. gasta más tiempo y 9 la actividad a la que Ud. le dedica menos tiempo. Por favor use cada número sólo una vez.

_____ Proponer leyes

_____ Vigilar las actividades de los órganos del gobierno

_____ Ayudar a los electores que tienen dificultades con las agencias del gobierno

_____ Defender los intereses de su distrito

_____ Defender los intereses de un grupo social particular

_____ Mantener contacto con las opiniones de sus electores

_____ Apoyar al gobernador

_____ Ayudar a los militantes de su partido

_____ Apoyar los intereses de su partido

_____ Otro _____

Si Ud. tiene otros comentarios sobre su participación como diputado local o sobre el cuestionario, por favor, escríbelos en otra página y entrégala con el cuestionario.

* *

MUCHAS GRACIAS POR SU COLABORACIÓN EN ESTE ESTUDIO ACADÉMICO.

* *

Si usted quiera un resumen de los resultados de esta encuesta, favor de llenar esta parte. (Para mantener su confidencialidad, Ud. puede entregar esta parte separado de la encuesta.)

Nombre:

Si, yo quiero un resumen de los resultados de esta encuesta

Notes to Chapter 2

1. Schumpeter and Mayhew emphasize competition between individual candidates rather than parties. Mayhew has no role for parties in his model, only competition between "single-minded seekers of reelection." In contrast, Schattschneider, Downs, and Schlesinger focus on parties and interparty competition. Apart from the unit of analysis, however, the theoretical arguments proposed by these authors are very similar.

2. According to Downs (1957), under simplified assumptions,

> the government subjects each decision to a hypothetical poll and always chooses the alternative which the majority of voters prefer. It must do so because if it adopts any other course, the opposition party can defeat it. For example, if the government acts as the majority prefers in everything except issue x, the opposition can propose a platform identical to the government's except for issue x, where it stands with the majority. Since the voters are indifferent between parties on all other issues, the whole contest narrows down to issue x, and the opposition, having supported the majority position, gains more votes than the incumbents. Thus to avoid defeat, the government must support the majority on every issue. (54–55)

3. Yet critics of this model argue that parties have goals beyond simply winning elections and therefore that party platforms do not always converge at the median voter. Also, voters' preferences may not be fixed, so parties and candidates can manipulate the mean voter. Furthermore, Arrow's paradox (1951) warns that if preferences are intransitive (i.e., a > b and b > c, but a ≯ c), new coalitions can be formed around alternative policies that are also preferred by a majority. Thus, we should expect to see unending cycles of new policies. In response to Arrow, scholars of the U.S. Congress have focused on the role of institutions in establishing policy stability. This research has established the basis for what is known as "rational choice institutionalism."

4. They summarize their argument:

At the ballot box, state electorates hold a strong control over the ideological direction of policies in their states. In anticipation of this electoral monitoring, state legislatures and other policymakers take public opinion into account when enacting state policy. These means of control are uncertain in any particular application but accumulate to create a striking correlation between the mean ideological preference of state electorates and the mean ideological tendency of state policy. (Erikson et al. 1993, 247)

5. In their classic formulation of political culture theory, Almond and Verba (1963) argued, "If the democratic model of the participatory state is to develop in these new nations, it will require more than the formal institutions of democracy—universal suffrage, the political party, the elective legislature. . . . A democratic form of participatory political system requires as well a political culture consistent with it" (3). A civic culture demonstrating high levels of interpersonal trust, feelings of efficacy, and a deep attachment to the political system is most conducive to stable democracy. Moreover, democracy is most likely in cultures that value participation rather than passive political behavior. Almond and Verba were not optimistic about the spread of civic culture to developing countries because of the difficulty in diffusing the subtle components of a civic culture and also because of the challenging economic conditions facing developing countries (4). What is needed to generate a democratic political culture, they argued, is "the simultaneous development of a sense of national identity, subject and participant competence, social trust, and civic cooperativeness" (373).

6. Key (1949) further argues that party systems influence policy outputs. He finds that interparty competition results in more organized politics, which in turn benefits lower-status groups, or, to use Key's terminology, the "have-nots." Key argues that the wealthy and powerful, the "haves," already have what they want. Therefore, the primary public policy goal of the "haves" is to obstruct change, whereas the "have-nots" seek to promote change. As organization is more important for promoting significant reforms than it is for simply obstructing change, the "have-nots" suffer in the context of disorganization. Disorganization promotes confusion among the electorate and creates issueless elections, making it difficult for lower-status groups to sort out their interests and vote for candidates that best represent them. Thus, the fluid factionalism that marked many of the one-party state governments studied by Key led to demagoguery, insufficient development of democratic institutions, lack of issue content in elections, and public policies that benefited powerful interests over the interests of the "have-nots."

7. Lockard (1959) concludes:

In the two-party states the anxiety over the next election pushes political leaders into serving the interests of the have-less element of society, thereby putting the party into the countervailing power operation. Conversely, in the one-party states it is easier for a few powerful interests to manage the government of the state without party interference since the parties are not representative of the particular elements that might pose opposition to the dominant interest groups. The parties do not represent the have-less element for the simple reason that politically there is no necessity to do so. (337)

Key's hypothesis and Lockard's findings inspired an ongoing effort to measure competition and statistically test the relationship between party competition and policy outputs across the U.S. states. Political scientists building on the so-called "Key hypothesis" argued that states with more competitive electoral systems are more likely to implement welfare and tax policies that favor lower-status groups. The results of this body of research have been mixed. Dawson and Robinson (1963) found a high bivariate correlation between interparty competition and policy outcomes that favor "have-nots" but also found that interparty competition has little independent impact on public policy outcomes when socioeconomic variables are controlled. Since the publication of Dawson and Robinson's findings, there has been an extensive debate over the hypothesized relationship. Some have found evidence to confirm the positive relationship between party competition and policy outcomes that favor the poor (Cnuddle and McCrone 1969; Holbrook and Van Dunk 1993; Sharkansky and Hofferbert 1969), while others have supported the findings of Dawson and Robinson that competition has no independent impact on policy outputs (Dye 1966; Fry and Winters 1970; Lewis-Beck 1977; Marquette and Hinckley 1981). These statistical studies focused on a greatly simplified version of Key's argument and left out the institutions highlighted by Key. For this reason, the results have not been robust.

8. A strong legislature has also been found to be important in constraining war (Morgan and Campbell 1991).

9. For example, Barbara Geddes (1996) argues that parties support institutional changes that maximize their capacity to rule. In the countries of Eastern Europe, institutional outcomes depended upon the perceived strength of the Communist party and the opposition parties. Communist parties preferred strong, popularly elected presidents in countries where they expected to win elections, whereas smaller parties preferred proportional representation (22).

10. In countries without single-member districts, the logic would obviously be different.

11. As Tsebelis (1990) notes, however, sometimes parties end up choosing unappealing candidates to fight competitive elections.

Notes to Chapter 3

1. Personal communication, September 24, 1998.

2. Parliamentary systems have very different institutional arrangements regulating the relationship between the executive and the legislature. Therefore, horizontal accountability in a parliamentary regime is very different from horizontal accountability in a presidential system.

3. For more on the effects of term limits, see Carey (1997).

4. The national congress as well as all the state congresses have mixed electoral systems. In all the legislatures, less than half of the seats are distributed through proportional representation. The rest are allocated in single-member districts. Proportional representation seats were added to the lower house of the national congress in 1964. Most state legislatures added proportional representation seats in the early 1980s. For an excellent analysis of electoral reforms at the national level, see Molinar Horcasitas (1996), and for reforms at the state level, see Crespo (1996).

5. While in the short-term context of the democratization process the relationship appears to be linear, over the long term it is likely that the relationship is actually curvilinear. Thus, extreme levels of competition may result in legislative deadlock and less effective institutions.

6. Arnulfo Vásquez Nieto, deputy, Guanajuato State Congress, interview by author, Guanajuato, Gto, June 19, 1998; Baltazar Reyna Reynosa, director of the Legislative Research Institute, San Luis Potosí State Congress, interview by author, San Luis Potosí, SLP, August 17, 1998.

7. For more on the 1991 election and the subsequent protest, see Valencia García (1993, 1994).

8. This time Nava was attempting to counter the domination of a new cacique, Jonguitud Barrios.

9. Nabor Centeno, deputy, Guanajuato State Congress, interview by author, Guanajuato, Gto, June 10, 1998; Eugenio Guadalupe Govea Arcos, deputy, San Luis Potosí State Congress, interview by author, San Luis Potosí, SLP, December 15, 1998; German Arce Martinez, deputy, Hidalgo State Congress, interview by author, Pachuca, Hgo, November 14, 1998.

10. Eugenio Guadalupe Govea Arcos, deputy, San Luis Potosí State Congress, interview by author, San Luis Potosí, SLP, December 15, 1998.

11. German Arce Martinez, deputy, Hidalgo State Congress, interview by author, Pachuca, Hgo, November 14, 1998.

12. Interview by author, Guanajuato, Gto, September 1, 1998.

13. Joel Sanchez Rodriguez, editor of *Avanzando,* interview by author, Pachuca, Hgo, November 6, 1998.

14. Andrés Manning Novales, interview by author, Pachuca Hgo, November 5, 1998.

15. Matias Cruz Mera, interview by author, Pachuca, Hgo, December 8, 1998.

16. Miguel Refugio Camarillo Salas, deputy, Guanajunto State Congress, interview by author, Guanajuato, Gto, June 3, 1998.

17. José Carmen Garcia Vázquez, interview by author, San Luis Potosí, SLP, June 1, 1998.

18. Fernando Hernández Ramírez, interview by author, Pachuca, Hgo, December 1, 1998.

19. Juan Manuel Menes Llaguno, interview by author, Pachuca, Hgo, November 4, 1998.

20. José Carmen Garcia Vázquez, interview by author, San Luis Potosí, SLP, June 1, 1998.

21. José López Garcia, deputy, Hidalgo State Congress, interview by author, Pachuca, Hgo, November 5, 1998.

22. Miguel Marquez Marquez and Ricardo Sheffield Padilla, interview by author, Guanajuato, Gto, August 11, 1998.

23. Miguel Refugio Camarillo Salas, interview by author, Guanajuato, Gto, June 3, 1998; Nabor Centeno, interview by author, June 10, 1998; Guanajuato, Gto, Guanajuato, Gto, August 12, 1998.

24. Interview by author, Guanajuato, Gto, June 10, 1998.

25. Isauro Villanueva Aguilar, director of Apoyo Parliamentario, Guanajuato State Congress, interview by author, Guanajuato, Gto, September 8, 1998.

26. Guadalupe Lemos Muñoz Ledo, legislative aide Guanajuato State Congress, interview by author, Guanajuato, Gto, April 2, 1998.

27. Isauro Villanueva Aguilar, director of Apoyo Parliamentario, Guanajuato State Congress, interview by author, Guanajuato, Gto, September 8, 1998.

28. Isauro Villanueva Aguilar, director of Apoyo Parliamentario, Guanajuato State Congress, interview by author, Guanajuato, Gto, August 12, 1998.

29. Miguel Refugio Camarillo Salas, interview by author, Guanajuato, Gto, June 3, 1998.

30. José Carmen Garcia Vázquez, interview by author, San Luis Potosí, SLP, June 1, 1998.

31. José Carmen Garcia Vázquez, interview by author, San Luis Potosí, SLP, June 1, 1998.

32. José Carmen Garcia Vázquez, interview by author, San Luis Potosí, SLP, June 1, 1998.

33. Gerardo Solís Monreal, interview by author, San Luis Potosí, SLP, December 15, 1998.

Notes to Chapter 4

1. The response rate was not spectacular but not particularly low compared with similar surveys of elites. Since very little information is available about state legislators in Mexico, it is hard to know what kind of bias was generated by the low response rate.

2. Data are not available for the states of Guerrero and Tamaulipas. The survey data presented in the following section *do* include Guerrero and Tamaulipas. The state of Mexico is also excluded from this analysis because it represents an extreme outlier. The most important expenditures for the state congresses are the salaries of the members. The state of Mexico dramatically increased the number of members in its congress over the time period studied here. In the 1996–1999 period, the state of Mexico had 75 members. The next largest legislature had only 42 members. The mean size of all the legislatures is 32.6. The standard deviation

is 10. The state of Mexico is more than three standard deviations away from the mean. Therefore, it is clearly an outlier.

3. A cross-sectional time series model allows for strong leverage in assessing both the significance of the relationship between the dependent and independent variables and the direction of causation (Finkel 1995). Unfortunately, a cross-sectional time series data set can also present significant difficulties when estimated with a traditional OLS model. Heteroskedasticity and serial correlation tend to be especially problematic in cross-sectional time series data. In the presence of heteroskedasticity and serial correlation, OLS estimation can produce unreliable standard errors, thus complicating hypothesis testing. The model, therefore is estimated using the GEE approach (Liang and Zeger 1986) with Stata's correction procedure for first-order autocorrelation, which allows for estimation in the presence of first-order autocorrelation within panels and cross-sectional correlation and/or heteroskedasticity across panels.

4. Missing data points have been estimated using Stata's linear interpolation technique.

5. When other variables are not held constant in a simple pairwise correlation, legislative budget and the number of members have a positive correlation of 0.45, which is statistically significant with 99 percent confidence.

6. Using OLS with ordinal data is problematic because the values assigned to each ranking are arbitrary. For example, in a scale from 1 to 5 in which "excellent" is 5, "good" is 4, and "average" is 3, we know that "excellent" is better than "good," but we do not know if the interval between "excellent" and "good" is equal to the interval between "good" and "average." The values 100, 23, and 5 may describe the intervals between these measurements better than 5, 4, and 3. With OLS, the actual values assigned to the rankings influence the estimates, whereas with ordered probit they do not.

7. See question 29 of the survey instrument in the Appendix.

8. See question 28 of the survey instrument in the Appendix.

9. See question 23 of the survey instrument in the Appendix.

10. See question 33 of the survey instrument in the Appendix. The rankings are coded from 1 to 9, with 1 as the activity to which the most time is dedicated and 9 as the activity to which the least time is dedicated. Therefore, the higher the value of the ranking, the less time the legislator devotes to the activity. To simplify interpretation of the results, I subtract the values for each ranking from 10 so that a higher number means a greater time commitment.

11. Caciques are local elites and political bosses who control local economics and politics.

12. See questions 27 and 28 of the survey instrument in the Appendix.

Notes to Chapter 5

1. *Precandidate* is the term used in Mexico for the politicians competing for the PRI's nomination.

2. Unfortunately, data on turnout were not available for all of the elections during the period covered in this data set, so the complete Vanhanen's index as used in the other chapters of this study could not be used.

3. The regressions were also calculated using gubernatorial election data, and the results were consistent with the results presented here.

Notes to Chapter 6

1. It should be noted that Garman et al. (2001) categorize the Mexican electoral system as a closed-list proportional representation system. They fail to mention that the majority of seats in the lower house are elected in single-member districts.

2. Roberto Madrazo Pintado was the governor of Tabasco, Francisco Labastida Ochoa the governor of Sonora, and Manuel Bartlett Diaz the governor of Puebla.

3. Ideally the analysis would include data on state spending in key policy areas such as education and health care. Unfortunately, the data are not available across all of the states, and the complexity of intergovernmental financing for education and health care makes it very difficult to analyze the data that do exist.

4. The term *maquila* is used in Mexico to refer to the manufacturing sector composed of foreign-owned factories that export the finished product.

5. Obviously, Mexico exports agricultural products and other goods that would not be captured by the *maquila* variable. Unfortunately, data for total exports disaggregated to the state level are not available. The *maquila* variable is therefore the best available indicator and, though clearly imperfect, demonstrates the significance of one important export sector.

6. Díaz-Cayeros, Magaloni, and Weingast (2000) examine a set of variables that are different from but related to those examined here. They argue that voters at the local level vote for the PRI even though they would prefer to be governed by the opposition. They do so because they fear that if an opposition party wins the local elections the state will be discriminated against in the allocation of federal funds. For this explanation to be convincing, we need evidence that states voting for the opposition are actually discriminated against in federal transfers. Also, if voting in local elections were dominated by concerns about federal transfers, we might expect those voters preferring the opposition to vote according to their preferences in presidential elections but not in local elections. Thus, we should see much greater opposition voting in federal elections than in local elections and widespread split-ticket voting. There is, however, very little evidence to suggest widespread split-ticket voting or vastly different voting behavior in local and federal elections.

7. The central argument I have made here is that political leaders in more competitive arenas face incentives to expand their control over less competitive arenas. In Mexico during the 1990s, this process resulted in decentralization because many states were more competitive than the national government. The 2000 presidential elections were the most competitive national elections in modern Mexican history. As a result, the asymmetry in the level of competitiveness has

shifted. After 2000, the national government became more competitive than many subnational governments. It is therefore likely that the same process described in this chapter will continue in the opposite direction. That is, the more competitive national government will exert control over those subnational governments with less competition, thus resulting in some centralization. While it is still too early to test this further proposition systematically, Fox's struggles with the state governments of Tabasco and Yucatán in 2001 suggest that the federal government is indeed exerting new influence over subnational authoritarian enclaves.

Notes to Chapter 7

1. See Remmer (1997) for a good review of the institutional literature.

2. Erikson et al.'s (1993) pathbreaking study of the relationship between public opinion and public policy in the United States provides an excellent example for comparativists interested in issues of democratic accountability. Unfortunately, sufficient survey data to replicate this study are not yet available in most newly democratized countries.

Agor, Weston H, ed. 1971. *Latin American Legislatures: Their Role and Influence, Analyses for Nine Countries.* New York: Praeger.

Aguilar-Barajas, Ismael, and Nigel Spence. 1988. "Industrial Decentralization and Regional Policy, 1970–1986: The Conflicting Policy Response." In *The Mexican Economy,* edited by George Philip. London: Routledge.

Alcocer V., Jorge. 1994. "Los partidos políticos y el poder legislativo (Reflexiones a partir de la experiencia mexicana)." In *El poder legislativo en la actualidad,* edited by Cámara de Diputados del H. Congreso de la Unión/Universidad Nacional Autónoma de México, 227–35. Serie G: Estudios doctrinales, no. 162. Mexico City: Instituto de Investigaciones Jurídicas.

Alemán Alemán, Ricardo. 1993. *Guanajuato: Espejismo electoral.* Mexico City: La Jornada.

Alesina, Alberto, and Howard Rosenthal. 1995. *Partisan Politics, Divided Government, and the Economy.* Cambridge: Cambridge University Press.

Almond, Gabriel A., and Sidney Verba. 1963. *The Civic Culture: Political Attitudes and Democracy in Five Nations.* Princeton, N. J.: Princeton University Press.

Alonso, Jorge, and Jaime Tamayo. 1997. "Jalisco." In *1994: Las elecciones en los estados,* edited by Silvia Gómez Tagle, 347–66. Mexico City: Centro de Investigaciones Interdisciplinarias en Ciencias y Humanidades, Universidad Nacional Autónoma de México.

Alvarado, Arturo. 1997. "El poder legislativo local ante el nuevo debate sobre el federalism." *Eslabones* 13:64–89.

Ames, Barry. 1987. *Political Survival: Politicians and Public Policy in Latin America.* Berkeley: University of California Press.

Amezcua, Adriana, and Juan E. Pardinas. 1997. *Todos los gobernadores del Presidente: Cuando el dedo de uno aplasta el voto popular.* Mexico City: Editorial Grijalbo.

Arrow, Kenneth Joseph. 1951. *Social Choice and Individual Values.* New York: John Wiley.

Aziz Nassif, Alberto. 1994. *Chihuahua: Historia de una alternativa.* Mexico D. F.: La Jornada Ediciones/Centro de Investigaciones y Estudios Superiores en Antropología Social.

————. 1996a. "Alternancia primero, gobierno dividido después: El caso de Chihuahua, 1992–1996." In *Poder legislativo: Gobiernos divididos en la Federación Mexicana,* edited by Alonso Lujambio. Mexico City: Colegio Nacional de Ciencias Políticas y Administración Pública, A. C., Universidad Autónoma Metropolitana, Instituto Federal Electoral.

————. 1996b. *Territorios de alternancia: El primer gobierno de oposición en Chihuahua.* Mexico City: Centro de Investigaciones y Estudios Superiores en Antropologia Social, Triana Editores.

Bailey, John. 1987. "Can the PRI Be Reformed? Decentralizing Candidate Selection." In *Mexican Politics in Transition,* edited by Judith Gentleman. Boulder, Colo.: Westview Press.

————. 1988. *Governing Mexico: The Statecraft of Crisis Management.* New York: St. Martin's Press.

Banamex. 1996. *Mexico social, 1994–1995 estadísticas seleccionadas.* Mexico City: Banco Nacional de Mexico, S. A.

Becerra, Ricardo, et al. 1996. *Así se vota en la Republica: Las elecciones legislativas en los estados: Un Análisis comparado.* Mexico D. F.: Instituto de Estudios para la Transición Democrática A. C.

Beck, Nathaniel, and Jonathan N. Katz. 1996. "Nuisance vs. Substance: Specifying and Estimating Time-Series-Cross-Section Models." *Political Analysis* 6 (July): 1–37.

Beltrán, Ulises et al. 1996. *Los Mexicanos de los noventa.* Mexico City: Instituto de Investigaciones Sociales, Universidad Nacional Autónoma de México.

Bezdek, Robert R. 1995. "Democratic Changes in an Authoritarian System: *Navismo* and Opposition Development in San Luís Potosí." In *Opposition Government in Mexico,* edited by Victoria E. Rodríguez and Peter M. Ward. Albuquerque: University of New Mexico Press.

Bill, Rebecca Ann. 2000. "A Tale of Two Provinces: Countervailing Power Centers and Judicial Autonomy in San Luis and Mendoza." Paper presented at the annual meeting of the Latin American Studies Association, Miami, Fla., March 16–18.

Binder, Sarah A. 1997. *Minority Rights, Majority Rule: Partisanship and the Development of Congress.* Cambridge: Cambridge University Press.

Bird, Richard M. 1993. "Threading the Fiscal Labyrinth: Some Issues in Fiscal Decentralization." *National Tax Journal* 46 (June): 207–27.

Black, Duncan. 1958. *The Theory of Committees and Elections.* Cambridge: Cambridge University Press.

Black, Gordon S. 1972. "A Theory of Political Ambition: Career Choices and the Role of Structural Incentives." *American Political Science Review* 64:865–78.

Brandenberg, Frank. 1964. *The Making of Modern Mexico.* Englewood Cliffs, N. J.: Prentice Hall.

Bratton, Michael, and Nicolas van de Walle. 1997. *Democratic Experiments in Africa: Regime Transitions in Comparative Perspective.* New York: Cambridge University Press.

Bruhn, Kathleen. 1996. "Social Spending and Politial Support: The 'Lessons' of the National Solidarity Program in Mexico." *Comparative Politics* 28:151–78.

—. 1997. *Taking on Goliath: The Emergence of a New Left Party and the Struggle for Democracy in Mexico.* University Park: Pennsylvania State University Press.

—. 1999. "PRD Local Governments in Michoacán: Implications for Mexico's Democratization Process. In *Subnational Politics and Democratization in Mexico,* edited by Wayne A. Cornelius, Todd A. Eisenstadt, and Jane Hindley. La Jolla: Center for U.S.-Mexican Studies, University of California, San Diego.

Burawoy, Michael, and Pavel Krotov. 1993. "The Economic Basis of Russia's Political Crisis." *New Left Review* 198:49–70.

Caballero, Alejandro. 1992. *Salvador Nava: Las últimas batallas.* Mexico City: La Jornada.

Cabrero Mendoza, Enrique. 1995. *La nueva gestion municipal: Análisis de experiencias innovadores en gobiernos locales.* Mexico City: Centro de Investigación y Docencia Económicas.

—. 1998. *Las políticas descentralizadoras en México (1983–1993): Logros y desencantos.* Mexico City: Centro de Investigación y Docencia Económicas.

Cabrero Mendoza, Enrique, and José Mejía Lira. 1998. "El estudio de las políticas descentralizadoras en México: Un reto metodológico." In *Las politicas descentralizadoras en México (1983–1993): Logros y desencantos,* edited by Enrique Mendoza Cabrero. Mexico City: Centro de Investigación y Docencia Económicas.

Cain, Bruce, John Ferejohn, and Morris Fiorina. 1987. *The Personal Vote: Constituency Service and Electoral Independence.* Cambridge, Mass.: Harvard University Press.

Calvillo Unna, Tomás. 1994. "San Luis Potosí." In *La República Mexicana: Modernización y democracia de Aguascalientes a Zacatecas,* vol. 3, edited by Pablo Gonzalez Casanova and Jorge Cadena Roa. Mexico City: La Jornada/Universidad Nacional Autónoma de México.

—. 1997. "San Luis Potosí." In *1994: Las elecciones en los estados,* edited by Silvia Gómez Talge. Mexico City: La Jornada Ediciones, Centro de Investigaciones Interdisciplinarias en Ciencias y Humanidades, Universidad Nacional Autónoma de México.

—. 1999. "A Case of Opposition Unity: The San Luis Potosí Democratic Coalition of 1991." In *Subnational Politics and Democratization in Mexico,* edited by Wayne A. Cornelius, Todd A. Eisenstadt, and Jane Hindley. La Jolla: Center for U.S.-Mexican Studies, University of California, San Diego.

Cámara de Diputados del H. Congreso de la Unión. 1994. *El poder legislativo en la actualidad.* Serie G: Estudios doctrinales, núm. 162. Mexico City: Universidad Nacional Autónoma de México, Instituto de Investigaciones Jurídicas.

Camp, Roderic Ai. 1977. "Losers in Mexican Politics: A Comparative Study of Official Party Precandidates for Gubernatorial Elections, 1970–1975." In *Quantitative Latin American Studies: Methods and Findings,* edited by James W.

Wilkie and Kenneth Ruddle. Los Angeles: UCLA Latin American Center Publications.

―――. 1995a. *Mexican Political Biographies, 1935–1993.* 3d ed. Austin: University of Texas Press.

―――. 1995b. "Mexico's Legislature: Missing the Democratic Lockstep?" In *Legislatures and the New Democracies in Latin America,* edited by David Close. Boulder, Colo.: Lynne Rienner.

―――. 1995c. *Political Recruitment across Two Centuries: Mexico, 1884–1991.* Austin: University of Texas Press.

―――. 1999. *Politics in Mexico: The Decline of Authoritarianism.* Oxford: Oxford University Press.

Campbell, Angus, et al. 1960. *The American Voter.* New York: John Wiley.

Cardoso, Fernando Herique, and Enzo Faletto. 1979. *Dependency and Development in Latin America.* Berkeley: University of California Press.

Carey, John M. 1996. *Term Limits and Legislative Representation.* Cambridge: Cambridge University Press.

―――. 1997. "Presidential and Political Parties in Costa Rica." In *Presidentialism and Democracy in Latin America,* edited by Scott Mainwaring and Matthew Soberg Shugart. Cambridge: Cambridge University Press.

Carmagnani, Marcello, ed. 1993. *Federalismos latinoamericanos: México, Brasil, Argentina.* Mexico City: El Colegio de México.

Carmines, Edward G. 1974. "The Mediating Influence of State Legislatures on the Linkage between Interparty Competition and Welfare Policies." *American Political Science Review* 68:1118–24.

Carpizo, Jorge. 1978. *El presidencialismo mexicano.* Mexico City: Siglo XXI.

Casar, Ma. Amparo. 1999. "El Congreso del 6 de Julio." In *1997: Elecciones y transición a la democracia en México,* edited by Luis Salazar. Mexico City: Cal y Arena.

Castellanos Hernández, Eduardo. 1997. *Formas de gobierno y sistemas electorales en México (1940–1994).* Mexico City: Centro de Investigación Científica Jorge C. Tamayo A. C.

Centeno, Miguel Ángel. 1994. *Democracy within Reason: Technocratic Revolution in Mexico.* University Park. Pennsylvania State University Press

Chalmers, Douglas A., et al., eds. 1997. *The New Politics of Inequality in Latin America: Rethinking Participation and Representation.* Oxford: Oxford University Press.

Chand, Vikram K. 2001. *Mexico's Political Awakening.* Notre Dame, Ind.: University of Notre Dame Press.

Chopra, Vir K. 1996. *Marginal Players in Marginal Assemblies: The Indian MLA.* New Delhi: Orient Longman.

Cinta, Alberto. 1999. "Uncertainty and Electoral Behavior in Mexico in the 1997 Congressional Elections." In *Towards Mexico's Democratization: Parties, Campaigns, Elections, and Public Opinion,* edited by Jorge I. Domínguez and Alejandro Poiré. New York: Routledge.

Close, David. 1995a. "Introduction: Consolidating Democracy in Latin America—What Role for Legislatures." In *Legislatures and the New Democracies in Latin America*, edited by David Close. Boulder, Colo.: Lynne Rienner.

———, ed. 1995b. *Legislatures and the New Democracies in Latin America*. Boulder, Colo.: Lynne Rienner.

Clubock, Alfred B., Norman B. Wilensky, and Forrest J. Berghorn. 1969. "Family Relationships, Congressional Recruitment and Political Modernization." *Journal of Politics* 31:1035–62.

Cnudde, Charles F., and Donald J. McCrone. 1969. "Party Competition and Welfare Policies in the American States." *American Political Science Review* 63:858–66.

Coleman, James S. 1990. *Foundations of Social Theory*. Cambridge, Mass.: Harvard University Press.

Collier, David, and Steven Levitsky. 1997. "Democracy with Adjectives: Conceptual Innovation in Comparative Research." *World Politics* 49:438–52.

Collier, Ruth Berins, and David Collier. 1991. *Shaping the Political Arena*. Princeton, N.J.: Princeton University Press.

Colton, Timothy J. 1996. "The Constituency Nexus in the Russian and Other Post-Soviet Parliaments." In *Democratization in Russia: The Development of Legislative Institutions*, edited by Jeffrey W. Hahn. Armonk, N.Y.: M. E. Sharpe.

Conaghan, Catherine M., James M. Malloy, and Luis A. Abugattas. 1990. "Business and the 'Boys': The Politics of Neoliberalism in the Central Andes." *Latin American Research Review* 25, no. 2:3–30.

Converse, Philip E. 1964. "The Nature of Belief System among Mass Publics." In *Ideology and Discontent*, edited by David Apter, 206–61. New York: Free Press.

Cook, Maria Lorena. 1990. "Organizing Opposition in the Teacher's Movement in Oaxaca." In *Popular Movements and Political Change in Mexico*, edited by Joe Foweraker and Ann L. Craig. Boulder, Colo.: Lynne Rienner.

———. 1996. *Organizing Dissent: Unions, the State, and the Democratic Teacher's Movement in Mexico*. University Park: Pennsylvania State University Press.

Coppedge, Michael. 1993. "Parties and Society in Mexico and Venezuela: Why Competition Matters." *Comparative Politics* 25:253–74.

———. 1994. *Strong Parties and Lame Ducks: Presidential Partyarchy and Factionalism in Venezuela*. Stanford, Calif.: Stanford University Press.

———. 1999. "Thickening Thin Concepts and Theories: Combining Large N and Small in Comparative Politics." *Comparative Politics* 31:465–76.

Cornelius, Wayne A. 1987. "Political Liberalization in an Authoritarian Regime: Mexico, 1976–1985." In *Mexican Politics in Transition*, edited by Judith Gentleman. Boulder, Colo.: Westview Press.

———. 1996. *Mexican Politics in Transition: The Breakdown of a One-Party-Dominant Regime*. La Jolla: Center for U.S.-Mexican Studies, University of California.

———. 1999. "Subnational Politics and Democratization: Tensions between Center and Periphery in the Mexican Political System." In *Subnational Politics and Democratization in Mexico*, edited by Wayne A. Cornelius, Todd A. Eisenstadt, and Jane Hindley. La Jolla: Center for U.S.-Mexican Studies, University of California, San Diego.

Cornelius, Wayne A., Todd A. Eisenstadt, and Jane Hindley, eds. 1999. *Subnational Politics and Democratization in Mexico*. La Jolla: Center for U.S.-Mexican Studies, University of California, San Diego.

Cornelius, Wayne A., Judith Gentleman, and Peter H. Smith, eds. 1989. *Mexico's Alternative Political Futures*. Monograph Series, no. 30. La Jolla: Center for U.S.-Mexican Studies, University of California, San Diego.

Cox, Gary W. 1990. "Centripetal and Centrifugal Incentives in Electoral Systems." *American Journal of Political Science* 34:903–35.

Cox, Gary W., and Scott Morgenstern. 2001. "Latin America's Reactive Assemblies and Proactive Presidents." *Comparative Politics* 33:171–90.

Craig, Ann L., and Wayne A. Cornelius. 1995. "Houses Divided: Parties and Political Reform in Mexico." In *Building Democratic Institutions: Party Systems in Latin America*, edited by Scott Mainwaring and Timothy R. Scully. Stanford, Calif.: Stanford University Press.

Crawford, Beverly, and Arend Lijphart. 1995. "Special Issue: Post Communist Transformation in Eastern Europe." *Comparative Political Studies* 28:171–314.

Crespo, José Antonio. 1995. "Governments of the Opposition: The Official Response." In *Opposition Government in Mexico*, edited by Victoria E. Rodríguez and Peter M. Ward. Albuquerque: University of New Mexico Press.

———. 1996. *Votar en los estados: Análisis comparado de las legislaciones electorales estatales en México*. Mexico City: Centro de Investigación y Docencia Económicas, Miguel Ángel Porrúa.

Crisp, Brian F. 1997. "Presidential Behavior in a System with Strong Parties: Venezuela, 1958–1995." In *Presidentialism and Democracy in Latin America*, edited by Scott Mainwaring and Matthew Soberg Shugart. Cambridge: Cambridge University Press.

Czudnowski, Moshe M. 1975. "Political Recruitment." In *Micropolitical Theory*, vol. 2 of *Handbook of Political Science*, edited by Fred I. Greenstein and Nelson Polsby, 155–242. Reading, Mass.: Addison-Wesley.

Dahl, Robert A. 1971. *Polyarchy: Participation and Opposition*. New Haven, Conn.: Yale University Press.

Davis, Charles L. 1989. *Working-Class Mobilization and Political Control: Venezuela and Mexico*. Lexington: University of Kentucky Press.

Dawisha, Karen, and Bruce Parrott, eds. 1997. *Democratic Changes and Authoritarian Reactions in Russia, Ukraine, Belarus, and Moldova*. Cambridge: Cambridge University Press.

Dawson, Richard E., and James A. Robinson. 1963. "Inter-Party Competition, Economic Variables, and Welfare Policies in the American States." *Journal of Politics* 25:265–89.

De Cordoba, Jose. 1998. "Mexico's Ruling Party Dabbles in Democracy to Stave off Decline." *Wall Street Journal*, July 1, 1998, A1.

De Cordoba, Jose, and Jonathan Friedland. 1999. "Mexican Governor Stirs Rebellion over Federal Jurisdiction on Cars." *Wall Street Journal*, April 30, 1999, A11.

De Tocqueville, Alexis. 1984. *Democracy in America*. New York: New American Library.

Destler, I. M. 1985. "Executive-Congressional Conflict in Foreign Policy: Explaining It, Coping with It." In *Congress Reconsidered,* 3d ed., edited by Lawrence C. Dodd and Bruce I. Oppenheimer, 343–63. Washington, D. C.: CQ Press.

Diaz, Christopher. 2000. "The Effects of Party Competition on the Quality of the PRI Candidates: An Analysis of Mexican Gubernatorial Elections 1989–1999." Paper presented at the annual meeting of the Latin American Studies Association, Miami, Fla., March 16–18.

Díaz-Cayeros, Alberto. 1995. *Desarrollo económico e inequidad regional: Hacia un nuevo pacto federal en México*. Mexico City: Centro de Investigación para el Desarrollo, A. C.

———. 1997. "Federalism and Veto Players: Equilibrium in Local Political Ambition in Mexico." Paper presented at the annual meeting of the American Political Science Association, Washington, D. C., August 28–31.

Díaz-Cayeros, Alberto, Beatriz Magaloni, and Barry Weingast. 2000. "Federalism and Democratization in Mexico." Paper presented at the annual meeting of the American Political Science Association, Washington, D. C., August 31 to September 3.

Domínguez, Jorge I., and James A. McCann. 1996. *Democratizing Mexico: Public Opinion and Electoral Choices*. Baltimore: Johns Hopkins University Press.

Doner, Richard F., and Eric Hershberg. 1996. "Flexible Production and Political Decentralization: Elective Affinities in the Pursuit of Competitiveness." Paper presented at the annual meeting of the American Political Science Association, San Francisco, August 30–September 2.

Downs, Anthony. 1957. *An Economic Theory of Democracy*. New York: Harper.

Dresser, Denise. 1996. "Mexico: The Decline of Dominant-Party Rule." In *Constructing Democratic Governance: Mexico, Central America, and the Caribbean in the 1990s,* edited by Jorge I. Domínguez and Abraham F. Lowenthal. Baltimore: Johns Hopkins University Press.

Ducatenzeiler, Graciela, and Philip Oxhorn. 1994. "Democracia, Autoritarismo y el Problema de la Gobernabilidad en América Latina." *Desarrollo Económico* 34:31–52.

Duverger, Maurice. 1959. *Political Parties: Their Organization and Activity in the Modern State,* translated by Barbara and Robert North. London: Methuen.

Dye, Thomas R. 1966. *Politics, Economics, and Public Policy in the American States*. Chicago: Rand McNally.

Easter, Gerald. 1997. "Preferences for Presidentialism: Postcommunist Regime Change in Russia and NIS." *World Politics* 49:184–211.

Eisenstadt, Todd A. 1999. "Electoral Federalism or Abdication of Presidential Authority? Gubernatorial Elections in Tabasco." In *Subnational Politics and Democratization in Mexico,* edited by Wayne A. Cornelius, Todd A. Eisenstadt, and Jane Hindley. La Jolla: Center for U.S.-Mexican Studies, University of California, San Diego.

Erikson, Robert S., Gerald C. Wright, and John P. McIver. 1993. *Statehouse Democracy: Public Opinion and Policy in the American States.* Cambridge: Cambridge University Press.

Espinoza Valle, Victor Alejandro. 1999. "Alternation and Political Liberalization: The PAN in Baja California." In *Subnational Politics and Democratization in Mexico,* edited by Wayne A. Cornelius, Todd A. Eisenstadt, and Jane Hindley. La Jolla: Center for U.S.-Mexican Studies, University of California, San Diego.

Fatton, Robert, Jr. 1999. "The Impairments of Democratization: Haiti in Comparative Perspective." *Comparative Politics* 31:209–30.

Fenno, Richard F. 1978. *Homestyle: House Members in Their Districts.* Boston: Little, Brown.

Figueroa Sepúlveda, Victor M., ed. 1993. *Elementos para una transformación democrática del estado y de la sociedad en Zacatecas.* Zacatecas, Mexico: Maestría en Ciencia Política, Universidad Autónoma de Zacatecas.

Finkel, Steven E. 1995. *Causal Analysis with Panel Data.* Thousand Oaks, Calif.: Sage.

Fiorina, Morris P. 1981. "Congressional Control of the Bureaucracy: A Mismatch of Incentives and Capabilities." In *Congress Reconsidered,* 2d ed., edited by Lawrence C. Dodd and Bruce I. Oppenheimer. Washington, D. C.: CQ Press.

———. 1992. *Divided Government.* New York: Macmillan.

———. 1994. "Divided Government in the American States: A Byproduct of Legislative Professionalism?" *American Political Science Review* 88:304–16.

Foweraker, Joe. 1993. *Popular Mobilization in Mexico: The Teacher's Movement, 1977–1987.* Cambridge: Cambridge University Press.

Fox, David J. 1992. "Decentralization, Debt, Democracy, and the Amazonian Frontierlands of Bolivia and Brazil." In *Decentralization in Latin America: An Evaluation,* edited by Arthur Morris and Stella Lowder. New York: Praeger.

Fox, Jonathan. 1994a. "The Difficult Transition from Clientelism to Citizenship: Lessons from Mexico." *World Politics* 46:151–84.

———. 1994b. "Latin America's Emerging Local Politics." *Journal of Democracy* 5, no. 2:105–16.

———. 1996. "How Does Civil Society Thicken? The Political Construction of Social Capital in Rural Mexico." *World Development* 24:1089–1103.

Fox, Jonathan, and Josefina Aranda. 1996. *Decentralization and Rural Development in Mexico: Community Participation in Oaxaca's Municipal Funds Program.* Monograph Series, no. 42. La Jolla: Center for U.S.-Mexican Studies, University of California, San Diego.

French, Howard W. 1996. "A Neglected Region Loosens Ties to Zaire." *New York Times,* September 18, 1996, A1.

Fry, Brian R., and Richard F. Winters. 1970. "The Politics of Redistribution." *American Political Science Review* 64:508–22.

Garman, Christopher, Stephen Haggard, and Eliza Willis. 2001. "Fiscal Decentralization: A Political Theory with Latin American Cases." *World Politics* 53:205–36.

Garmendia G., Marina. 1996. "Un gobierno dividido fugaz: La historia de la VII Legislatura de Baja California Sur, 1993–1996." In *Poder legislativo: Gobiernos divididos en la Federación Mexicana,* edited by Alonso Lujambio. Mexico City: Colegio Nacional de Ciencias Políticas y Administración Pública, A. C., Universidad Autónoma Metropolitana, Instituto Federal Electoral.

Garrido, Luis Javier. 1989. "The Crisis of *Presidencialismo.*" In *Mexico's Alternative Political Futures,* edited by Wayne Cornelius, Judith Gentleman, and Peter Smith. La Jolla: Center for U.S.-Mexican Studies, University of California, San Diego.

Gay, Robert. 1994. *Popular Organization and Democracy in Rio de Janiero: A Tale of Two Favelas.* Philadelphia: Temple University Press.

Geddes, Barbara. 1994. *Politician's Dilemma: Building State Capacity in Latin America.* Los Angeles: University of California Press.

———. 1995. "A Comparative Perspective on the Leninist Legacy in Eastern Europe." *Comparative Political Studies* 28:239–74.

———. 1996. "Initiation of New Democratic Institutions in Eastern Europe and Latin America." In *Institutional Design in New Democracies: Eastern Europe and Latin America,* edited by Arend Lijphart and Carlos H. Waisman. Boulder, Colo.: Westview Press.

Geddes, Barbara, and John Zaller. 1989. "Sources of Popular Support for Authoritarian Regimes." *American Journal of Political Science* 33:319–47.

Gentleman, Judith, ed. 1987. *Mexican Politics in Transition.* Boulder: Westview Press.

Gershberg, Alec Ian. 1993. "Fiscal Decentralization, Intergovernmental Relations, and Education Finance: Welfare and Efficiency Considerations in Educational Expenditures and Outcomes in Mexico." Ph.D. diss., University of Pennsylvania.

González Block, Miguel Angel. 1991. "Economic Crisis and the Decentralization of Health Services in Mexico." In *Social Responses to Mexico's Economic Crisis of the 1980's,* edited by Mercedes González de la Rocha and Agustín Escobar Latapí. San Diego: Center for U.S.-Mexican Studies, University of California, San Diego.

González Casanova, Pablo. 1970. *Democracy in Mexico.* Translated by Danielle Salti. New York: Oxford University Press.

González Oropeza, Manuel. 1987. *La intervención federal en la desaparición de poderes,* 2d ed. Mexico City: Universidad Nacional Autónoma de México.

———. 1994. "Las comisiones del Congreso de la Unión en México." In *El poder legislativo en la actualidad,* edited by Cámara de Diputados del H. Congreso de la Unión. Serie G: Estudios doctrinales, núm. 162. Mexico City: Instituto de Investigaciones Jurídicas, Universidad Nacional Autónoma de México.

Graham, Lawrence S. 1971. *Mexican State Government: A Prefectural System in Action.* Austin: University of Texas, Institute of Public Affairs.

Granados Chapa, Miguel Ángel. 1992. *¡Nava sí, Zapata no!: La hora de San Luis Potosí de una lucha que triumfó.* Mexico City: Editorial Grijalbo.

Greene, W. H. 1993. *Econometric Analysis.* 2d ed. Englewood Cliffs, N. J.: Prentice Hall.

Grindle, Merilee S. 1977. *Bureaucrats, Politicians, and Peasants in Mexico: A Case Study in Public Policy.* Berkeley: University of California Press.

————. 1996. *Challenging the State: Crisis and Innovation in Latin America and Africa.* Cambridge: Cambridge University Press.

————. 2000. *Audacious Reforms: Institutional Invention and Democracy in Latin America.* Baltimore: Johns Hopkins University Press.

Guillén López, Tonatiuh. 1993. *Baja California 1989–1992: Balance de la transición democrática.* Tijuana: El Colegio de la Frontera.

————. 1995. "Alternancia y nuevas prácticas del poder político: Las elecciones de 1994 desde la experiencia regional." In *La voz de los votos: Un análisis crítico de las elecciones de 1994,* edited by Germán Pérez Fernández de Castillo, Arturo Alvarado M., and Arturo Sánchez Gutiérrez. Mexico City: Facultad Latinoamericana de Ciencias Sociales.

————. 1996. "Gobierno dividido en Baja California: Integración y dinámica legislativa en el periodo 1989–1995." In *Poder legislativo: Gobiernos divididos en la Federación Mexicana,* edited by Alonso Lujambio. Mexico City: Colegio Nacional de Ciencias Políticas y Administración Pública, A. C., Universidad Autónoma Metropolitana, Instituto Federal Electoral.

Gujarati, Damodar N. 1988. *Basic Econometrics.* 2d ed. New York: McGraw-Hill.

Gunder Frank, Andre. 1969. *Latin America: Underdevelopment or Revolution.* New York: Monthly Review Press.

Gutiérrez Mejía, Irma. 1990. *Hidalgo: Sociedad, economía, política y cultura.* Mexico City: Centro de Investigaciones Interdisciplinarias en Humanidades, Universidad Nacional Autónoma de México.

Gutiérrez Mejía, Irma, and E. Pablo Vargas González. 1994. "Hidalgo." In *La República Mexicana: Modernización y democracia de Aguascalientes a Zacatecas,* vol. 2, edited by Pablo Gonzalez Casanova and Jorge Cadena Roa. Mexico City: La Jornada/Universidad Nacional Autónoma de México.

Gwynne, Robert N. 1992. "Industrial Decentralization in Mexico in Global Perspective." In *Decentralization in Latin America: An Evaluation,* edited by Arthur Morris and Stella Lowder. New York: Praeger.

Haggard, Stephan, and Robert R. Kaufman. 1995. *The Political Economy of Democratic Transitions.* Princeton, N. J.: Princeton University Press.

Hagopian, Frances. 1996. *Traditional Politics and Regime Change in Brazil.* Cambridge: Cambridge University Press.

————. 1996a. "The Development of Local Legislatures in Russia: The Case of Yaroslavl." In *Democratization in Russia: The Development of Legislative Institutions,* edited by Jeffrey W. Hahn. Armonk, N.Y.: M. E. Sharpe.

Hahn, Jeffrey W. 1996b. "Introduction: Analyzing Parliamentary Development in Russia." In *Democratization in Russia: The Development of Legislative Institutions,* edited by Jeffrey W. Hahn. Armonk, N.Y.: M. E. Sharpe.

Hall, Peter A., and Rosemary C. R. Taylor. 1996. "Political Science and the Three New Institutionalisms." *Political Studies* 44:936–57.

Hansen, Roger D. 1971. *The Politics of Mexican Development.* Baltimore: Johns Hopkins University Press.

Harris Armengol, Lilian. 1993. "San Luis Potosí." In *Elecciones de 1991: La recuperación oficial,* edited by Silvia Gómez Talge. Mexico City: La Jornada.

Harvey, Neil. 1990. "Peasant Strategies and Corporatism in Chiapas." In *Popular Movements and Political Change in Mexico,* edited by Joe Foweraker and Ann L. Craig. Boulder, Colo.: Lynne Rienner.

Helmke, Gretchen. 1998. "Toward a Formal Theory of an Informal Institution: Insecure Tenure and Judicial Independence in Argentina, 1976–1995." Paper presented at the 21st International Congress of the Latin American Studies Association, Chicago, September 24–26.

Heredia, Blanca. 1994. "Making Economic Reform Politically Viable: The Mexican Experience." In *Democracy, Markets, and Structural Reform in Latin America: Argentina, Bolivia, Brazil, Chile, and Mexico,* edited by William C. Smith, Carlos H. Acuña, and Eduardo A. Gamarra. Coral Gables, Fla.: North-South Center, University of Miami.

Herman, Edward S., and Frank Brodhead. 1984. *Demonstration Elections: U.S.-Staged Elections in the Dominican Republic, Vietnam, and El Salvador.* Boston: South End Press.

Hibbing, John R. 1988. "Legislative Institutionalization with Illustrations from the British House of Representatives." *American Journal of Political Science* 32:681–712.

Higley, John, and Richard Gunther, eds. 1992. *Elites and Democratic Consolidation in Latin America and Southern Europe.* Cambridge: Cambridge University Press.

Hofferbert, Richard I. 1966. "The Relation between Public Policy and Some Structural and Environmental Variables in the American States." *American Political Science Review* 60:73–82.

Holbrook, Thomas M., and Emily Van Dunk. 1993. "Electoral Competition in the American States." *American Political Science Review* 87:955–62.

Huber, Evelyne, Dietrich Rueschemeyer, and John D. Stephens. 1997. "The Paradoxes of Contemporary Democracy: Formal, Participatory, and Social Democracy." *Comparative Politics* 29:323–42.

Hunter, Wendy. 1997. *Eroding Military Influence in Brazil: Politicians against Soldiers.* Chapel Hill: University of North Carolina Press.

Huntington, Samuel P. 1965. "Political Development and Political Decay." *World Politics* 17:386–430.

Hurtado, Javier. 1998. "Los gobiernos divididos y las elecciones de 1998 en México." *Este Pais,* April, 46–53.

Instituto de Investigaciones Jurídicas, Universidad Nacional Autónoma de México. 1997. "Las constituciones de México y sus estados." December 12. Retrieved from http://info.juridicas.unam.mx/cnsinfo/#INICIO.

Instituto de Investigaciones Legislativas del Congreso del Estado de San Luis Potosí. 1998. "Reseña del Instituto de Investigaciones Legislativas de Congreso del Estado de San Luis Potosí." Paper presented at the Primer Foro Regional sobre Temas Legislativos, October 9–10, San Luis Potosí, SLP.

Instituto Federal Electoral. 1997. "Elecciones federales, 1997: Senadores votos acreditados y porcentajes." October 6. Retrieved from http://mxelections.tracesc.com/prep/reportes/senavoto.html.

Instituto Nacional de Estadística, Geografía e Informática. 1986. *Finanzas públicas estatales y municipales de México, 1975–1984.* Aguascalientes, Mexico: INEGI.

———. 1991. *Finanzas públicas estatales y municipales de México, 1979–1988.* Aguascalientes, Mexico: INEGI.

———. 1992. *XI censo de poblacion y vivienda, 1990.* Aguascalientes, Mexico: INEGI.

———. 1994. *Finanzas públicas estatales y municipales de México, 1989–1992.* Aguascalientes, Mexico: INEGI.

———. 1996. *Sistema de cuentas nacionales de Mexico: Producto interno bruto por entidad federativa, 1993.* Aguascalientes, Mexico: INEGI.

———. 1998. *Finanzas públicas estatales y municipales de México, 1992–1996.* Aguascalientes, Mexico: INEGI.

_____. 2000. "El INEGI en su entidad." Retrieved from www.inegi.gob.mx.

Inter-American Development Bank. 1997. *Latin America after a Decade of Reforms: Economic and Social Progress, 1997 Report.* Washington, D. C.: Inter-American Development Bank.

International Monetary Fund. 1992. *International Financial Statistics Yearbook, 1991.* Washington, D. C.: IMF.

———. 1999. *International Financial Statistics Yearbook, 1998.* Washington, D. C.: IMF.

Jacobson, Gary C. 1992. *The Politics of Congressional Elections.* 3d ed. New York: Harper Collins.

Jewell, Malcolm E., and Marcia Lynn Whicker. 1994. *Legislative Leadership in the American States.* Ann Arbor: University of Michigan Press.

Jones, Mark P. 1994. "Presidential Election Laws and Multipartism in Latin America." *Political Research Quarterly* 47, no. 1: 41–57.

———. 1995. *Electoral Laws and the Survival of Presidential Democracies.* Notre Dame, Ind.: University of Notre Dame Press.

Joseph, Richard. 1999. "Democratization in Africa after 1989: Comparative and Theoretical Perspectives." In *Transitions to Democracy,* edited by Lisa Anderson. New York: Columbia University Press.

Juárez, Miguel Ángel. 1998. *Revolución del Teítupelu . . . en el principio era el Caos: El nacimiento de la democracia en México.* Mexico City: Grupo Resistencia.

Karl, Terry Lynn. 1986. "Imposing Consent? Electoralism vs. Democratization in El Salvador." In *Elections and Democratization in Latin America, 1980–1985,* edited by Paul W. Drake and Eduardo Silva, 9–36. San Diego: Center for Iberian and Latin American Studies, University of California, San Diego.

———. 1990. "Dilemmas of Democratization in Latin America." *Comparative Politics* 23:1–21.

Karl, Terry Lynn, and Philippe C. Schmitter. 1991. "Modes of Transition in Latin America, Southern and Eastern Europe." *International Social Science Journal* 128 (May): 269–84.

Key, V. O., Jr. 1949. *Southern Politics in State and Nation.* New York: Vintage Books.

King, Gary, Robert O. Keohane, and Sidney Verba. 1994. *Designing Social Inquiry: Scientific Inference in Qualitative Research.* Princeton, N. J.: Princeton University Press.

Koelble, Thomas A. 1995. "The New Institutionalism in Political Science and Sociology." *Comparative Politics* 27:231–43.

Kohli, Atul. 1987. *The State and Poverty in India.* Cambridge: Cambridge University Press.

Kornberg, Allan, ed. 1973. *Legislatures in Comparative Perspective.* New York: David McKay.

Kornberg, Allan, and Lloyd D. Musolf. 1970. *Legislatures in Developmental Perspective.* Durham, N. C.: Duke University Press.

Kraemer, Moritz. 1999. *One Decade of Decentralization: An Assessment of the Venezuelan Experiment.* Washington, D. C.: Inter-American Development Bank.

Krehbiel, Keith. 1991. *Information and Legislative Organization.* Ann Arbor: University of Michigan Press.

Laing, Kung-Yee, and Scott L. Zeger. 1986. "Longitudinal Data Analysis Using Generalized Linear Models." *Biometrika* 73:13–22.

Langston, Joy. 2001. "Why Rules Matter: Changes in Candidate Selection in Mexico's PRI, 1988–2000." *Journal of Latin American Studies* 33:485–511.

Lewis-Beck, Michael S. 1977. "The Relative Importance of Socioeconomic and Political Variables for Public Policy." *American Political Science Review* 71:559–66.

———. 1986. "Interrupted Time Series". In *New Tools for Social Scientists: Advances and Applications in Research Methods,* edited by William D. Berry and Michael S. Lewis-Beck. Beverly Hills, Calif.: Sage.

Liebert, Ulrike, and Maurizio Cotta, eds. 1990. *Parliament and Democratic Consolidation in Southern Europe: Greece, Italy, Portugal, Spain and Turkey.* London: Pinter.

Lijphart, Arend. 1975. "The Comparable-Cases Strategy in Comparative Research." *Comparative Political Studies* 8, no. 2:158–77.

———. 1984. *Democracies: Patterns of Consensus Government in Twenty-One Countries.* New Haven, Conn.: Yale University Press.

———. 1994. *Electoral Systems and Party Systems: A Study of Twenty-Seven Democracies, 1945–1990.* Oxford: Oxford University Press.

Lijphart, Arend, and Carlos H. Waisman, eds. 1996. *Institutional Design in New Democracies: Eastern Europe and Latin America.* Boulder, Colo.: Westview Press.

Ling Altamirano, Ricardo Alfredo. 1992. *Vamos por Guanajuato.* Mexico City: Estudios y Publicaciones Económicas y Sociales.

Linz, Juan J. 1994. "Democracy, Presidential or Parliamentary: Does It Make a Difference?" In *The Failure of Presidential Democracy,* edited by Juan J. Linz and Arturo Valenzuela, 3–87. Baltimore: Johns Hopkins University Press.

Linz, Juan J., and Amando de Miguel. 1966. "Within-Nation Differences and Comparisons: The Eight Spains." In *Comparing Nations: The Use of Quantitative Data in Cross-National Research,* edited by Richard L. Merritt and Stien Rokkan. New Haven, Conn.: Yale University Press.

Linz, Juan J., and Alfred Stepan. 1992. "Political Identities and Electoral Sequences: Spain, the Soviet Union, and Yugoslavia." *Daedalus* 121:123–40.

———. 1996. *Problems of Democratic Transition and Consolidation: Southern Europe, South America, and Post-Communist Europe.* Baltimore: Johns Hopkins University Press.

Linz, Juan J., and Arturo Valenzuela, eds. 1994. *The Failure of Presidential Democracy.* Baltimore: Johns Hopkins University Press.

Lions, Monique. 1974. *El poder legislativo en América Latina.* Mexico City: Instituto de Investigaciones Jurídicas, Universidad Nacional Autónoma de México.

Lockard, Duane. 1959. *New England State Politics.* Princeton, N. J.: Princeton University Press.

Loewenberg, Gerhard, and Samuel C. Patterson. 1979. *Comparing Legislatures.* Boston: Little, Brown.

Lujambio, Alonso. 1995. *Federalismo y congreso en el cambio político de México.* Mexico City: Instituto de Investigaciones Jurídicas, Universidad Nacional Autónoma de México.

———. 1996a. "Estudio Introductorio." In *Poder legislativo: Gobiernos divididos en la Federación Mexicana,* edited by Alonso Lujambio. Mexico City: Colegio Nacional de Ciencias Políticas y Administración Pública, A. C., Universidad Autónoma Metropolitana, Instituto Federal Electoral.

———, ed. 1996b. *Poder legislativo: Gobiernos divididos en la Federación Mexicana.* Mexico City: Colegio Nacional de Ciencias Políticas y Administración Pública, A. C., Universidad Autónoma Metropolitana, Instituto Federal Electoral.

———. 1998. "Mexican Parties and Congressional Politics in the 1990s." In *Governing Mexico: Political Parties and Elections,* edited by Mónica Serrano. London: Institute of Latin American Studies, University of London.

Magaloni, Beatriz. 1999. "Is the PRI Fading? Economic Performance, Electoral Accountability, and Voting Behavior in the 1994 and 1997 Elections." In *Towards Mexico's Democratization: Parties, Campaigns, Elections, and Public Opinion,* edited by Jorge I. Domínguez and Alejandro Poiré. New York: Routledge.

Mainwaring, Scott. 1999. *Rethinking Party Systems in the Third Wave of Democratization: The Case of Brazil.* Stanford, Calif.: Stanford University Press.

Mainwaring, Scott, Guillermo O'Donnell, and Samuel J Valenzuela, eds. 1992. *Issues in Democratic Consolidation: The New South American Democracies in Comparative Perspective.* Notre Dame, Ind.: University of Notre Dame Press.

Mainwaring, Scott, and Timothy Scully, eds. 1995. *Building Democratic Institutions: Party Systems in Latin America.* Stanford, Calif.: Stanford University Press.

Mainwaring, Scott, and Matthew Soberg Shugart, eds. 1997. *Presidentialism and Democracy in Latin America.* Cambridge: Cambridge University Press.

Marquette, Jesse F., and Katherine A. Hinckley. 1981. "Competition, Control and Spurious Covariation: A Longitudinal Analysis of State Spending." *American Journal of Political Science* 25:362–75.

Martínez Assad, Carlos, and Álvaro Arreola Ayala. 1987. "El poder de los gobernadores." In *La vida política mexicana en la crisis,* edited by Soledad Loaeza and Rafeal Segovia. Mexico City: El Colegio de Mexico.

Mayhew, David. 1974. *Congress: The Electoral Connection*. New Haven, Conn.: Yale University Press.

Méndez, Juan E., Guillermo O'Donnell, and Paulo Sergio Pinheiro, eds. 1999. *The (Un)rule of Law and the Underprivileged in Latin America*. Notre Dame, Ind.: University of Notre Dame Press.

Meyer, Lorenzo. 1989. "Democratization of the PRI: Mission Impossible?" In *Mexico's Alternative Political Futures*, edited by Wayne A. Cornelius, Judith Gentleman, and Peter H. Smith. Monograph Series, no. 30. La Jolla: Center for U.S.-Mexican Studies, University of California, San Diego.

———. 1994. "Prólogo." In *Chihuahua: Historia de una alternativa*, by Alberto Aziz Nassif. Mexico City: La Jornada Ediciones/Centro de Investigaciones y Estudios Superiores en Antropología Social.

———. 1995. "El municipio mexicano al final del siglo XX: Historia, obstáculos, y posibilidades." In *En busca de la democracia municipal: La participación ciudadana en el gobierno local mexicano*, edited by Mauricio Merino. Mexico City: El Colegio de Mexico.

———. 1998. "Mexico: Economic Liberalism in an Authoritarian Polity." In *Market Economics and Political Change: Comparing China and Mexico*, edited by Juan D. Lindau and Timothy Cheek. Lanham, Md.: Rowman and Littlefield.

Middlebrook, Kevin. 1995. *The Paradox of Revolution: Labor, the State, and Authoritarianism in Mexico*. Baltimore: Johns Hopkins University Press.

Mitchell, Neil J., and James M. McCormick. 1988. "Economic and Political Explanations of Human Rights Violations." *World Politics* 40:476–98.

Mizrahi, Yemile. 1994. "Rebels without a Cause? The Politics of Entrepreneurs in Chihuahua." *Journal of Latin American Studies* 26:137–59.

———. 1995a. "Conciliation against Confrontation: How Does the Partido Acción Nacional Rule in Chihuahua?" CIDE Working Paper. Mexico City: Centro de Investigación y Docencia Económicas.

———. 1995b. "Democracia, eficiencia y participación: Los dilemas de los gobiernos de oposicion en México." *Política y Gobierno* no. 2, 2:177–205.

———. 1995c. "Entrepreneurs in the Opposition: Modes of Political Participation in Chihuahua." In *Opposition Government in Mexico*, edited by Victoria E. Rodríguez and Peter M. Ward. Albuquerque: University of New Mexico Press.

———. 1998. "The Costs of Electoral Success: The Partido Acción Nacional in Mexico." In *Governing Mexico: Political Parties and Elections*, edited by Mónica Serrano. London: Institute of Latin American Studies, University of London.

Molinar Horcasitas, Juan. 1991. *El Tiempo de la legitimidad*. Mexico City: Cal y Arena.

———. 1996. "Changing the Balance of Power in a Hegemonic Party System: The Case of Mexico." In *Institutional Design in New Democracies: Eastern Europe and Latin America*, edited by Arend Lijphart and Carlos H. Waisman. Boulder, Colo.: Westview Press.

Molinar Horcasitas, Juan, and Jeffrey A. Weldon. 1994. "Electoral Determinants and Consequences of National Solidarity." In *Transforming State-Society Relations in Mexico: The National Solidarity Strategy*, edited by Wayne A. Cornelius,

Ann L. Craig, and Jonathan Fox. La Jolla: Center for U.S.-Mexican Studies, University of California, San Diego.

Morgan, T. Clifton, and Sally Campbell. 1991. "Domestic Structure, Decisional Constraints and War: So Why Kant Democracies Fight?" *Journal of Conflict Resolution* 35:187–211.

Morris, Arthur. 1992. "Decentralization: The Context." In *Decentralization in Latin America: An Evaluation,* edited by Arthur Morris and Stella Lowder. New York: Praeger.

Morris, Stephen D. 1995. *Political Reformism in Mexico: An Overview of Contemporary Mexican Politics.* Boulder, Colo.: Lynne Rienner.

Munck, Gerardo L., and Jay Verkuilen. 2002. "Conceptualizing and Measuring Democracy: Evaluating Alternative Indices." *Comparative Political Studies* 35:5–34.

Nacif-Hernández, Benito. 1998. "Legislative Parties in the Mexican Chamber of Deputies." Presented at the annual meeting of the American Political Science Association. September 3–6, Boston.

Nacional Financiera. 1995. *La economía mexicana en cifras, 1995.* 14th ed. Mexico City: Nacional Financiera.

———. 1998. *La economía mexicana en cifras, 1998.* 15th ed. Mexico City: Nacional Financiera.

Needler, Martin C. 1995. *Mexican Politics: The Containment of Conflict.* Westport, Conn: Praeger.

North, Douglass C. 1990. *Institutions, Institutional Change and Economic Performance.* Cambridge: Cambridge University Press.

Oates, Wallace E. 1972. *Fiscal Federalism.* New York: Harcourt Brace Jovanovich.

———. 1993. "Fiscal Decentralization and Economic Development." *National Tax Journal* 46:237–43.

O'Connor, Patrick F. 1982. "The Legislature." In *Louisiana Politics: Festival in a Labyrinth,* edited by James Bolner. Baton Rouge: Louisiana State University Press.

O'Donnell, Guillermo. 1993. "On the State, Democratization, and Some Conceptual Problems: A Latin American View with Glances at Some Postcommunist Countries." *World Development* 21:1355–69.

———. 1994. "Delegative Democracy." *Journal of Democracy* 5, no. 1: 55–69.

———. 1996. "Illusions about Consolidation." *Journal of Democracy* 7, no. 2: 34–51.

———. 1998. "Horizontal Accountability in New Democracies." *Journal of Democracy* 9, no. 3: 112–26.

O'Donnell, Guillermo, and Philippe C. Schmitter. 1986. *Transitions from Authoritarian Rule: Tentative Conclusions about Uncertain Democracies.* Baltimore: Johns Hopkins University Press.

O'Donnell, Guillermo, Philippe C. Schmitter, and Laurence Whitehead, eds. 1986. *Transitions from Authoritarian Rule.* Baltimore: Johns Hopkins University Press.

Olson, David M., and Philip Norton, eds. 1996. *The New Parliaments of Central and Eastern Europe.* Portland, OR: Frank Cass.

O'Neill, Kathleen, M. 2000. "Tugging at the Purse Strings: Fiscal Decentralization and State Discretion." Paper presented at the annual meeting of the Latin American Studies Association, Miami, Fla., March 16–18.

Ordeshook, P. C. 1986. *Game Theory and Political Theory.* Cambridge: Cambridge University Press.

Organisation for Economic Co-operation and Development. 1998. *Decentralization and Local Infrastructure in Mexico: A New Policy for Development.* London: OECD.

Ornelas, Carlos. 1995. *El sistema educativo mexicano: La transición de fin de siglo.* Mexico City: Centro de Investigación y Docencia Económicas.

Orozco, Víctor. 1997. "Chihuahua." In *1994: Las elecciones en los estados,* edited by Silvia Gómez Tagle, 211–29. Mexico City: Centro de Investigaciones Interdisciplinarias en Ciencias y Humanidades, Universidad Nacional Autónoma de México.

Oxhorn, Philip D. 1995. *Organizing Civil Society: The Popular Sectors and the Struggle for Democracy in Chile.* University Park: Pennsylvania State University Press.

———. 1998. "Is the Century of Corporatism Over? Neoliberalism and the Rise of Neopluralism." In *What Kind of Democracy? What Kind of Market? Latin America in the Age of Neoliberalism,* edited by Philip D. Oxhorn and Graciela Ducatenzeiler. University Park: Pennsylvania State University Press.

Oxhorn, Philip D., and Graciela Ducatenzeiler. 1998. "Conclusions: What Kind of Democracy? What Kind of Market?" In *What Kind of Democracy? What Kind of Market? Latin America in the Age of Neoliberalism,* edited by Philip D. Oxhorn and Graciela Ducatenzeiler. University Park: Pennsylvania State University Press.

Palacios Roji García, Augustín, and Joaquín Palacios Roji García. 1998. *Guia Roji por las carreteras de México 1998.* Mexico City: Guia Roji.

Pansters, Will G. 1996. "Citizens with Dignity: Opposition and Government in San Luis Potosí, 1938–93." In *Dismantling the Mexican State?* edited by Rob Aitken, Nikki Craske, Gareth A. Jones, and David E. Stansfield. New York: St. Martin's Press.

Patterson, Samuel C. 1996. "Legislative Politics in the States." In *Politics in the American States: A Comparative Analysis,* edited by Virginia Grey and Herbert Jacob. Washington, D. C.: CQ Press.

Patterson, Samuel C., and Gregory A. Caldeira. 1984. "The Etiology of Partisan Competition." *American Political Science Review* 78:691–706.

Pérez Arce, Francisco. 1990. "The Enduring Union Struggle for Legality and Democracy." In *Popular Movements and Political Change in Mexico,* edited by Joe Foweraker and Ann L. Craig, 105–20. Boulder, Colo.: Lynne Rienner.

Peterson, George E. 1997. *Decentralization in Latin America: Learning through Experience.* Washington, D. C.: World Bank.

Petras, James, and Fernando Ignacio Leiva. 1994. *Democracy and Poverty in Chile: The Limits to Electoral Politics.* Boulder, Colo.: Westview Press.

Pinheiro, Paulo Sergio. 1999. "The Rule of Law and the Underprivileged in Latin America: Introductions." In *The (Un)rule of Law and the Underprivileged in Latin America,* edited by Juan E. Mendez, Guillermo O'Donnell, and Paulo Sergio Pinheiro. Notre Dame, Ind.: University of Notre Dame Press.

Poe, Steven C., and C. Neal Tate. 1994. "Repression of Human Rights to Personal Integrity in the 1980s: A Global Analysis." *American Political Science Review* 88:853–72.

Poiré, Alejandro. 1999. "Retrospective Voting, Partisanship, and Loyalty in Presidential Elections: 1994." In *Towards Mexico's Democratization: Parties, Campaigns, Elections, and Public Opinion,* edited by Jorge I. Domínguez and Alejandro Poiré. New York: Routledge.

Polsby, Nelson W. 1968. "The Institutionalization of the U.S. House of Representatives." *American Political Science Review* 62:144–68.

———. 1975. "Legislatures." In *Handbook of Political Science,* vol. 5, edited by Fred Greenstein and Nelson Polsby. Reading, Mass.: Addison-Wesley.

———. 1986. *Congress and the Presidency.* 4th ed. Englewood Cliffs, N.J.: Prentice Hall.

Presidencia de la República, Unidad de la Crónica Presidencial. 1987. *Diccionario biográfico del gobierno mexicano 1987.* Mexico City: Fondo de Cultura Económica.

———. 1989. *Diccionario biográfico del gobierno mexicano 1989.* Mexico City: Fondo de Cultura Económica.

———. 1992. *Diccionario biográfico del gobierno mexicano 1992.* Mexico City: Fondo de Cultura Económica.

———. 1993. *Diccionario biográfico del gobierno mexicano 1993, addenda.* Mexico City: Fondo de Cultura Económica.

Preston, Julia. 1999. "The Elites' Choice Heads to Victory in Mexico Primary." *New York Times,* November 8, 1999, A1.

Prud'homme, Jean-François. 1999. "State Electoral Conflicts and National Interparty Relations in Mexico, 1988–1994." In *Subnational Politics and Democratization in Mexico,* edited by Wayne A. Cornelius, Todd A. Fisenstadt, and Jane Hindley. La Jolla: Center for U.S.-Mexican Studies, University of California, San Diego.

Przeworski, Adam. 1991. *Democracy and the Market: Political and Economic Reforms in Eastern Europe and Latin America.* Cambridge: Cambridge University Press.

Przeworski, Adam, Susan C. Stokes, and Bernard Manin, eds. 1999. *Democracy, Accountability, and Representation.* Cambridge: Cambridge University Press.

Putnam, Robert D. 1993. *Making Democracy Work: Civic Traditions in Modern Italy.* Princeton, N.J.: Princeton University Press.

Ranney, Austin. 1976. "Parties in State Politics." In *Politics in the American States: A Comparative Analysis,* edited by Herbert Jacob and Kenneth N. Vines. Boston: Little, Brown.

Reding, Andrew. 1996. "The Next Mexican Revolution." *World Policy Journal* 13, no. 3: 61–71.

Rejai, Mostafa. 1969. "Toward the Comparative Study of Political Decision-Makers." *Comparative Political Studies* 2:353–54.

Remington, Thomas F., ed. 1994. *Parliaments in Transition: The New Legislative Politics in the Former USSR and Eastern Europe.* Boulder, Colo.: Westview Press.

Remmer, Karen L. 1978. "Evaluating the Policy Impact of Military Regimes in Latin America." *Latin American Research Review* 13, no. 2: 39–54.

———. 1985–86. "Exclusionary Democracy." *Studies in Comparative International Development* 20, no. 4: 64–85.

———. 1986. "The Politics of Economic Stabilization: IMF Standby Programs in Latin America, 1954–1984." *Comparative Politics* 19:1–24.

———. 1990. "Democracy and Economic Crisis: The Latin American Experience." *World Politics* 42:315–35.

———. 1995. "New Theoretical Perspectives on Democratization." *Comparative Politics* 28:103–22.

———. 1997. "Theoretical Decay and Theoretical Development: The Resurgence of Institutional Analysis." *World Politics* 50:34–61.

Remmer, Karen L., and Erik Wibbels. 2000. "The Subnational Politics of Economic Adjustment: Provincial Politics and Fiscal Performance in Argentina." *Comparative Political Studies* 33:419–51.

Reyes Rodríguez, Andrés. 1996. "Gobierno dividido y convivencia política en Aguascalientes, 1995–1996." In *Poder legislativo: Gobiernos divididos en la Federación Mexicana,* edited by Alonso Lujambio. Mexico City: Colegio Nacional de Ciencias Políticas y Administración Pública, A. C., Universidad Autónoma Metropolitana, Instituto Federal Electoral.

Riker, William H. 1964. *Federalism: Origin, Operation, Significance.* Boston: Little, Brown.

———. 1980. "Implications from the Disequilibrium of Majority Rule for the Study of Institutions." *American Political Science Review* 75:432–47.

Rionda, Luis Miguel. 1996. "Guanajuato: Gobierno dividido y cohabitación bipartidista, 1991–1996." In *Poder legislativo: Gobiernos divididos en la Federación Mexicana,* edited by Alonso Lujambio. Mexico City: Colegio Nacional de Ciencias Políticas y Administración Pública, A. C., Universidad Autónoma Metropolitana, Instituto Federal Electoral.

———. 1997. "Guanajuato." In *1994: Las elecciones en los estados,* edited by Silvia Gómez Talge. Mexico City: La Jornada Ediciones, Centro de Investigaciones Interdisciplinarias en Ciencias y Humanidades, Universidad Nacional Autónoma de México.

———. 1998. *Origen y evolución de los partidos políticos en el estado de Guanajuato.* Guanajuato, Mexico: Instituto Electoral del Estado de Guanajuato.

Roberts, Kenneth M. 1998. *Deepening Democracy? The Modern Left and Social Movements in Chile and Peru.* Stanford, Calif.: Stanford University Press.

Robinson, James. 1970. "Staffing the Legislatures." In *Legislatures in Developmental Perspective,* edited by Allan Kornberg and Lloyd Musolf. Durham, N.C.: Duke University Press.

Rodríguez, Victoria E. 1993. "The Politics of Decentralisation in Mexico: From *Municipio Libre* to *Solidaridad.*" *Bulletin of Latin American Research* 12:133–145.

———. 1997. *Decentralization in Mexico: From Reforma Municipal to Solidaridad to Nuevo Federalismo.* Boulder, Colo.: Westview Press.

Rodríguez, Victoria E., and Peter M. Ward. 1992. *Policymaking, Politics, and Urban Governance in Chihuahua: The Experience of Recent Panista Governments.* Austin: LBJ School of Public Affairs, University of Texas at Austin.

———. 1994. *Political Change in Baja California: Democracy in the Making?* Monograph Series, no. 40. San Diego: Center for U.S.-Mexican Studies, University of California, San Diego.

———. 1995a. "Introduction: Governments of the Opposition in Mexico." In *Opposition Government in Mexico,* edited by Victoria E. Rodríguez and Peter M. Ward. Albuquerque: University of New Mexico Press.

———. 1995b. *Opposition Government in Mexico.* Albuquerque: University of New Mexico Press.

Roeder, Philip G. 1993. *Red Sunset: The Failure of Soviet Politics.* Princeton, N.J.: Princeton University Press.

Rogowski, Ronald. 1995. "The Role of Theory and Anomaly in Social-Scientific Inference." *American Political Science Review* 89:467–71.

Rosenthal, Alan. 1990. *Governors and Legislatures: Contending Powers.* Washington, D. C.: CQ Press.

Rossiter, Clinton, ed. 1961. *The Federalist Papers.* New York: New American Library.

Ruble, Blair A. 1996. "Local Policy Making: Lessons from Urban Planning in Yaroslavl." In *Democratization in Russia: The Development of Legislative Institutions,* edited by Jeffrey W. Hahn. Armonk, N.Y.: M. E. Sharpe.

Rueschemeyer, Dietrich, Evelyne Huber Stephens, and John D. Stephens. 1992. *Capitalist Development and Democracy.* Chicago: University of Chicago Press.

Ruíz Massieu, José Francisco. 1995. *El parlamento.* Guanajuato, Mexico: LVI Legislatura H. Congreso del Estado de Guanajuato.

Russett, Bruce. 1993. *Grasping the Democratic Peace: Principles for a Post-Cold War World.* Princeton, N.J.: Princeton University Press.

Sartori, Giovanni. 1976. *Parties and Party Systems: A Framework for Analysis.* New York: Cambridge University Press.

———. 1997. *Comparative Constitutional Engineering: An Inquiry into Structures, Incentives, and Outcomes.* New York: New York University Press.

Schattschneider, E. E. 1942. *Party Government.* New York: Holt, Rinehart and Winston.

Schedler, Andreas, Larry Diamond, and Marc F. Plattner, eds. 1999. *The Self-Restraining State: Power and Accountability in New Democracies.* Boulder, Colo.: Lynne Rienner.

Schlesinger, Joseph A. 1966. *Ambition and Politics: Political Careers in the United States.* Chicago: Rand McNally.

———. 1991. *Political Parties and the Winning of Office.* Ann Arbor: University of Michigan Press.

Schmitter, Philippe C. 1999. "The Limits of Horizontal Accountability." In *The Self-Restraining State: Power and Accountability in New Democracies,* edited by Andreas Schedler, Larry Diamond, and Marc F. Plattner. Boulder, Colo.: Lynne Rienner.

Schneider, Ben Ross. 1995. "Democratic Consolidations: Some Broad Comparisons and Sweeping Arguments." *Latin American Research Review* 30:215–34.

Schofield, N. 1993. "Party Competition in a Spatial Model of Coalition Formation." In *Political Economy: Institutions, Competition, and Representation,* edited by W. Barnett et al. Cambridge: Cambridge University Press.

Schumpeter, Joseph A. 1942. *Capitalism, Socialism and Democracy.* New York: Harper and Brothers.

Sharkansky, Ira, and Richard I. Hofferbert. 1969. "Dimensions of State Politics, Economics, and Public Policy." *American Political Science Review* 63:867–79.

Shirk, David. 1999. "Democratization and Local Party Building: The PAN in León, Guanajuato." In *Subnational Politics and Democratization in Mexico,* edited by Wayne A. Cornelius, Todd A. Eisenstadt, and Jane Hindley. La Jolla: Center for U.S.-Mexican Studies, University of California, San Diego.

Shirk, Susan. 1993. *The Political Logic of Economic Reform in China.* Berkeley: University of California Press.

Shugart, Matthew Soberg, and John M. Carey. 1992. *Presidents and Assemblies: Constitutional Design and Electoral Dynamics.* Cambridge: Cambridge University Press.

Shugart, Matthew Soberg, and Scott Mainwaring. 1997. "Presidentialism and Democracy in Latin America: Rethinking the Terms of the Debate." In *Presidentialism and Democracy in Latin America,* edited by Scott Mainwaring and Matthew Soberg Shugart. Cambridge: Cambridge University Press.

Smith, Peter H. 1979. *Labyrinths of Power: Political Recruitment in Twentieth-Century Mexico.* Princeton, N. J.: Princeton University Press.

Smith, William C., and Carlos H. Acuña. 1994. "Future Politico-Economic Scenarios for Latin America." In *Democracy, Markets, and Structural Reform in Latin America: Argentina, Bolivia, Brazil, Chile, and Mexico,* edited by William C. Smith, Carlos H. Acuña, and Eduardo A. Gamarra. Miami, Fla.: University of Miami North-South Center.

Snyder, Richard. 1999a. "After Neoliberalism: The Politics of Reregulation in Mexico." *World Politics* 51:173–204.

———. 1999b. "After the State Withdraws: Neoliberalism and Subnational Authoritarian Regimes in Mexico." In *Subnational Politics and Democratization in Mexico,* edited by Wayne A. Cornelius, Todd A. Eisenstadt, and Jane Hindley. La Jolla: Center for U.S.-Mexican Studies, University of California, San Diego.

————. 2001a. *Politics after Neoliberalism: Reregulation in Mexico.* Cambridge: Cambridge University Press.

————. 2001b. "Scaling Down: The Subnational Comparative Method." *Studies in Comparative International Development* 36:93–110.

Snyder, Richard, and David Samuels. 2001. "Devaluing the Vote in Latin America." *Journal of Democracy* 12, no. 1: 146–59.

SourceMex. Various. "SourceMex: Economic and Political News on Mexico." Latin American Data Base, Latin American Institute, University of New Mexico. Retrieved from http://ladb.unm.edu.

Squire, Peverill. 1992. "The Theory of Legislative Institutionalization and the California Assembly." *Journal of Politics* 54:1026–54.

Stallings, Barbara, and Robert Kaufman, eds. 1989. *Debt and Democracy in Latin America.* Boulder, Colo.: Westview Press.

Stansfield, David E. 1992. "Decentralization in Mexico: The Political Context." In *Decentralization in Latin America: An Evaluation,* edited by Arthur Morris and Stella Lowder. New York: Praeger.

Stokes, Susan. 1997. "Democratic Accountability and Policy Change: Economic Policy in Fujimori's Peru." *Comparative Politics* 29:209–28.

————. 1999. "What Do Policy Switches Tell Us about Democracy?" In *Democracy, Accountability, and Representation,* edited by Adam Przeworski, Susan C. Stokes, and Bernard Manin. Cambridge: Cambridge University Press.

————. 2001. *Mandates and Democracy: Neoliberalism by Surprise in Latin America.* Cambridge: Cambridge University Press.

Stoner-Weiss, Kathryn. 1996. "Conflict and Consensus in Russian Regional Government: The Importance of Context." In *Democratization in Russia: The Development of Legislative Institutions,* edited by Jeffrey W. Hahn. Armonk, N.Y.: M. E. Sharpe.

————. 1997. *Local Heroes: The Political Economy of Russian Regional Governance.* Princeton, N.J.: Princeton University Press.

Tarkowski, Jacek. 1990. "Endowment of Nomenklatura, or Apparachiks Turned into Enterpreneurchiks, or from Communist Ranks to Capitalist Riches." *Innovation* 1990:89–105.

Tarrow, Sidney. 1994. *Power in Movement: Social Movements, Collective Action and Politics.* Cambridge: Cambridge University Press.

————. 1995. "Bridging the Quantitative-Qualitative Divide in Political Science." *American Political Science Review* 89:471–75.

Taylor-Robinson, Michelle M., and Christopher Diaz. 1999. "Who Gets Legislation Passed in a Marginal Legislature and Is the Label 'Marginal Legislature' Still Appropriate? A Study of the Honduran Congress." *Comparative Political Studies* 32:589–625.

Tendler, Judith. 1997. *Good Government in the Tropics.* Baltimore: Johns Hopkins University Press.

Thomas, Sue. 1994. *How Women Legislate.* New York: Oxford University Press.

Thompson, Ginger. 2002. "Congress Shifts Mexico's Balance of Power." *New York Times,* January 21, 2002.

Tiebout, Charles. 1956. "A Pure Theory of Local Expenditures." *Journal of Political Economy* 64:416–24.

Tokman, Victor E., and Guillermo O'Donnell, eds. 1998. *Poverty and Inequality in Latin America: Issues and New Challenges.* Notre Dame, Ind.: University of Notre Dame Press.

Trejo, Guillermo, and Claudio Jones. 1998. "Political Dilemmas of Welfare Reform: Poverty and Inequality in Mexico." In *Mexico under Zedillo,* edited by Susan Kaufman Purcell and Luis Rubio, 67–101. Boulder, Colo: Lynne Rienner.

Tsebelis, George. 1990. *Nested Games: Rational Choice in Comparative Politics.* Berkeley: University of California Press.

————. 1995. "Decision Making in Political Systems: Veto Players in Presidentialism, Parliamentarism, Multicameralism and Multipartyism." *British Journal of Political Science* 25 (July):289–325.

Tulchin, Joseph S. 1995. *The Consolidation of Democracy in Latin America.* Boulder, Colo.: Lynne Rienner.

Turner, Brian. 1998. "The Impact of Decentralization on Political Parties: Political Careers and Party-Building at the Subnational Level." Paper presented at the annual meeting of the Latin American Studies Association, Chicago, September 24–26.

Ugalde, Antonio. 1970. *Power and Conflict in a Mexican Community: A Study of Political Integration.* Albuquerque: University of New Mexico Press.

Uslaner, Eric. 1978. "Comparative State Policy Formation, Interparty Competition and Malapportionment: A New Look at V. O. Key's Hypotheses." *Journal of Politics* 40:409–32.

Valencia García, Guadalupe. 1993. "Guanajuato." In *Elecciones de 1991: La recuperación oficial,* edited by Silvia Gómez Tagle. Mexico City: García y Valadés Editores and Demos, Desarrollo de Medios, La Jornada Ediciones.

————. 1994. "Guanajuato." In *La República Mexicana: Modernización y democracia de Aguascalientes a Zacatecas,* vol. 2, edited by Pablo González Casanova and Jorge Cadena Roa. Mexico City: Centro de Investigaciones Interdisciplinarias en Humanidades, Universidad Nacional Autónoma de México.

————. 1998. *Guanajuato: Sociedad, economía, política, cultura.* Mexico City: Centro de Investigaciones Interdisciplinarias en Ciencias y Humanidades, Universidad Nacional Autónoma de México.

Vanderbush, Walt. 1999. "Assessing Democracy in Puebla: The Opposition Takes Charge of Municipal Government." *Journal of Interamerican Studies and World Affairs* 41, no. 2: 1–27.

Vanhanen, Tatu. 1990. *The Process of Democratization: A Comparative Study of 147 States, 1980–88.* New York: Crane Russak.

————. 2000. "A New Dataset for Measuring Democracy, 1810–1998." *Journal of Peace Research* 37:251–65.

Vargas González, Pablo. 1991. "La insurgencia en las elecciones de 1984 y 1987." In *Insurgencia democrática: Las elecciones locales,* edited by Jorge Alonso and Silvia Gómez Tagle. Guadalajara: Universidad de Guadalajara.

————. 1993. "Hidalgo." In *Elecciones de 1991: La recuperación oficial,* edited by Silvia Gómez Tagle. Mexico City: García y Valadés Editores and Demos, Desarrollo de Medios, La Jornada Ediciones.

————. 1996. *Opinión pública y cultura política en el estado de hidalgo.* Pachuca, Mexico: Centro de Estudios de Población, Universidad Autónoma del Esatdo de Hidalgo.

————. 1997. "Hidalgo." In *1994: Las Elecciones en los Estados,* edited by Silvia Gómez Talge. Mexico City: La Jornada Ediciones, Centro de Investigaciones Interdisciplinarias en Ciencias y Humanidades, Universidad Nacional Autónoma de México.

————. 1998. *Hidalgo: Las dificultades de la transición política.* Pachuca, Mexico: Universidad Autónoma del Estado de Hidalgo.

Veltmeyer, Henry, and James Petras. 2000. *The Dynamics of Social Change in Latin America.* New York: St. Martin's Press.

von Mettenheim, Kurt, and James Malloy. 1998. *Deepening Democracy in Latin America.* Pittsburgh, Pa.: University of Pittsburgh Press.

Ward, Peter M., and Victoria Rodríguez. 1999. "New Federalism, Intra-Governmental Relations and Co-Governance in Mexico." *Journal of Latin American Studies* 31:673–710.

Wasserman, Mark. 1993. *Persistent Oligarchs: Elites and Politics in Chihuahua, Mexico 1910–1940.* Durham, N. C.: Duke University Press.

Weffort, Francisco C. 1998. "New Democracies and Economic Crisis in Latin America." In *What Kind of Democracy? What Kind of Market? Latin America in the Age of Neoliberal Reform,* edited by Philip D. Oxhorn and Graciela Ducatenzeiler. University Park: Pennsylvania State University Press.

Weingast, Barry, and William Marshall. 1988. "The Industrial Organization of Congress." *Journal of Political Economy* 96:132–63.

Weldon, Jeffrey. 1997. "Political Sources of *Presidencialismo* in Mexico." In *Presidentialism and Democracy in Latin America,* edited by Scott Mainwaring and Matthew Soberg Shugart. Cambridge: Cambridge University Press.

Weyland, Kurt. 1996. *Democracy without Equity: Failures of Reform in Brazil.* Pittsburgh, Pa.: University of Pittsburgh Press.

————. 1997. " 'Growth with Equity' in Chile's New Democracy." *Latin American Research Review* 32, no. 1: 37–67.

Wiarda, Howard J. 1973. "Toward a Framework for the Study of Political Change in the Iberic-Latin Tradition: The Corporative Model." *World Politics* 25:206–35.

Willis, Eliza, Christopher da C. B. Garman, and Stephan Haggard. 1999. "The Politics of Decentralization in Latin America." *Latin American Research Review* 34, no. 1: 7–56.

Wong-Gonzalez, Pablo. 1992. "International Integration and Locational Change in Mexico's Car Industry: Regional Concentration and Deconcentration." In *Decentralization in Latin America: An Evaluation,* edited by Arthur Morris and Stella Lowder. New York: Praeger.

Wood, B. Dan, and Richard W. Waterman. 1994. *Bureaucratic Dynamics: The Role of the Bureaucracy in a Democracy.* Boulder, Colo.: Westview Press.

Woodruff, David. 1999. "Exchange Rate Politics and the Fracture of Monetary Order in Russia." Paper presented at the annual meeting of the American Political Science Association, Atlanta, Ga., September 2–5.

Wright, Deil S. 1978. *Understanding Intergovernmental Relations: Public Policy and Participants' Perspectives in Local, State, and National Governments.* North Scitrate, Mass.: Duxbury Press.

Ziccardi, Alicia, ed. 1995. *La tarea de gobernar: Gobiernos locales y demandas ciudadanas.* Mexico City: Instituto de Investigaciones Sociales, Universidad Nacional Autónoma de México.

CAROLINE C. BEER is assistant professor of political science at the University of Vermont.